C000080078

Next Generation Entrepreneur

Live Your Dreams and Create a Better World through Your Business

Success Factor Modeling
Volume I

by
Robert B. Dilts

Design and illustrations by
Antonio Meza

Published by:

Dilts Strategy Group
P. O. Box 67448
Scotts Valley CA 95067
USA
Phone: (831) 438-8314
E-Mail: info@diltstrategygroup.com
Homepage: http://www.diltstrategygroup.com

Copyright © 2015 by Robert Dilts and Dilts Strategy Group. All right reserved.
Printed in the United States of America. All rights reserved. This book or parts thereof may not be reproduced in any form without written permission of the Publisher.

Library of Congress Control Number: 2015904441

I.S.B.N. 978-0-9962004-0-0

Next Generation Entrepreneurs

Live Your Dreams and Create a Better World through Your Business

Success Factor Modeling
Volume I

by
Robert B. Dilts

Design and illustrations by
Antonio Meza

Table of Contents

Dedication   i

Acknowledgments   iii

Preface   v

Introduction — A Changing World   2

A Changing World   4

Meeting the Challenges of Change   5

Modeling   6

Success Factor Modeling™   7

Basic Steps of the Success Factor Modeling Process   10

Chapter 1 — From Vision to Action: Key Levels of Success Factors   12

Key Levels of Success Factors   14

Summary of Success Factors   17

Critical Success Factors Questionnaire   18

The Allegory of the Six Stone-Workers   20

Holons and Holarchies   22

Ego and Soul   24

Vision, Mission, Ambition and Role   28

The Example of the "Miracle on the Hudson"   30

Aligning Ego and Soul   32

Exercise: The COACH State –
Integrating Ego and Soul into a "Holon"   34

Ego, Soul and Organizations   36

Defining Vision, Mission, Ambition and Role   41

Vision   41

Mission   45

Ambition   47

Role   52

Exploring Your Own Vision, Mission, Ambition and Role   56

Ego and Soul Worksheet for Individuals   57

Reflections and Conclusion   58

Chapter 2 — Next Generation Entrepreneurship and the SFM Circle of Success™   60

The Silicon Valley Phenomenon   62

Entrepreneurship   64

A New Generation of Entrepreneurs   66

The "Three Jewels" of Zentrepreneurship   70

Five Keys to "Creating a World to Which People Want to Belong"   72

Modeling Next Generation Entrepreneurs   74

The SFM Circle of Success™   76

The SFM Circle of Success and the Five Keys to
Creating a World to Which People Want to Belong   78

Integrating Passion, Vision, Mission, Ambition and Role
with the SFM Circle of Success   80

Self and Identity   82

Table of Contents

Customers and Market 84

Team Members and Employees 87

Stakeholders and Investors 89

Partners and Alliances 91

Example of the SFM Circle of Success 95

The Influence of Context and the "Field of Innovation"
on the Circle of Success 96

The Law of Requisite Variety and the Field of Innovation 100

Success Factor Case Example: Powerset's Barney Pell 102

Barney Pell's Circle of Success 111

Success Factor Case Example: IBM's Samuel Palmisano 116

Samuel Palmisano's Circle of Success 120

Conclusion: Starting Your Own Circle of Success 122

References and Further Readings 125

Chapter 3 – Becoming a Success 126

What is Success? 128

Win-Win Results 130

Success and "Self" 131

The "Spirit" of Prosperity 133

Being True to Yourself and Your Dreams 136

Taking Risks and Facing Failure 137

Famous Failures 138

Perceiving Failure as Feedback 141

Finding Support and Sponsorship 144

Gathering Your Allies 147

Dealing with Uncertainty and Getting "Lucky" 148

The Importance of Preparation and Practice 149

Cultivating Your "Luck Factor" 150

Success Factor Case Example:
Tidal Wave Technologies' Mark Fitzpatrick 156

Mark Fitzpatrick's Circle of Success 160

Success Factor Case Example:
Xindium Technologies' Cindana Turkatte 163

A Pattern of Success 165

Critical Success Factors 166

The Role of Women as Entrepreneurs 169

Cindana Turkatte's Circle of Success 170

Reflections on the Success Factor Case Examples 172

Knowing Yourself and Finding Your Passion 172

Identity Level Elicitation Process 175

Expressing and Anchoring Your Passion 178

Exploring the Center of Your Circle of Success
Through the Identity Matrix 180

Generative Complementarities 182

Transforming Polarities into Generative Complementarities 186

The Identity Assessment Template 187

Chapter Summary 188

References and Further Readings 189

Table of Contents

Chapter 4 — Creating the Future   **190**

The Journey of Identity   192

Entrepreneurial Vision   193
    Identifying Potential Customers and Their Needs   196
    Generative Vision Exercise   200
    Creativity Catalysts   202
    "More of/Less of" Chart   206
    Formulating a Vision Statement   208
    Connecting Your Vision with Your Charisma   210
    Communicating Your Vision with Authentic Charisma 212

Clarifying the Mission of Your Venture or Team   213
    Identifying Potential Team Members   216
    Communicating Your Mission   218
    Mission Statement Worksheet   220

Ambition, Vision and Motivation   221
    Setting Your Ambitions   222
    Ambition, Passion and the Identity Matrix   225
    Role Models, Competitors and Advisors   229
    Identifying Potential Stakeholders   231
    Assessing Motivation Worksheet   233

Establishing the Role of Your Project or Venture   236
    Identifying Potential Partners   238
    Exploring Win-Win Partnerships   240

Vision and Ambition Worksheet
    for New Ventures and Projects   245

Enriching Your Circle of Success   246
    Examples of Defining a Generative Circle of Success 248

Success Factor Case Example: Apple's Steve Jobs   252
    Changing the World for the Better Through Technology 253
    My Journey with Apple   254
    A Transformational Leader   256
    Seeing the Future Before It Becomes Obvious   259
    A Passion for Perfection   261
    In Service of Something Bigger   262
    Creating an Environment of Excellence   263
    An Orchestrator of Innovation   266
    Open Innovation and the Power of Partnerships   268
    The iPod and the Expansion of Apple's Mission   270
    The Importance of Aesthetic Intelligence   271
    Summary of Steve Jobs' Success Factors   273
    Steve Jobs' Circle of Success   275
    Concluding Comments on Steve Jobs   280

Chapter Summary   281

References and Further Readings   283

Conclusion – Making Your "Elevator Pitch"   **284**

What is an Elevator Pitch?   286

Preparing Your Pitch   288

Example of Pitch Preparation for the "Generative Venture Community" 289

Presenting With Passion   291

Next Steps   292

Table of Contents

Afterword   293

Appendix: Ongoing Success Factor Modeling Projects   297

Glossary   300

About the Author and Illustrator   316

Dedication

This book is dedicated with much love and appreciation to

John Dilts

May his enthusiasm for the spirit of entrepreneurship inspire
the readers of this work to take the chance to live your dreams
and make a better world through your visions and ventures.

Acknowledgements

I would like to gratefully acknowledge Benoit Sarazin, Michael Dilts, Glenn Bacon and Antonio Meza for their time and efforts in reading over the initial draft of this book and offering their feedback and suggestions. Due to them, this is much better book than it would have been.

Of course, a special additional acknowledgment goes to Antonio Meza for his work on the design of the layout of the book and for the brilliance and amazing creativity of his illustrations. This would be a much less rich and interesting book without them. Antonio has also been a valued advisor throughout the process of bringing this book to publication.

This book would clearly not exist without the many "next generation" entrepreneurs – such as Steve Jobs, Elon Musk, Richard Branson, Jeff Bezos, Muhammed Yunus, Blake Mycoskie, Marwan Zebian, Ronald Burr, Ed Hogan, Brian Chesky, Joe Gebbia and Samuel Palmisano – whose efforts inspired this work. I would like to especially acknowledge Barney Pell, Mark Fizpatrick, Cindana Turkatte, Steig Westerberg, Steve Artim and Don Pickens for the extended interviews they gave for our Success Factor Case Examples and for the experience and knowledge they generously shared. They all took risks and blazed new trails with their vision, ambition and heart.

Last but certainly not least, I would like to acknowledge my brother John Dilts whose passion for creating a world of visionary entrepreneurs was the foundation and remains the spirit of Success Factor Modeling.

Preface

This book is the fulfillment of a dream that began in 1999 when my brother John and I founded the *Dilts Strategy Group*. John had been working in a Silicon Valley law firm that represented venture backed start-up companies as well as handling mergers, acquisitions, and initial public offerings. As a result, John had gathered a lot of experience sitting on both sides of negotiations between hopeful entrepreneurs and potential investors. He began to notice that, after an unsuccessful meeting with an entrepreneur, a potential investor might say something like, "If they had only had addressed X or demonstrated Y, I would have been interested." John began to wonder, "Well, why don't you tell them that so that they have the opportunity to respond to the feedback and get a chance to make adjustments?" It occurred to him that nobody was really providing this type of coaching for prospective entrepreneurs and that it could be very valuable knowledge. It could also possibly be quite lucrative, especially for ventures that had the potential to make it big.

During these meetings, John also became increasingly aware of the importance of the entrepreneur's ability to communicate his or her vision in a way that inspired others, rather than just present their product or financial plan. He realized that venture capitalists and business angels rarely chose to invest in an idea, product or plan alone. Rather, they invested in the entrepreneur and his or her vision and commitment to make things happen. Investors didn't want to take a chance on a single product or a particular plan, they wanted to invest in a business; which in a rapidly changing environment takes much more than a plan or product. The plan and product were important, but ultimately investors invested in people.

These experiences began to seed in John the idea of a special type of "venture catalyst." A *venture catalyst* is an individual or collection of individuals that puts both money and other resources into a start-up company in order to accelerate its growth and increase its chances of success. John's idea was not only to put money into small start-ups with high potential and support them with legal and financial planning, but also coach the entrepreneurs in the behavioral and management skills they needed to grow their business.

That was where I came in. I had been working with companies and organizations for almost 20 year by that point, usually in the area of behavioral skill development. I had written several books on leadership, innovation and effective presentation and communication skills. My background is in NeuroLinguistic Programming, which supports both personal and professional development through a process known as modeling – a methodology that examines, uncovers and identifies the patterns of thought and behavior of exceptional performers.

John Dilts
Co-Founder Dilts Strategy Group

When we would talk about what we were observing and experiencing with respect to our work with our clients (and with respect to our own entrepreneurial activities), John and I frequently found ourselves speculating about what types of skills, tools and support it took to make a truly successful venture. We had both grown up in the Silicon Valley and had witnessed the phenomenal successes of companies like Apple, Yahoo, Hewlett Packard, Oracle, Cisco and many others. I had even done consulting and training for some of theses companies. Our father was a patent attorney who was an advanced electronics specialist and had moved to the San Francisco Bay Area in the late 1950s at the beginning of the technology revolution. His work brought him into contact with many entrepreneurs and start-up companies. So we spent much of our lives exposed to the stories of technology developments and hugely successful ventures that had begun as scribbles on a paper napkin. Of course, there were also the stories of those should have made it but didn't because they lacked some key element.

The late 1990s was right in the heart of the Internet explosion and the technology "bubble." John and I were both fascinated by the fact that seemingly average people could create a wildly successful venture so quickly. What used to take years was happening in months or even weeks. It was also obvious that not everyone succeeded. In fact, there were more failures than successes. The questions we began to explore were: "What is the difference that makes the difference?" "What are the critical success factors related to starting or building a business." We started by looking at some of the obvious Silicon Valley success stories and by interviewing some of our clients and acquaintances who had built successful ventures.

As we shared what we were learning with our colleagues and friends, they became fascinated and wanted to know what we were doing and what we called it. We decided to call this exploration *"Success Factor Modeling."*

It was an exhilarating time and an exciting endeavor. We began to experiment with our ideas and put them into action. John and I would both interview and coach entrepreneurs who were interested in getting funding for their ideas. It began to become more and more obvious what successful entrepreneurs did, how they thought and what motivated them. This, in turn, made us even more and more passionate about what were doing. We came to view an explosion of visionary entrepreneurs as being the most certain way to bring positive change into the world; in a way that governments, religions, big businesses and other large institutions would never be able to accomplish. We both shared a love of new ideas and felt deeply inspired to help others reach their dreams.

John eventually left his law firm to start a small early stage investment fund. And we formed Dilts Strategy Group as a way to support the companies in which he was investing and to share the success strategies we were discovering with our clients and others who wanted to create and launch successful ventures.

I began the first draft of this book in 2001 in order to explain the process of Success Factor Modeling and record the discoveries we were making. Since then, there have been two major global financial recessions and many changes and new developments in technology, business, society and the world. The foundations of what John and I synthesized as a result of our initial Success Factor Modeling work have withstood the test of time. We also continued to apply the Success Factor Modeling process to new generations of entrepreneurs. John even launched his own business angel investor group called Maverick Angels, which he ran until his sudden and untimely passing in the summer of 2010.

John's vision for Success Factor Modeling has lived on, however, and this work is a testament to that. By the time I finished the preliminary draft for this current embodiment of Success Factor Modeling in 2013, it had reached several hundred pages. I sent the draft out to a number of family members and colleagues in order to get feedback and suggestions including my older brother Michael Dilts, my father in law Glenn Bacon and my colleague Benoit Sarazin, who had collaborated on several projects with Dilts Strategy Group. I also sent it to Antonio Meza, a colleague, friend and a gifted illustrator and cartoonist as well as a trainer and coach. Antonio began to make suggestions for cartoons to illustrate the fundamental principles and ideas in the book that made them much more clear, accessible and entertaining. As you will see, Antonio's work has become a major contribution to this project and makes the ideas and models easy to understand. Antonio has also provided invaluable input into the structure and organization of the work, including the suggestion to divide it into three volumes.

This first volume *Next Generation Entrepreneurship: Living Your Dreams and Making a Better World through Your Business* captures the spirit and exhilaration (as well as the commitment and skill) related to launching a venture based on your passion and vision. Future volumes will explore *The Power of Generative Collaboration* and *Rebounding from Adversity by Developing Resilience and Leadership*.

This publication also marks a type of relaunch of the Dilts Strategy Group following John's passing. I have already begun to offer certification programs in Success Factor Modeling in different countries throughout the world. These programs provide participants with the road maps and tools necessary to support and develop – in themselves and others – the confidence, competence and resources necessary to launch a successful project or venture. I plan to renew the worldwide network of consultants and coaches that John and I had begun to build in the period before his death. This network will help "spread the word" and meet the increasing global demand for the tools and strategies provided by Success Factor Modeling.

I have also initiated several new Success Factor Modeling research projects centered in different parts of the world. One on "next generation entrepreneurship" is being sponsored by Institut REPERE in Paris. Another on "collective intelligence in organizations" is sponsored by Vision 2021 in Avignon. In fact, some of the findings of those studies have already been incorporated into this book. (Information on these projects is provided in the Appendix.)

I hope you find this world of Success Factor Modeling and next generation entrepreneurship as exciting and rewarding to explore as John and I have. May it bring you much success and satisfaction as you live your dreams and make a better world through your business.

Robert Dilts
Santa Cruz, California

Introduction
A Changing World

Things are always changing . . . but they are not always progressing.
Anthony Robbins

*The people who are crazy enough to think they can change the world
are usually the ones who do.*
Steve Jobs

Be the change you wish to see in the world.
Mahatma Ghandi

ANTONIO MEZA

A Changing World

Social, industrial and economic developments are constantly bringing about changes in the world of business and the way in which people, teams and organizations, old and new, must operate. Technological progress is continually "pushing the edge of the envelope," creating both opportunities and challenges for new ventures and forcing traditional companies to adapt.

The last decades have seen dramatic increases in the speed of change and the demand for response. As a result of "internet time," or "web speed," changes that once took years now routinely occur in a matter of months. Rapid technical change puts increased emphasis on the need for individuals and organizations to constantly innovate and "learn to learn," in order to keep up with continuing advances.

Recurring global economic fluctuations create additional challenges for businesses attempting to cope with change, requiring them to accomplish more with fewer resources. Companies need to rely more and more on strategic alliances and outsourcing to conduct key aspects of their business. As a result, the boundaries between synergistic companies are becoming more flexible, leading to the notions of the "extended organization" and "open innovation." This puts an increased emphasis on relationship building and alliances; which calls for the ability to create effective "win-win" partnerships.

Such rapid technical, social and economic changes place an increased demand on individuals and companies to respond quickly and innovatively in order to keep pace with fresh developments, manage resources more efficiently and stay ahead of competition.

These changes also open up opportunities for innovative individuals and organizations to envision new solutions and create revolutionary products and services that will truly change the world. If you have the proper combination of vision, motivation and skill today there are endless possibilities to fulfill your dreams.

This book is about how to do just that – develop and apply the imagination, passion and capabilities necessary to live your dreams and create a better world through your business.

Meeting the Challenges of Change

Entrepreneurs, teams and organizations face numerous challenges as they attempt to adapt to and take advantage of the changing economy and the transformations in business methods and standards that accompany it. The size of many larger, established companies, for instance, make it difficult to change rapidly, and they frequently lack the flexibility to respond quickly to a dynamic environment. Many organizations, for example, develop cultures emphasizing stability and security. This tends to counteract attempts to increase flexibility and diversity.

It has been said that "if you always do what you've always done, you'll always get what you've always got." One implication of this statement is that if you want to get something different, you should promote change. However, it is also important to realize that, in a changing world, doing what you used to do doesn't even get you the results you used to get. If companies try to operate in the same ways that were successful 20 years ago, they will not be successful today.

An obvious example is a company like Apple Inc. Twenty years ago the company name was Apple *Computer*. Today, its primary products are no longer computers but instead smart phones, tablets and MP3 players. The company has had to change its name to reflect this evolution. If the company was still trying to survive by selling the Macintosh computer of 20 years ago, it would be bankrupt by now. Companies like Apple have survived and flourished because of their ability to rapidly adapt and innovate.

Other companies that are global leaders today, like Google, Facebook and PayPal, etc., did not even exist 20 years ago. Their success has come because innovative entrepreneurs saw opportunities to create something new that opened up increased possibilities for new generations of potential customers.

All of this raises key questions, such as "How do we keep up in a rapidly changing world?" "How do we find the formulas for success in today's economy?"

Entrepreneurs and organizations must learn to embrace diversity and foster innovation in order to survive and succeed in a rapidly changing global economy.

It is in response to the needs imposed by an increasingly complex and continually evolving environment that Success Factor Modeling™ has developed.

When Steve Jobs introduced the Macintosh computer in 1984 the company's name was "Apple Computer."

When Steve Jobs introduced the iPad in 2010 the company's name had changed to "Apple Inc."

Modeling

Webster's Dictionary defines a *model* as "a simplified description of a complex entity or process"—such as a "computer model" of the circulatory and respiratory systems. The term comes from the Latin root *modus*, which means "a manner of doing or being; a method, form, fashion, custom, way, or style." More specifically, the word "model" is derived from the Latin *modulus*, which essentially means a "small" version of the original mode. A "model" of an object, for example, is typically a miniature version or representation of that object. A "working model" (such as that of a machine) is something which can do on a small scale the work which the machine itself does, or is expected to do.

The notion of a "model" has also come to mean "a description or analogy used to help visualize something (as an atom) that cannot be directly observed." It can also be used to indicate "a system of postulates, data, and inferences presented as a formal description of an entity or state of affairs."

Thus, a miniature train, a map of the location of key train stations, or a train schedule, are all examples of different possible types of models of a railway system. Their purpose is to emulate some aspect of the actual railway system and provide useful information to better manage interactions with respect to that system. A miniature train set, for instance, may be used to assess the performance of a train under certain physical conditions; a map of key train stations can help to plan the most effective itinerary to reach a particular city; a train schedule may be used to determine the timing required for a particular journey. From this perspective, the fundamental value of any type of model is its *usefulness*.

A "model" can be a miniature version of a system that helps us explore and understand how the dynamics work on a small scale.

A model can also be a type of map that helps us to manage our interaction with a particuar system.

Success Factor Modeling™

Success Factor Modeling™ (SFM) is a methodology developed by myself and my brother John in order to identify, understand and apply the critical success factors that drive and support successful people and organizations. Success Factor Modeling™ is founded upon a set of principles and distinctions which are uniquely suited to analyze and identify crucial patterns of *business practices* and *behavioral skills* used by successful individuals, teams and companies. The SFM™ process is used to identify key characteristics and capabilities shared by successful entrepreneurs, teams and ventures and then to define specific models, tools and skills that can be used by others to greatly increase their chances of producing impact and achieving success.

By examining successful businesses, projects and ventures and observing the behavior of high performing individuals and teams, SFM™ helps people and organizations to distinguish the factors that have created a particular legacy of success and to identify the trends necessary to extend that legacy into the future. These factors can then be "baked into" people's daily activities by providing the appropriate strategies, tools and support.

One of the strengths of the SFM™ process is its integration of effective business practices with key behavioral skills. Benoit Sarazin, former Marketing Manager for the Communications Solutions Services Division at Agilent Technologies, points out, "Many methodologies exist to help people with effective business practices. If you go to a library or bookstore, you can find all types of resources for making business plans, forming marketing strategies, protecting intellectual property, etc. But there are no methodologies for the behavioral skills. This is what makes Success Factor Modeling totally unique."

Modeling behavioral skills involves observing and mapping the crucial mental and physical processes that produce a successful or remarkable performance of some type. The goal of the behavior modeling process is to identify the essential elements of thought and action required by an individual or group to produce the desired response or outcome—i.e., discovering what is *"the difference that makes the difference."* It is the process of taking a complex performance or interaction and breaking it into small enough chunks so that it can be recapitulated in some way. The purpose of behavior modeling is to create a pragmatic map or "model" of that behavior which can be used to reproduce or simulate some aspect of that performance by anyone who is motivated to do so. Thus, it involves benchmarking behaviors and ideas, as well as business practices.

Success Factor Modeling™ explores the question, "What is the difference that makes the difference?" in order to find the success factors that distinguish between poor, average and remarkable performance.

Poor, average or remarkable performance?

Skills

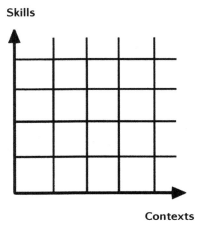

Contexts

Success Factor Modeling™ links behavioral skills to relevant contexts.

An effective model provides a description of the lock (strategic challenges and objectives) and the key which opens it (skills and actions).

A number of the key distinctions used in Success Factor Modeling™ come from the field of Neuro-Linguistic Programming. *Neuro-Linguistic Programming* (NLP) is a method for better understanding and using your brain and nervous system — especially your sensory representational systems (visualization, sound, feeling, etc.) — and linguistic processes, such as persuasion, negotiation and other forms of verbal influence. NLP tools and skills have been used to help people overcome fears, increase their personal productivity and success, recover from serious health problems, start successful businesses, and grow personally in many ways. NLP models and methods have been used as the basis for many behavior change programs by a number of successful groups and organizations such as Apple Inc., IBM, Hewlett Packard, Fiat, The World Bank, Weight Watchers, the US Army, as well as individuals, including numerous sports figures and the internationally known motivational speaker Anthony Robbins.

NLP techniques were developed as the result of modeling what successful people do to reach their outcomes (see *Modeling with NLP*, Dilts, R., 1998.). Applying the distinctions of NLP, I myself have studied healers, innovators, business leaders, and some of the world's most famous geniuses (Einstein, Mozart, Leonardo da Vinci and Walt Disney to name a few).

The objective of the modeling process is not to end up with the one "right" or "true" description of a particular person's, team's or organization's process, but rather to make an *instrumental map* that allows us to apply the strategies that we have modeled in some useful way. An "instrumental map" is one that allows us to act more effectively— the "accuracy" or "reality" of the map is less important than its "usefulness." Thus, the instrumental application of the behaviors or strategies modeled from a particular individual or group of individuals involves putting them into structures that allow us to use them for some practical purpose. This purpose may be similar to or different from that for which the individual or group initially used them.

Success Factor Modeling™ extends the behavioral modeling process by placing the actions and skills to be modeled within a relevant context. Thus, Success Factor Modeling™ links particular behavioral skills to the context or activity which they most directly support and for which they are most needed in order to be successful.

We can liken Success Factor Modeling™ to the process of finding the right key to unlock a particular door. Life circumstances present us with doorways leading to different areas of success. The locks on these doorways are the critical issues and contextual constraints we must address in order to reach our goal in those particular circumstances. The "key" to a particular "lock" is the appropriate combination of behaviors required to effectively address those issues and constraints.

A key that successfully unlocks one door will not necessarily unlock another one, even if it worked perfectly for the previous door. Thus, in order to address changing contexts, an effective model would provide not only a description of the key, but also include a description of the lock which that key fits.

Seen from the organizational and entrepreneurial perspective, the locks that must be opened in order to pass through the doorways to success are described in the form of strategic challenges and objectives. The keys that open the locks are defined by the behaviors and practices of the individuals and teams. They are the "key" actions necessary to meet strategic challenges and achieve strategic goals (the "locks") within their particular context and marketplace.

As we pointed out earlier, the objective of the Success Factor Modeling™ process is to make an *instrumental map*—one supported by a variety of exercises, formats and tools that allows people to apply the factors that have been modeled in order to reach key outcomes within the chosen context. This is another important implication of the analogy of a key. People must be able to use it to get through the door. Thus, identifying and creating tools and techniques which allow others to succeed is also fundamental to the Success Factor Modeling™ process.

In summary, the goals of Success Factor Modeling™ are to:

- Identify key factors associated with successful performance.
- Organize those factors into a comprehensive and comprehensible model.
- Define specific tools and skills with which to transfer the key success factors encompassed by the model to others.
- Support the implementation of critical success factors through a variety of development paths that serve to create a dynamic and sustainable trajectory of progress.

WRONG CONTEXT   RIGHT SKILLS

RIGHT CONTEXT   RIGHT SKILLS

RIGHT CONTEXT   WRONG SKILLS

It is important to apply the right skills to the right context.

Everybody is a genius. But if you judge a fish by its ability to climb a tree, it will live its whole life believing that it is stupid.

– Albert Einstein

Basic Steps of the Success Factor Modeling™ Process

The basic steps of the SFM™ process are:

1. Conducting a *needs analysis* to determine the specific issues, contexts and skills to be addressed. The first step involves identifying "success stories" to determine their desired state of success and selecting the individuals or teams to be modeled.

2. Setting up and carrying out *research* through modeling interviews, case studies and other information-gathering procedures in order to identify the capabilities or performance to be examined and collect relevant data.

3. *Determining relevant patterns* in the behavior, strategies and beliefs of the individuals and teams who have been modeled, which sets the benchmark for successful actions in the venture's future.

4. *Organizing the patterns* that have been discovered into a descriptive and prescriptive structure; i.e., a "model." This involves constructing a customized model and defining the supporting skills and competencies.

5. Designing effective *installation/intervention procedures and tools* in order to transfer or apply the key elements of the model to others. This involves completing the instructional design and development of the assessment tools and competency development paths for different individuals and teams.

Over the past decade and a half, my brother John and I have gone through these steps with countless entrepreneurs, leaders and organizations and built a coaching and consulting practice – *The Dilts Strategy Group* – from the results that we have discovered. In this book, I will share with you how we have used the Success Factor Modeling™ process to identify the critical factors for success in a number of different areas. I will also show how we have formed them into models and tools that you can use to achieve success in your own ventures.

The main purpose of all of this is for you to learn and apply the skills and success factors necessary to reach success in your own projects, ventures or businesses and, in doing so, live your dreams and make a better world.

Throughout this book you will find case examples, principles, models and tools that will guide and support you to think and act like a successful entrepreneur. In doing so, be prepared for one of the most exciting and life-changing journeys of your life.

Let's begin!

The steps of Success Factor Modeling are designed to identify and transfer the key patterns in the behavior, strategies and beliefs of successful individuals, teams and organizations.

Dilts
Strategy Group

The main purpose for studying Success Factor Modeing is to be able to learn and apply the skills and success factors necessary to reach success in your own projects, ventures or businesses and, in doing so, live your dreams and make a better world.

BASIC STEPS OF THE SUCCESS FACTOR MODELING™ PROCESS

1. Conduct a needs analysis. What is success for them? What do they want to achieve more of?

2. Gather information through interviews, case studies and identify their current capabilities.

3. Determine relevant patterns in behavior, strategies and beliefs to be modeled.

4. Organize the patterns into a descriptive "model".

5. Design effective procedures to transfer the key elements of the model to others.

From Vision to Action
Key Levels of Success Factors

"I slept and dreamt that life was joy.
I awoke and saw that life was service.
I acted and behold, service was joy."
Rabindranath Tagore

"Being the richest man in the cemetery doesn't matter to me.
Going to bed at night saying we've done something wonderful...
...that's what matters to me."
Steve Jobs

ANTONIO MEZA

Environment: *Our holistic orchard network focuses on sharing sustainable fruit growing techniques that emphasize orchard soil health which in turn makes for healthy trees and thus healthy apples and healthy people.*

Behavior: *Our activities cover everything needed to bring our juice from our farms to our customers, including juicing, packing and distribution.*

Key Levels of Success Factors

According to SFM™, effective and successful performance and change involves a number of levels of success factors. These factors relate to our **environment** (*where* and *when we act*), our **behavior** (*what* we do), our **capabilities** (*how* we think and plan), our **values and beliefs** (*why* we think and act the way we do), and our **identity** (*who* we perceive ourselves to be) and our sense of **purpose** (for *whom* and for *what* we dedicate ourselves). The life of people in a team or organization, and indeed, the life of the team or organization itself, takes place on all of these different levels.

The primary level is the *environment* in which individuals and organizations act and interact—i.e., *when* and *where* the operations and relationships within a venture or organization take place. Environmental factors determine the external context and create the opportunities and constraints within which people operate. A team's or organization's local environment is made up of such things as the geographical locations of its operations, the buildings and facilities which define the "work place," office and factory design, etc. The wider environment includes such things as market trends, global financial conditions, social structure, technology developments, etc. Depending on the state of these factors, opportunities that open doors and new possibilities may emerge. At other times, such as during an economic downturn, people and companies have to contend with restrictions or disruptions. Responding creatively and wisely to the evolving state of the environment is probably the main determining factor in the success of a venture or organization. In fact, the primary definition of intelligence is: *The ability to interact successfully with one's world, especially in the face of challenge or change.*

In addition to the influence environmental factors have on people and organizations, it is also important to examine the influence and impact that people and organizations have upon their environment. This includes the products or creations that they bring into the environment and the consequences those creations have on the external environment.

At another level, we can examine the specific *behaviors* and actions of an organization, team or individual—i.e., *what* the person, team or organization does within their environment in order to respond to it or change it. This has to do with the particular patterns of work, interaction and communication. On the individual level, behaviors take the form of specific work routines, working habits or job-related activities. For a venture or organization, behaviors may be defined in terms of the activities required to make its products or deliver its services. Thus, behaviors are the concrete activities that we take to respond to constraints or take advantage of opportunities.

Another level of process explored in Success Factor Modeling involves the strategies, skills and *capabilities* by which a venture, team or individual selects and directs their behaviors and actions within their environment—i.e., *how* they generate and guide their behaviors within a particular context. For an individual, capabilities include cognitive strategies and skills such as learning, memory, decision-making and creativity, which facilitate the performance of a particular behavior or task. On an organizational level, capabilities relate to the infrastructures available to support communication, innovation, planning and decision-making between members of the organization. Such capabilities are critical to the ability of an individual or organization to succeed in their environments. Without the proper capabilities we are unable to concretely respond appropriately and effectively to the challenges and changes in our environments.

These various levels of process (environments, behaviors and capabilities) are shaped by *values* and *beliefs*, which provide the motivation and guidelines behind the strategies and capabilities used to accomplish behavioral outcomes in the environment—i.e., *why* people do things the way they do them in a particular time and place. Our values and beliefs provide the reinforcement (*motivation and permission*) that supports or inhibits our use of particular capabilities and behaviors. Values such as *quality, ease of use, security, customer service, promoting greater health*, etc., determine which types of capabilities are likely to be developed and put into action. Values establish priorities and give guidance and direction to people as to where to focus their attention and how to conduct their interactions.

Beliefs are related to values and also serve to establish and shape what is considered to be possible, appropriate and important. Beliefs such as "We are capable to adapt," "We are responsible for our success," "It is important for us to innovate," "Customers come first," "It is possible for us to be a market leader," etc., determine which capabilities and behaviors will receive focus and how much effort will be exerted. Thus, values and belief are the primary influences on judgment and culture.

Beyond values and beliefs is the individual's, team's or organization's sense of *identity*—i.e., the *who* behind the why, how, what, where and when. The identity of an individual or organization includes and transcends all of the previous levels and integrates them into a single entity. It is our perception of our identity that organizes our beliefs, capabilities and behaviors into a single system. To a certain degree, identity relates to role and brand, but it is also more than that. Like the DNA of our bodies, the sense of identity of an individual or organization provides the deep structure and fundamental organizing principles that aggregates all of the other success factors.

Capabilities: *We have developed an innovative system to organize our fleet of electrical trucks so that we can distribute our juice without preservatives in a fast and clean way.*

Values: *Have you guessed? Our values are quality, taste, health and ecology. They guide our decisions as an organization.*

Identity: *We see ourselves as being like a modern "Johnny Appleseed" who was known for his kind, generous ways and his leadership in conservation, and because of the symbolic significance of apples to health.*

Purpose: *And we want our community to benefit from our work by inspiring people with our values and providing the best apple juice!*

Successful companies like Apple, Disney, Google, BMW, etc., have a clear sense of identity that encompasses, aligns, and synthesizes specific and recognizable values, capabilities and behaviors within the changing landscape of the environment in which they operate.

There is a final level of success factors that can best be referred to as the level of *spirit* or *purpose*. This level has to do with people's visions and perceptions relating to the larger systems to which they belong and within which they participate. These perceptions relate to a person's or organization's sense of *for whom* or *for what* their actions are directed, providing a sense of meaning and purpose for their actions, capabilities, beliefs and identity. This sense of a larger system can extend from one's family to one's profession, one's community and all the way to the planet.

In summary, Success Factor Modeling™ takes into account the following levels of behavioral factors related to success:

- **Environmental factors** which determine the external opportunities or constraints which individuals and organizations must recognize and to which they must react. They involve considering *where* and *when* success occurs.
- **Behavioral factors** relating to the specific action steps taken in order to reach success. They involve *what*, specifically, must be done or accomplished in order to succeed.
- **Capabilities** which make up to the mental maps, plans or strategies that lead to success. They direct *how* actions are selected and monitored.
- **Beliefs and values** which provide the reinforcement that supports or inhibits particular capabilities and actions. They relate to *why* a particular path is taken and the deeper motivations which drive people to act or persevere.
- **Identity factors** relating to people's sense of their role and unique distinguishing characteristics. These factors are a function of *who* a person or group perceives themselves to be.
- **Vision and purpose** which relate to people's view of the larger system of which they are a part. These factors involve *for whom* or *for what* a particular action step or path has been taken

Summary of Success Factors

While all the levels of success factors are important, it seems clear that the higher levels exert progressively greater influence on the likelihood of a successful venture. Without a clear sense of purpose, identity, direction and priorities it is easy to get lost, lose focus and motivation, and become confused and conflicted, especially when things become challenging and difficult.

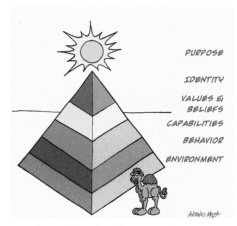

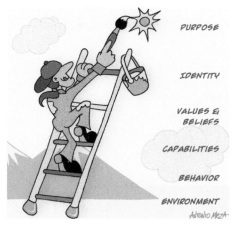

The relationship between the various levels of success factors can be represented as a pyramid. The environment forms the foundation upon which the other levels are built, with the vision as the pinnacle of the structure.

Still another way to view the relationships of this group of success factors is as a ladder. The lower levels serve as the rungs of the ladder which are necessary in order to climb to the top and reach the vision.

Yet another way to perceive the relationship of these various factors is as concentric circles with the vision in the center, like a target with the vision as the "bulls eye."

We will be referring to these various levels of success factors throughout the remainder of this book, so finding the way of representing them to yourself that works best for you makes it easy to keep the different levels and their relationship in mind.

Critical Success Factors Questionnaire

To get a personal sense of these various levels of success factors, take a few moments and go over the following *Critical Success Factors Questionnaire*.

Identify a project or venture that you were personally involved with that has already been successfully achieved. To bring the critical success factors out more clearly, it is useful to have a contrast. In this regard it can be useful to identify a project or venture that you were personally involved with that was not so successful or maybe even failed. What were some of the differences that made a difference?

Successful Project/Venture: _____

Model some of the Critical Success Factors by considering the following SFM questions:

	Not Important	Somewhat Important	Very Important

1. What part did *vision* play in reaching success?

   How important was it to the successful project or venture for there to be a clear vision or purpose?

1	2	3	4	5

   What was the vision or purpose?

2. What *identity* factors were involved in the success?

   How important to the success of the project or venture was having and communicating a clear sense of brand or identity?

1	2	3	4	5

   How would you describe your identity and distinguishing characteristics? What would be a good symbol or metaphor for your identity and unique qualities?

3. What *values and beliefs* supported achieving the success?

   a. How important to the success of the project or venture was having and communicating core values?

1	2	3	4	5

   What were those values?

	Not Important		Somewhat Important		Very Important

b. How important to the success of the project or venture was it for people to believe in what they were doing?

| 1 | 2 | 3 | 4 | 5 |

What beliefs supported or motivated people to follow through and succeed?

4. What competencies and *capabilities* contributed to the success of the project or venture?

| 1 | 2 | 3 | 4 | 5 |

How important to the success of the project or venture was having particular skills and capabilities?

Which skills and capabilities were most significant?

5. What specific *behavioral* steps and actions were most responsible for the success?

| 1 | 2 | 3 | 4 | 5 |

How important to the success of the project or venture was having a specific behavioral plan?

Which actions were most important? Where was it important to be flexible in the action plan?

6. What *environmental* opportunities and influences were part of the success?

| 1 | 2 | 3 | 4 | 5 |

How important to the success of the project or venture was reacting to the environment (opportunities and constraints)?

Which environmental factors were most significant?

7. Reflect upon what you learned from going over these questions.
Were some levels of factors more critical for success at different stages of the project or venture?
Were there any combinations of factors that seemed particularly important at certain times?
How would you summarize what you have learned?
How can you use what you've learned in order to be more likely to succeed in future projects and initiatives?

The Allegory of the Six Stone-Workers

A good illustration of the influence of these levels on motivation and performance is the allegory of the six stone-workers. The allegory focuses on six individuals whose work ranges from poor to excellent as does their level of satisfaction. As they work, the lowest performing and least satisfied worker is asked, "What are you doing?"

Looking at the clock, he grumbles, "I am waiting for my time here to be through so I can go home and do something I care about."

The next stone-worker, who performs a little better and is not so completely bored, is asked, "What are you doing?" He looks up from his task. "What does it look like I'm doing. I am hitting a rock," he answers, slightly annoyed.

The next stone-worker, who does average work and is somewhat more engaged in what he is dong, is asked, "What are you doing?" "I am using my skills to craft this block of stone," is his matter-of-fact reply.

The fourth stone-worker, who is quite motivated and doing decent work, is asked, "What are you doing?" He responds with determination, "I am earning a living to support my family and put my children through school. That's what I am doing."

The fifth stone-worker, who is not only doing excellent work but also looking over the others to be sure that their work is adequate, is asked, "What are you doing?" "I am a master stone mason and I am building a cathedral," he responds with enthusiasm.

The sixth and most accomplished stone-worker is completely involved and present in each movement he makes. He constantly surveys the work of the others and does his best to keep them focused and interested as well. When asked, "What are you doing?" he says with deep reverence, "I am creating a sacred space to help people to connect with their souls."

These responses reflect the six levels of factors we have been exploring in this book.

- The first response, "waiting for my time here to be through so I can go home," is about the *environment* (the where and when).
- The second response, "hitting a rock" is about the specific *behavior* (what).
- The third answer, "using my skills to craft a block," is about *capability* (how).
- The fourth reply, "earning a living for my family," is about *values* (why).
- The fifth response, "a master stone mason building a cathedral," is about *identity* (the who).
- The sixth answer, "creating a sacred space to help people to connect with their souls," is about the deeper *purpose and vision* (for whom and for what).

Each level brings greater meaning, motivation and presence into the same activity. Clearly, the deepest levels have the greatest influence on motivation, performance and ultimately the sense of success. In the coming chapters we will continue to explore and examine how to identify and put into place critical success factors at each of these levels, beginning with the most profound and influential: purpose and identity.

Holons and Holarchies

Our reflections on the various levels of success factors and the allegory of the six stone workers highlight an intriguing fact of our existence. On the one hand we are whole and independent beings. On the other hand, we are also part of systems that are bigger than us. Arthur Koestler used the term *holarchy* to describe the dynamics of this relationship. In *The Act of Creation* (1964, p. 287) Koestler explained:

> *A living organism or social body is not an aggregation of elementary particles or elementary processes; it is an integrated hierarchy of semiautonomous sub-wholes, consisting of sub-sub-wholes, and so on. Thus the functional units on every level of the hierarchy are double-faced as it were: they act as whole when facing downwards, as parts when facing upwards.*

So something that integrates parts on the level below into a larger whole becomes a part itself for the level above it. Water, for instance, is a unique entity that emerges from the integration of hydrogen and oxygen. Water itself, however, can become a part of many other larger entities from orange juice to oceans to the human body. Thus, water is both a whole and a part of other larger wholes.

In *A Brief History of Everything* (1996) transformational teacher and author Ken Wilber described this relationship in the following way:

> *Arthur Koestler coined the term "holon" to refer to an entity that is itself a whole and simultaneously a part of some other whole. And if you start to look closely at the things and processes that actually exist, it soon becomes obvious that they are not merely wholes, they are also parts of something else. They are whole/parts, they are holons.*

> *For instance, a whole atom is part of a whole molecule, and the whole molecule is part of the whole cell, and the whole cell is part of a whole organism, and so on. Each of these entities is neither a whole nor a part, but a whole/part, a holon.*

Each person is a whole, made up of wholes (cells, organs, psychological states, etc.) and part of a greater whole (e.g. family, group, community, etc.).

According to Wilber, each new whole *includes* yet transcends the parts on the level below it. It is important to point out that, in a holarchy, if a lower level of such a system is not present the levels above it will not be able to be fully expressed. The lower levels are the necessary components of all higher levels.

Each of us, then, is a holon. We are made up of whole atoms, which make up whole molecules, that combine to create whole cells, which join together to make whole organs and a whole interconnected nervous system from which our whole body is formed. We in turn are part of progressively larger wholes: a family, a professional community, the whole system of living creatures on this planet and ultimately the whole universe.

Ego and Soul

Viewed from this perspective, we can say that our lives and motivations are primarily driven by these two complementary aspects of our identities: those emerging from our existence as a separate, independent whole and those arising from our existence as a part of a larger whole (e.g., family, profession, community, etc.). The part of our existence that we experience as an individual *whole* we typically call our *ego*. The part of our existence that we experience as a *holon* (part of a larger whole) can be referred to as our *soul*.

If we revisit the previous allegory of the six stone-workers, it also becomes clear that the first three responses to the question "What are you doing?" – "I am waiting for my time here to be through so I can go home," "I am hitting a rock" and "I an using my skills to craft a block" – all come from the perspective of the *ego* (a separate individual).

The second three responses – "I am earning a living for my family," "I am a master stone mason building a cathedral," and "I am creating a sacred space to help people to connect with their souls" – come from the *soul* (i.e., the perspective of being part of something bigger than oneself). There is a movement toward a successively larger scope of contribution.

According to psychoanalysis, the *ego* is "the part of the psyche that mediates between the conscious and the unconscious and is responsible for reality testing and a sense of personal identity." Thus, the ego has to do with the development and preservation of our sense of a separate self, perceiving reality from our own independent and individualistic perspective.

At the level of environment, the ego tends to operate from the so-called "pleasure principle"; pursuing those things that bring personal gain and satisfaction and avoiding experiences that bring pain or discomfort. Consequently, at the level of behavior, the ego tends to be more reactive to external conditions and can be particularly attuned to shorter-term opportunities as well as dangers and constraints. The capabilities associated with the ego are generally those connected with the conscious cognitive intellect such as analysis and strategy. At the level of beliefs and values (*why*) the ego focuses on safety, security, approval, control, achievement and self-benefit. A sense of permission is typically needed in order to engage fully in some activity. This relates to the sense that one "should," "shouldn't," "needs to" or "must not" do something. At the identity level (*who*), our ego relates to our social roles and who we feel we should be or need to be to get approval or acknowledgement. At the level of purpose (*for whom and for what*), the ego is oriented toward survival, recognition and personal ambition.

"I AM CREATING A SACRED SPACE TO HELP PEOPLE TO CONNECT WITH THEIR SOULS."

"I AM A MASTER STONE MASON AND I AM BUILDING A CATHEDRAL."

"I AM EARNING A LIVING TO SUPPORT MY FAMILY".

I AM USING MY SKILLS TO CRAFT THIS BLOCK OF STONE.

"I AM HITTING A ROCK!"

"I AM WAITING FOR MY TIME HERE TO BE THROUGH"

EGO
Separate
Whole

SOUL
Integrated
Holon

Oriented toward survival, recognition and personal **ambition**.

PURPOSE
For Whom?
For What?

*Oriented toward our **vision** of what we want to create in the world through us but that is beyond us.*

Relates to social **roles** and who we feel we should be or need to be to get approval or acknowledgement.

IDENTITY
Who?

*Relates to our **mission** and the unique gifts that we bring into the world.*

Focused on **permission**, safety, security, approval, control, achievement and self-benefit.

VALUES & BELIEFS
Why?

*Focused on **motivations** such as service, contribution, connection, being, expansion and awakening.*

Application of **analysis** and **strategy**.

CAPABILITIES
How?

*Expression of **energy** and **emotional intelligence***

Respond **reactively** to external conditions.

BEHAVIOR
What?

*Respond **proactively** toward desired goals*

Sort for **dangers** and **constraints**

ENVIRONMENT
Where? When?

*Sort for **opportunities** for expression and contribution*

From the NLP perspective, the ego can be considered a cognitively constructed map or model of one's "self" as a separate entity and a natural developmental process. These notions of "reality" and "self" associated with the ego, however, are influenced by external factors such as social norms, cultural values and family patterns. Like all maps or models, our self-concept is necessarily incomplete. It can never be 100% accurate. If distortions in our sense of ourselves create too much disconnection and separation from who we really are and potentially could become, they can create symptoms. Some characteristics of an unhealthy ego take the form of either *self-inflation*—pride, arrogance, self-importance, narcissism and self-infatuation—or *self-depreciation*—self-judgment, depression, self-criticism, lack of self-worth and self-confidence, etc. These can lead us to become overly gripped by greed, fear and survival strategies (fight, flight, freeze).

Our "ego" is our sense of being a separate self, individual identity and separate whole.

Our "soul" emerges from our experience of being part of someting bigger than ourselves as an integrated holon.

"Soul" is a term used to refer to the deepest part of a person's nature and is expressed as a special quality of "emotional or intellectual energy or intensity." Our *soul* is the unique life force, essence or energy that we come into the world with and that comes into the world through us. As a newborn baby, for instance, we do not yet have an ego, but we have a unique energy and being that is the foundation for our identity. This energy is expressed through our bodies and our interface with the larger systems surrounding us. Because our soul is an energetic "deep structure," it is not associated with any particular content—and therefore is not constructed from influences such as society, culture and family. It does, however, express itself in the form of contribution to these as larger systems. Thus, rather than being an objectified or separate self, the soul is our expression of an unfolding, connected being.

At the level of environment, our soul tends to focus on opportunities for expression and contribution. As a result, at the level of behavior the soul tends to respond more proactively to external conditions. The capabilities associated with the soul are generally those related to the perception and expression of energy and emotional intelligence. At the level of beliefs and values, the soul focuses on internal motivations such as service, contribution, connection, being, expansion and awakening. At the identity level, soul relates to our mission and the unique gifts that we bring into the world. At the level of spirit or purpose, the soul is oriented toward our vision of what we want to create in the world through us but that is beyond us.

In the words of modern dance pioneer Martha Graham:

Martha Graham

There is a vitality, a life force, a quickening [energy] that is translated through you into action, and because there is only one of you in all time, this expression is unique. If you block it, it will never exist through any other medium and be lost. The world will not have it. It is not yours to determine how good it is; nor how it compares with other expressions. It is your business to keep the channel open.

From this perspective, we can say that the ego creates the "channel" through which the "vitality" and "life force" of the soul is expressed into the world. When the ego is healthy aligned with our soul, the channel is open. When the ego is inflated, deflated, rigid or gripped by survival strategies, the channel is constricted or closed.

Vision, Mission, Ambition and Role

Clearly, both of these aspects of ourselves, ego and soul, are necessary for a healthy and successful existence. The primary questions relating to our *ego* are about what we want to achieve for ourselves in terms our *ambition* and *role*: "What type of life do I want to create for myself?" and "What type of person do I need to be in order to create the life I want?" These are about living out our dreams for ourselves. The primary questions with respect to the *soul* are those related to our *vision* and *mission* for the larger systems of which we are a part: "What do I want to create in the world through me that is beyond me?" and "What is my unique contribution to bringing that vision into expression?"

We can add these distinctions of *ego* (one's self as an independent whole) and *soul* (ourselves as holons that are a part of a bigger system) to our earlier representation of the various levels of success factors as shown in the following diagram.

The complementary dimensions of ego and soul tend to bring out a different emphasis for each level. The ego side accentuates ambition, role, the importance of permission, strategy and appropriate reactions to constraints and potential dangers in the environment. The soul side puts priority on vision, mission, inner motivation and activating the energy and emotional intelligence needed to proactively take advantage of environmental opportunities.

Clearly our periods of highest performance occur when the levels of success factors related to both ego and soul are balanced, aligned and integrated.

Our highest level of performance and greatest satisfaction come when we balance and align the motivations of our ego and our soul; embracing the dual realities that we are simultaneously separate wholes and integrated holons.

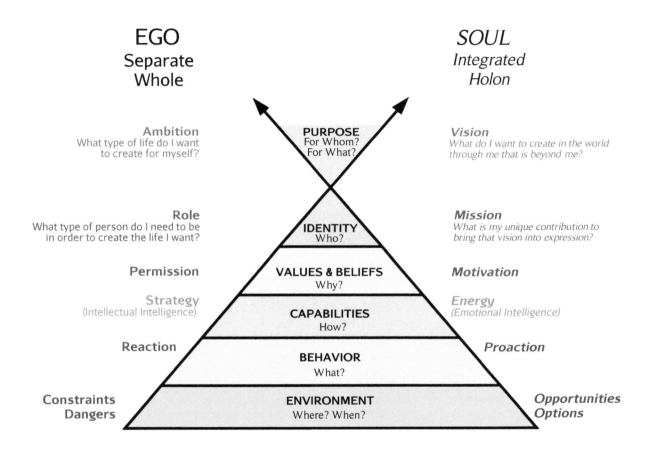

EGO
Separate
Whole

SOUL
Integrated
Holon

Ambition
What type of life do I want
to create for myself?

PURPOSE
For Whom?
For What?

Vision
What do I want to create in the world
through me that is beyond me?

Role
What type of person do I need to be
in order to create the life I want?

IDENTITY
Who?

Mission
What is my unique contribution to
bring that vision into expression?

Permission

VALUES & BELIEFS
Why?

Motivation

Strategy
(Intellectual Intelligence).

CAPABILITIES
How?

Energy
(Emotional Intelligence)

Reaction

BEHAVIOR
What?

Proaction

Constraints
Dangers

ENVIRONMENT
Where? When?

*Opportunities
Options*

The Example of the "Miracle on the Hudson"

Consider the case of the so-called "miracle on the Hudson." On January 15, 2009, US Airways flight 1549 was forced to land in the Hudson river in New York City after running into a flock of geese and losing all the power in both engines. Due to the capability of the captain and crew to stay calm and focused, all 155 occupants made it safely off of the airliner and were rescued by nearby watercraft, making it the most successful emergency landing in aviation history.

Maintaining his composure and remaining calm in an unexpected and extremely challenging situation, Captain Chesley Sullenberger was able to glide the Airbus 320 to an unprecedented emergency water landing. There were only three minutes between the time the birds hit the engines and the plane touched down on the water. Having twice walked the length of the cabin to confirm that no one remained inside after the plane had been evacuated, the captain was the last person to leave the aircraft.

Widely praised for his poise and calm demeanor during the crisis, Sullenberger was asked how he felt during the ordeal. The captain reported, "Calm on the outside, turmoil inside." Sullenberger claimed that he never felt more nervous in his life, but that he had simultaneously never been more calm in his life.

When asked how he had managed to stay calm in spite of having never felt more nervous in his life, the captain gave several answers that point to significant success factors for both leaders and entrepreneurs. The first was preparation and practice. As Sullenberger put it, "One way of looking at this might be that for 42 years, I've been making small, regular deposits in this bank of experience, education and training. And on January 15 the balance was sufficient so that I could make a very large withdrawal."

The second answer was that he connected to a mission beyond himself. He pointed out that he was "the captain" and it was his mission to "land the aircraft" and "look after the safety of the crew and passengers." Sullenberger's actions demonstrate an important distinction between role and mission. Role is about one's status and capabilities. Mission is about service to something beyond yourself. In contrast to Sullenberger's miracle landing, for instance, consider the disaster of the Italian cruise ship *Costa Concordia* in January 2012. In the disaster, the captain of the ship, after causing the wreck by steering too close to the shore, abandoned the craft while there were still as many as 300 passengers on board. He only returned when ordered by the Coast Guard.

Chesley Sullenberger
Pilot of US Airways Flight 1549
"The Miracle on the Hudson"

"Miracle on the Hudson" pilot Sullenberger was able to maintain a remarkable degree of composure by connecting to a sense of mission beyond his individual identity. This state allowed him to creatively apply his skill and knowledge as a pilot and inspire others to remain calm and resourceful.

In Sullenberger's words, *mission* is about "service above self." This implies a linking to a "larger Self" beyond his own individual ego.

Sullenberger's third answer was that he was able to stay so calm was because his crew remained so cool and composed and the passengers remained calm. Interestingly, the crew claimed they were able to remain calm because the captain was so confident and in control and that the passengers were calm and cooperative. Similarly, the passengers reported that the demeanor of the pilot and crew prompted them to remain calm. This is what we would call a resourceful or generative "field" of support in SFM. The focal point, however, remains upon the leader.

Intriguingly, a final success factor influencing Sullenberger related to a personal tragedy; his father's suicide some years before. "I was angry, hurt and devastated," he said about his father's death. "It was very difficult. But, it gave me a better sense of the fleeting nature of life and led me to want to preserve life at all costs." "That was with me that day," Sullenberger reported. "Because I couldn't save my father, I did everything I could to save everyone on that flight. . . I'm willing to work very hard to protect people's lives, to be a good Samaritan, and to not be a bystander, in part, because I couldn't save my father."

Again, Sullenberger's comments point to a connection to larger purpose for a bigger system. This allowed him to transform his anger, hurt and devastation relating to a personal tragedy into a mission of service for something bigger than himself.

Sullenberger applied the same view about turning difficulties into opportunities to the situation surrounding the Miracle on the Hudson itself. "While the event was certainly traumatic for those of us involved, it ultimately was the source for a lot of wonderful opportunities," he said. "It turned out, for many of us, our lives were preparation for this event and its aftermath without us really knowing about it."

While entrepreneurs and business leaders don't usually face situations as overtly dramatic as Captain Sullenberger did, there will be times when the "engines" of their venture lose power (financial or otherwise) and they need to keep their crew (team) and passengers (customers) calm and cooperative. As we will see, the four factors cited by Sullenberger also play a significant role in the success of entrepreneurial ventures:

1. Preparation and practice
2. A sense of mission that connects one to a larger Self beyond the individual ego
3. The creation and nurturing of a resourceful and generative "field" of support
4. A sense of a greater purpose, often as a compensation for personal trauma or tragedy

Aligning Ego and Soul

Sullenberger's remarkable feat was dependent on the alignment and integration of both his ego and his soul. When our ego and soul are out of alignment and our ambition is at odds with our mission and vision, it produces conflict and struggle. Charisma, passion and presence emerge naturally when these two forces (ego and soul; mission and ambition) are aligned. Optimum performance comes when the ego is in service of the soul. When we "sell our soul" for ego benefits, we may have short-term success but are heading for a crisis in the long run. The most powerful motivations are those that combine and align our vision, mission, ambition and role.

As an illustration, I was recently coaching a young man who was outwardly very successful. Before reaching the age of 40, he had already achieved the level of General Manager of a major division within his organization. With $2 billion in revenue and more than 9,000 employees worldwide, the company was doing very well and had even been growing and prospering during a time of global financial crisis. He pointed out that he had a secure position, was well paid and had exceptional financial stability. There was no higher position for him to go within the division.

The challenge he faced, however, was that he felt that something was deeply missing in his life. As he put it, "I am not going to work with a sparkle in my eye anymore." He realized that he could have potentially twenty more years in that position and couldn't imagine going the rest of his career without that "sparkle."

As we explored the situation, it became clear that he had been very driven by what he believed to be his duty and responsibility to achieve and to provide for his family. He had an image of an "ideal" self as a successful businessman that would fulfill the expectations of his family and the culture in which he grew up.

When I asked what would bring the sparkle back, he revealed that he had a "crazy" dream to quit his job, give up his possessions and go and help alleviate suffering for people who were unable to help themselves. The problem, of course, was the potentially disastrous consequences that would have on his career and his wife and three children. So he immediately rejected it as ridiculous.

I told him that, rather than discount this dream, he might realize that contained within it were the seeds of a very important sense of vision and mission and the key to getting his sparkle back. Rather than needing to choose between being the duty driven, high-powered general manager or the penniless saintly server who wanted to help people in need, he could hold both of these seeming polarities as what could be called "generative

When we become disconnected from the life force and vitality that comes from our soul and sense of purpose, there is no longer a "sparkle in our eyes."

complementarities" and find an expression that could satisfy both his ambition and his sense of vision and mission. It was not a matter of "either or." There were probably many variations in between the two extremes that could potentially integrate key aspects of both.

I invited him to take some time and start exploring and noting what things, no matter how large or how small, brought a "sparkle" to his eye. I encouraged him to start establishing practices for himself that had nothing directly to do with his family or his profession. The purpose was to bring more of a sense of inspiration as well as aspiration into his life and practice living more from his soul.

I also had him write a resume for himself focusing as much or more on what mattered to him personally (his soul) as on his professional experience. Interestingly, as he wrote about himself, his deep intuitive sense of balance between his ego and soul began to become more and more clear as is illustrated in the following excerpt from his resume.

> I am results driven with high energy and positive forward thinking. I possess the ability to make complex decisions by using my brain, heart and guts.
>
> I genuinely believe that successful leadership must be built on strong values, vision, authenticity, integrity and ability to care for others. My leadership is also about inspiring and empowering people to create value to the company beyond just doing their jobs.

As a result of these practices and exercises, he began to discover a renewed sense of himself; and his company began to appreciate his contributions even more. As this happened, many interesting and unexpected coincidences and synchronicities began to emerge in his life, including offers from other companies. Instead of jumping at the first opportunities, however, he took his time to deeply consider what really matched all of his needs and values, including his responsibility to his original company.

As he became clearer, more integrated and more aligned within himself, his feeling of dissatisfaction diminished. He began to realize that his degree of happiness and satisfaction was not so much determined by his external surroundings, but rather by how he was able to creatively respond to those circumstances as a whole person and as a "holon." He became aware that there were many opportunities for him to live his dreams and make a better world, and he became committed to take advantage of those opportunities where he found them.

Ultimately, he ended up getting the sparkle back in his eye and staying with his current company. His reinvigorated commitment and energy led a short time later to his being selected as president of the most important sector within the organization, where he continues to flourish.

When we reconnect to our soul and experience ourselves as an integrated holon, we become aware of opportunities and resources (on multiple levels) that are available in the bigger systems of which we are a part.

Exercise: The COACH State
Integrating Ego and Soul into a "Holon"

A common thread between the success of Captain Chesley Sullenberger and my client in the previous example is the ability to reconnect and stay connected to the experience of being a "holon"; of being both a whole and connected to something beyond ourselves that gives us purpose and energy. Achieving this, of course, is not always very easy, especially in challenging situations. Sullenberger talked about the importance of lots of practice and experience.

One of the exercises I do regularly myself, and that I assign to my coaching clients like the young man in the previous story, is to practice aligning my personal experience of being both a whole and a holon. It is something I recommend as a daily exercise for every individual and group that I work with. It is a simple but powerful process that you can do in a matter of a few minutes or even seconds. The basic steps can be summarized by the acronym COACH:

Center yourself, especially in the "gut" (your belly center)

Open your field of awareness

Attend to what is going on within you and around you with mindfulness

Connect to yourself and to the larger system(s) of which you are a part

Hold whatever is happening from a state of resourcefulness and curiosity

One procedure to accomplish this begins by sitting or standing in a comfortable position with both feet flat on the floor and your spine erect but relaxed (i.e., "in your vertical axis").

1. Bring your attention to your belly center (just below the naval and in the physical center of your body) and breathe into it.
2. Breathe into your chest and open your attention to include your whole body and your surroundings.
3. Become aware of the three-dimensional volume of your body; then continue to expand your awareness to include the space below your feet, above your head, behind you, in front of you, to your left and to your right.
4. Experience a sense of connection inwardly (being sure to include your head, heart, belly and feet) and outwardly (to the Earth through your feet, to the cosmos through the top of your head, and to the environment around you) so that you feel both being whole and part of something larger than you.
5. Imagine projecting a sense of calm, confidence and curiosity into the space (holding environment) you sense around you.

When we are in the COACH state, our "channel is open."

In a COACH state you are centered, open, aware, connected and holding your context with curiosity.

There are, of course, many other ways to achieve the equivalent of the COACH state. Meditation and other mindfulness practices can lead to similar experiences of being simultaneously an independent whole and a holon. The best approach is to find what works for you and practice it regularly. As the example of Captain Sullenberger illustrates, in the complex, challenging, unpredictable and changing circumstances around us, we need to constantly be prepared to be the best of ourselves if we are to succeed.

In summary, in order to progress through change, it is important to cultivate qualities such as flexibility and stability, balance and the ability to let go. This comes from being centered and in ourselves and connected with something beyond the confines of our egos. As the example of Sullenberger and the miracle on the Hudson illustrates, the most important thing to remember when you are in an unexpected crisis (i.e., birds have shut down both engines) is, paradoxically, to relax.

The opposite of this occurs when we can collapse into an inner stuck state that can be summarized by the letters CRASH:

Contraction
Reactivity
Analysis Paralysis
Separation
Hurting or Hating

When we "CRASH," we no longer perceive ourselves as a holon. We lose our connection to our soul, and everything becomes more difficult. When we confront an outer obstacle from the CRASH state, we experience it as an impossible problem. If Sullenberger had tensed up, panicked and "CRASHed," it is very likely that the aircraft he was flying would have literally crashed as well, and instead of a miracle the situation would have become a disaster.

When we CRASH our "channel is closed."

In a CRASH state you are contracted, reacting to the environment, analysing, separated and feeling hurt or hate.

Ego, Soul and Organizations

The dynamic between ego and soul (whole and holon) operates in a similar way in a company or organization. The ego of the company is made up of the owners and shareholders, whose concern is with the survival, financial profitability ("bottom line") and return on investment. This is reflected by the ambition of the organization and its members in terms of status and level of performance.

The dynamic between "ego" and "soul" also takes place within organizations. A company is a separate entity or whole, made up of wholes (divisions, teams people, etc.) and part of successively larger wholes (community, market, environment, etc.).

The soul of the organization is the value it provides for customers and the larger social and physical environment. This is created by the vision of the organization and the unique contribution and mission of the organization and its members with respect to the larger systems which it serves.

Team members and employees clearly operate in the middle of these two dimensions and need to find the proper balance between the two in order to effectively do their jobs and serve their purpose.

When an organization leans more to the "ego" side, emphasis is more on management and efficiency. Environmental constraints and dangers take priority and the company starts to focus on reacting properly, analyzing situations correctly and following the proper plans and strategies. Permission and appropriate approval are required before any action can be taken and team members must stick to their prescribed roles.

When an organization is more "soul" leaning, emphasis goes more toward leadership and entrepreneurial activities. The environmental focus is more on opportunities and proactive, enterprising risk-taking is encouraged. Energy and emotional intelligence are as much a part of guiding decision-making process as strategy. Values related to a customer-focused vision and mission determine the priorities, which create the inspiration and motivation for action.

To thrive, ventures must balance self-protection, self-benefit and growth with contribution to their customers and larger eco-system.

In both individuals and organizations it is important to keep a balance between the two. The bigger your vision, the more ambition you need in order to reach it. Similarly, the bigger your ambition, the more important it is for your vision to expand. Soul without ego can lead to impotence and "burnout." Ego without soul creates "blind ambition." In fact, it could be said that the global economic crisis that spread through the world in the period following 2008 was partially created because of too much "ego" and not enough "soul" in many financial institutions and organizations. An imbalance in either direction can have serious consequences.

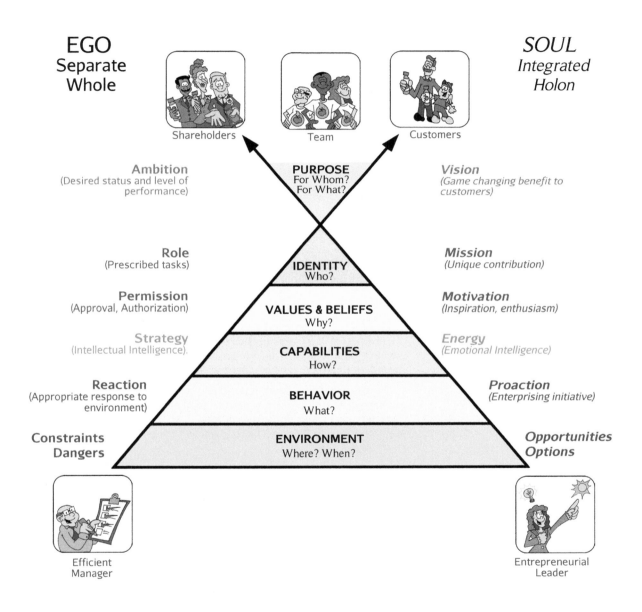

EGO
Separate
Whole

SOUL
Integrated
Holon

Shareholders — Team — Customers

Ambition
(Desired status and level of performance)

PURPOSE
For Whom?
For What?

Vision
(Game changing benefit to customers)

Role
(Prescribed tasks)

IDENTITY
Who?

Mission
(Unique contribution)

Permission
(Approval, Authorization)

VALUES & BELIEFS
Why?

Motivation
(Inspiration, enthusiasm)

Strategy
(Intellectual Intelligence).

CAPABILITIES
How?

Energy
(Emotional Intelligence)

Reaction
(Appropriate response to environment)

BEHAVIOR
What?

Proaction
(Enterprising initiative)

Constraints
Dangers

ENVIRONMENT
Where? When?

Opportunities
Options

Efficient
Manager

Entrepreneurial
Leader

Individuals, roles, teams, divisions and even an entire organizational culture can be more "ego" oriented (security, profit, ambition, etc.) or more "soul" oriented (contribution, service, vision, etc.). This affects what priorities are established and how and which decisions are made.

Consider the example of one of my recent company clients. An internationally known brand, this company was started by a family who had a passion for winter sports. This passion led them to a vision of winter sports equipment (skis, boots, bindings, clothing, etc.) that they believed should significantly improve the quality of individual performance and experience of their customers, and at the same time feel like a natural extension of the user's body. The company gained a reputation for their innovativeness and the level of the performance, style and ease of use of their products. The passion for the products was also shared by the company's employees who were all winter sports fanatics. This led the company to maintain many years as a market leader.

At a certain point, the founders, who were getting older, wanted to step back from being so involved in running the company. They also realized that, in order to grow the company to the next level, they needed to bring in more resources in the form of investment. Through a series of events, the company ended up being acquired by a large venture capital firm.

In a move to protect their investment, the venture capital firm replaced key top management positions and members of the board of directors with their own people. These new individuals had little interest in winter sports. They had no time for winter sports. They were interested in money not winter sports, and their priority was ensuring the financial performance of the company rather than the innovativeness, style and performance of the products.

The culture of the organization began to change. In earlier times, it was no problem if a team took several years to develop a product. Suddenly, if a product was not producing revenue within six to nine months it was shelved.

In the past, it had been a company policy that it was "the right and the duty of all employees to find interesting new market opportunities and share them with the right decision makers inside the company." After the acquisition, this was no longer so. Employees had to get permission to spend time on something other than what was in their job description.

The employees began to wonder what company they were working for. Motivation, productivity and innovation began to wane. The company was losing its "soul" and that was creating confusion and dissention among the employees and affecting the popularity of the company's products with its customers.

I was brought in to do some visioning work with one of the divisions of the company, but realized right away that the issue was with the bigger vision and mission of the organization. When I asked the members of the board of directors what their vision was, they responded, "We want to build the biggest sports equipment empire in the world." I pointed out that that was a great ambition and asked again about their vision. Again, they answered that they wanted to be the biggest sports equipment conglomerate in the world.

Like many people in top management that I have met, they did not understand the difference between vision, mission and ambition. For them, these were all the same thing. They were just abstract concepts that didn't really matter that much.

It took a while, but I was finally able to get them to understand and realize the importance of knowing and communicating the actual vision and mission of the company – what they wanted to create more of in the world and for their customers and what their unique contribution was to that – and make that the focus of their culture.

As a result, the company was able to "recover its soul," make a turn around and regain their former standing as an innovative leader in their industry.

Another company client I worked with had the opposite problem. They were a "clean energy" company who called themselves a "micro multinational" because, even though they only had about 200 actual employees, they had projects all over the world. They were able to accomplish this largely by partnering with governments and other organizations in order to put their projects into action. Their vision and mission was absolutely clear. They wanted to see a world in which people used "green," sustainable energy. And their mission was to "convert waste into energy through innovative technologies."

Their problem was getting the resources that they needed in order to expand their operations in a way that would allow them to move to the next level in bringing their vision and mission more fully into the world. They always seemed to be struggling to get by and were frustrated in their ability to grow beyond being a relatively small organization.

What they needed in order to get their vision out to the world was to get substantial investment in addition to their partnering efforts. However, they were having big difficulties raising the funds and maintaining good relationships with potential investors. They couldn't understand why investors didn't naturally want to support their vision. I pointed out to them that, even though potential investors might appreciate their vision and mission, that was not their main concern. Investors would want to know about their ambitions.

Ventures, new and old, must constantly strive to maintain the balance between "ego" and "soul." As a company's vision expands, its ambition must also get bigger. As a company increases its ambition, its vision must extend and broaden as well.

When I asked about their ambition, their first response was "to save the planet." I pointed out that this was actually an extension of their vision and mission. Investors wanted to know how the company would create value for them in return for their investment. This had to do with their aspirations as a company. "Are you happy to stay a 'micro' organization?" "Do you want to be a 100 million dollar company, a half a billion dollar company, a billion dollar company?" "Are you striving to be the first? The best? The biggest?" This is what investors wanted to know.

My point was that, if you have a big vision, your ambition needs to be equally large in order to attract the support necessary to implement it. If the company's top management was not striving to have the organization become a recognized world player, the company (no matter how important or relevant their vision was) would likely remain "small potatoes." They needed to think as "big" about their company as they did about their vision and technology.

Of course, part of this meant some soul searching and confidence building in their belief about themselves and what they were doing. Clarifying their ambition meant taking a bigger risk. Taking a bigger risk, in turn, meant a greater conviction in their vision and mission.

As a result of these deliberations, they made the decision to broaden the company's focus from essentially assisting its partners in developing clean energy project solutions to also becoming an owner and operator of projects in its own right. They even altered their name to reflect this shift in ambition and identity. This decision ended up opening the door to millions of dollars more in investments, and the company still continues to grow today.

Bigger visions and ambitions lead to greater risks and demand more effort. Success in achieving them both requres strong belief in oneself, one's team and one's purpose.

Defining Vision, Mission, Ambition and Role

The most powerful motivations are those that combine and align our vision, mission, ambition and role. This is a core theme that has arisen from our Success Factor Modeling work. We will be revisiting and refining this principle throughout this book. To begin, let's take a closer look at each of these key success factors.

Vision

For our purposes *vision* can best be defined as *"a mental image of what the future will or could be like."* Our capacity for vision involves "the ability to think about or plan the future with imagination or wisdom." The creative vision of successful entrepreneurs has to do with this ability to imagine and focus on longer-term possibilities. It involves the ability to see beyond the confines of the "here and now" and imagine future scenarios. It also involves the capacity to set and stay focused on longer-term goals, adopting long-term plans and a holistic view. As the great psychologist William James pointed out, "In all ages the person whose determinations are swayed by reference to the most distant ends has been held to possess the highest intelligence."

A key characteristic of the vision of successful next generation entrepreneurs and leaders is that it is always directed outward beyond themselves (i.e., it is a product of their "soul"). That is, it is about what they want to see more of or different in the world – it is about "creating a world to which people want to belong." This world (hopefully) includes oneself but is not inherently about oneself. Thus, entrepreneurial vision involves the answers to the questions:

- *What do you want to create in the world through you that is beyond you?*
- *What do you want to see more of and less of in the world?*
- *What is the world to which you want to belong?*

A good example of this is the vision of highly successful entrepreneur Elon Musk, who is clear about his determination to transform the way people live today. Musk founded his first company (*Zip2* – a website that provided online content publishing software for various news organizations) at the age of 23 and sold it for $300 million. His next venture was the online payment platform *PayPal* which allows users to safely buy and sell online. Since then, Musk has continued to expand his vision to include affordable solar energy for the public through his company *SolarCity*, and has made the

Imagination is more important than knowledge. Knowledge is limited. Imagination encircles the world.
– Albert Einstein

Vision is "a mental image of what the future will or could be like." The visions of the most successful entrepreneurs and leaders are those of "game changing" developments that contribute to "creating a world to which people want to belong."

Elon Musk
Founder of PayPal, SolarCity, Tesla Motors and SpaceX

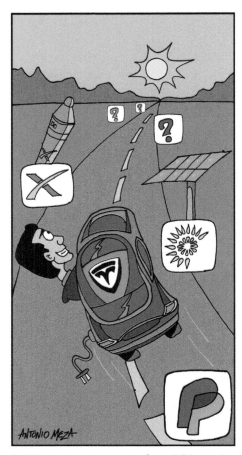

A vision creates at type of vanishing point towards which all of the efforts of an entrepreneur are focused. For Elon Musk, it is about creating companies that help to "increase the scope and scale of human consciousness".

dream of an electric car possible and inexpensive with *Tesla Motors*. Beyond that, his *SpaceX* space travel company created the first privately funded liquid-fuelled vehicle to put a satellite into Earth orbit and became the first commercial company to launch and dock a vehicle to the International Space Station.

Musk overtly and intentionally focuses his vision on things that he believes will most positively affect the future of humanity: The internet; clean energy; and space exploration. Interestingly, his passion for these areas emerged as a result of an existential crisis he experienced as a teenager. Reading philosophers like Hegel, Schopenhauer and Nietzsche during his mid-teens led him to do some intense soul searching. He reports that he became deeply depressed by the lack of answers to the large questions of life, such as the purpose of existence. In a manner parallel to Captain Sullenberger's transformation of his devastation over his father's suicide, Musk's crisis and depression became the foundation for a profound commitment to the expansion of global consciousness. In the same way that Sullenberger transformed his grief into the awareness of the "fleeting nature of life" and the commitment to "preserve life at all costs," "be a good Samaritan" and "not be a bystander," Musk became convinced that if global consciousness can be expanded, perhaps in the future mankind would be able to ask the right questions. As he put it:

> I came to the conclusion that we should aspire to increase the scope and scale of human consciousness in order to better understand what questions to ask. Really, the only thing that makes sense is to strive for greater collective enlightenment.

Musk considers the internet, renewable energy and space exploration as the methods which have the potential to make the most impact in this regard. To him, the internet can serve as a global nervous system, renewable energy can expand the timeframe within which mankind can try to ask the right questions before running into economical or ecological collapse, and space exploration can serve as a backup for life itself. Musk also considers becoming a spacefaring civilization as an important step in evolution itself, akin to life first crawling onto land.

It is clear that Musk's vision for his ventures come more from the perspective of being a holon (a part of something bigger than himself) than from the perspective of an isolated ego. His vision emerges from a deep passion, intention and commitment to change things for the better. Vision of this type is inherently *generative*. This means that it continues to create specific new future scenarios as the territory in which we are operating changes and evolves. It is not fixed upon the details or contents of any particular context or circumstances.

This type of vision does not focus on any one specific destination. Rather, its purpose is to provide a direction from which any number of new specific ventures and products may emerge. Musk's passion and intention to "increase the scope and scale of human consciousness" and "strive for greater collective enlightenment" have continued to spawn a series of successive ventures, and new ones will most likely continue to emerge and evolve as the world continues to change.

We can make an analogy to taking a journey. As we look far ahead in the direction that we are heading, it is difficult to see the details of our destination. In fact, sometimes the destination is beyond the horizon and not visible to our eyes at all and we follow more of a felt sense, like an inner compass.

Even though our direction is clear, we cannot always see the details of the ultimate destination that is beyond the vanishing point on the horizon. As we continue to travel, however, landmarks, milestones and other interesting sites come into view and we see them more and more clearly as we approach them. Some are expected. Others are a surprise.

Similarly, the image of a particular project or venture is the product of such a journey toward a larger generative vision. As an example, in 1941 (shortly after the release of *Fantasia*) Walt Disney was asked about his vision for the future of his company and his industry. Disney mentioned that he had several other animated films planned for the coming years, including *Pinocchio* and *Bambi*. Beyond that, however, he said it was difficult to say anything specific. As he put it, *"What I see way off is too nebulous to describe. But it looks big and glittering."*

Disney did not mention specific plans for *Disneyland*, *Mary Poppins*, *The Wonderful World of Disney* television program, the *Epcot Center*, *the Disney Channel*, etc., because he didn't know yet that he would create them. Television did not yet even exist. Plans for Disneyland were still 15 years away. But that does not mean that Disney had no direction.

The words "big and glittering" are not specifications for a particular objective. They evoke emotions and qualities more than contents. While there was no content in Disney's answer, it provided powerful guidance with respect to the direction he would take his venture. When we think of Disney productions, they are all to some degree "big and glittering."

When Disney applied his vision to live-action films or television, he began to see something more specific emerging from the "big and glittering" future. Similarly, when he applied his vision to making an amusement park or a ride at the amusement park, what emerged was "big and glittering." As the world and technology evolved, Disney's generative vision continued to create new products defined by the direction his bigger vision took him.

Your vision will become clear only when you look into your heart. Who looks outside, dreams. Who looks inside, awakens.

– Carl Jung

A "generative" vision is one that provides a clear direction rather than end at any particular destination.

Walt Disney's game changing success in a variety of different industries is a good illustration of the power of a generative vision.

Walt Disney

"What I see way off is too nebulous to describe. But it looks big and glittering".
Walt Disney

Thus, a vision is not limited to one specific goal or objective. Goals and objectives tend to be too short-term and too specific. They are the products of vision and on a different level than the deeper passion and intention that generates the vision. Vision is connected more to the "life force" and "vitality" mentioned by Martha Graham that is "translated through us into action." Vision is a generative process that is constantly renewing itself; integrating our current knowledge of what is with our imagination of what could be in order to create something new.

This brings up the importance of the "creative unconscious" in achieving success. We are not always conscious of all of the dimensions we must manage to create and manifest a successful project or venture. There are frequently a number of "weak signals" we must juggle and integrate that are not possible to keep track of or even perceive consciously. In fact, visions often begin as dreams. Dreams arise from the creative unconscious, not out of our cognitive rational mind.

When we dream, the cognitive mind is not a direct participant in generating the dream, but can afterwards become a witness.

Visions emerge as the cognitive mind (ego) joins and helps direct the dreams that arise from the creative unconscious (soul) in response to perceived opportunities or obstacles or through creative exchange with others. United by the vision, these two forces (ego and soul) ultimately produce specific projects and objectives. These projects and objective then become primarily driven by the cognitive mind in a more rational progression; with less contribution from the creative unconscious.

We will be exploring this process and the role of the creative unconscious more deeply in the coming chapters.

Mission

The mission of an individual or organization has to do with their contribution to manifesting a particular vision. In fact, *mission* is defined in the dictionary as *"an important assignment carried out for political, religious, or commercial purposes."* It is typically defined as coming from *"a strongly felt aim or calling."* The word comes from the Latin *missio*, which means "the act of sending." It is derived from the Latin *mittere*, meaning "to send," and shares a common root with the words "message" and "missile." A "missive," for example, is a communication which is to "be sent."

Like an entrepreneur's vision, then, his or her sense of mission comes from the perspective of being a "holon." A mission is always defined with respect to a system beyond the individual or group who is carrying it out. It is in service of the vision that unites those who are in that system. The mission of individual within an organization has to do with his or contribution to that organization and its vision. Similarly, an organization's mission will be with respect to the larger system of its customers and their needs.

Thus, a mission relates to the purpose that an individual or organization serves with respect to a bigger system — i.e., *for whom* and *for what* their capabilities and actions are directed. Such larger systems may include: family, colleagues, contemporaries, society and culture, the planet, universe, etc.

The notion of mission is clearly expressed in John F. Kennedy's famous statement, *"My fellow Americans, ask not what your country can do for you, ask what you can do for your country. My fellow citizens of the world, ask not what America will do for you, but what together we can do for the freedom of man."*

Mission is ultimately in the service of vision (which, in the case of Kennedy's statement, is "the freedom of man"). The long-term vision of an individual or group provides the guidance and direction for its mission in a particular area. A vision is typically very broad and involves many others outside of the individual or group who are holding the vision. Missions, however, are a function of our personal relationship to that vision. One's vision is more detached and distant than one's mission. A mission comes from one's personal involvement in pursuing a larger vision. Thus, mission has to do with the questions:

- *What is your service to the bigger system and vision?*
- *What is your unique contribution to making the vision happen?*
- *What are the special gifts, resources, capabilities and actions that you bring to the larger system in order to help reach the vision?*

Mission comes in the form of a "strongly felt aim or calling."

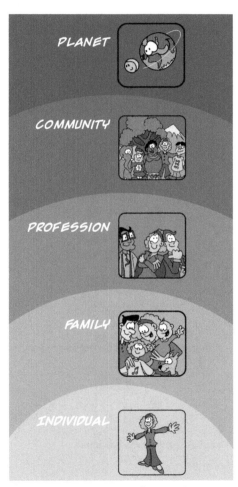

A mission relates to one's contribution to the larger systems of which he or she is a member.

A rat is on one place of the electrified grid. Food is on the other side.

The rat tries to get the food...

...but gets discouraged.

However, if baby rats are placed on the other side of the grid...

... the rat crosses despite getting an electric shock...

...and never gets discouraged.

Missions will always be stated in the form of actions such as: provide, create, support, build, develop, guide, lead, serve, defend, etc. The mission of Elon Musk's Tesla Motors is to "design and build high performing, affordable electric cars." This serves the larger vision of helping humanity to break away from its dependency on fossil fuels and create a cleaner and more sustainable environment. Musk's personal mission with respect to Tesla Motors is to "lead and oversee the product design and quality" of the cars manufactured by the company.

Our missions connect us to something bigger than ourselves, activating our core motivations and our core competences and directing them toward the vision. They are extremely motivating, providing us with the energy and courage to take risks and inciting a strong sense of desire to give and do our best. As Elon Musk commented about his work with designing the Tesla vehicles, *"You want to be extra rigorous about making the best possible thing you can, find everything that's wrong with it and fix it. Seek negative feedback, particularly from friends."*

There is an informative study that behavioral psychologists have done with rats that illustrates the power of a sense of mission and the dynamic between what we have called the "ego" and the "soul" in Success Factor Modeling. In the experiment, laboratory rats were placed on one side of an electrified grid. Various items, such as food, water, a sexual partner and other types of stimuli were placed at different times on the other side of the grid. To get to the object, the rats had to endure the pain and discomfort caused by the electrical shock of crossing the grid. The researchers noted how many times the animals would cross the painful barrier to achieve satisfaction.

Observations revealed that mother rats were consistently willing to sustain more electric shocks to get their young than for any other type of motivator provided in the study.

One mother crossed the grid a total of 58 times to get her babies (and only stopped because the experiment was terminated).

Moreover, not only did the rats retrieve their own babies, they "rescued" unrelated babies just as quickly, including baby mice, rabbits, chicks and even kittens. Surprisingly, female rats who weren't mothers often retrieved the helpless young, risking painful electric shocks to help even the young of natural enemies (kittens).

These experiments illustrate the relationship between our two realities as living beings – one as a separate whole (ego) and one as a holon that serves something larger than ourselves (soul). In these examples, items that appeal to the ego and provide self-benefit and personal gratification such as food, water, sexual partners, etc., are motivations for the rat that will get it to take a certain level of risk and endure a certain level of pain. When the level of electricity was turned up high enough, however, rats would not cross the grid even for food. Yet, at the same level of electrical shock, they would cross to get their babies.

Clearly, the deepest motivation for the rat is to protect and care for its young (and even the young of other species); something to which it devotes itself that is beyond itself. This is an example of what is meant by *mission*.

While this type of behavior is often called "instinctual" by behavioral scientists, implying that it is not truly an issue of choice, it is still triggered by the rat's deep intuitive sense of being a "holon" and its connection to something bigger than itself.

These experiments provide a powerful metaphor for a fundamental success factor for leaders and entrepreneurs. The electrified grid in the studies symbolize the risks and challenges that the leader or entrepreneur must face. The items on the other side represent various types of goals and motivations. Stimuli such as food and sex represent motivations relating to the ego – our smaller self as a separate whole. The babies represent motivations coming from our larger Self (or soul) and the felt experience that we are a holon.

If we make the analogy between the rats crossing the wire and the Captain Sullenberger (from The Miracle on the Hudson") responding to the difficulties that befell their various crafts, it is easy to see the parallel between the mother rat's willingness to cross the electrified wire for her babies and the Sullenberger's capacity to stay calm, pilot the airliner and care for the crew and passengers even though he was afraid for his own life.

If babies of other species are placed on the other side of the grid, even kittens...

...the rat continues to cross the grid despite the electricity...

...to "rescue" them.

Ambition

At the same time that we are holons, we are also wholes in and of ourselves and have our own individual dreams and desires for our lives. While vision and mission have to do with what a person or organization wants to create in the world that is beyond them, *ambition* is a result of the desire and determination to achieve success and recognition for oneself. Vision and mission are about creating a better world. Ambition is about living your dreams for your life and achieving a level of success recognized by others.

Ambition is defined in the dictionary as *"a strong desire to do or to achieve something, typically requiring determination and hard work"* that brings us personal benefit. Our ambitions in the form of dreams and aspirations for our lives arise from a healthy ego and come from the *drive for growth and mastery.*

Ambition is "a strong desire to achieve something." It takes the form of our dreams and aspirations for out own lives and comes from our innate drive for growth and mastery.

Ambition is frequently directed toward attaining a certan level of acknowledgement and recognizable "status" as a consequence of our achievments.

Richard Branson
Founder of The Virgin Group

My interest in life comes from setting myself huge, apparently unachievable challenges and trying to rise above them . . . From the perspective of wanting to live life to the full, I felt that I had to attempt it.

It is interesting to note that the word "ambition" comes from the Latin *ambitio*, which literally meant to "go around" canvassing for votes. [In Latin, *ambi* means to surround or go around.] It was the term used to describe the actions of candidates for office in Rome soliciting votes. So, "ambition" originally implied a desire to be recognized in order to be elected to a government position. Today, the notion of ambition still indicates the desire to achieve a certain level of recognizable "status" and also includes the aspiration to achieve. Ambition has to with such questions as:

- *What type of life do you want to create for yourself?*
- *What do you want to accomplish? What type of status and performance do you want to achieve with respect to yourself and others?*
- *What would you like to be recognized and/or remembered for? What would like to be able to add to your resume or biography?*

Ambitions arise from our personal dreams, desires, drives and needs. In addition to making a reasonable or good living from our endeavors, for example, we may have a desire for growth, a drive for mastery or a need for recognition and approval. The healthy ambition of a successful athlete, for instance, could be to win a tournament or place first in a competition. Successful writers want to have their books published and perhaps make the list of top sellers or win a prize for their work. Musicians and performers want to win awards and achieve a certain degree of celebrity and fame. Companies like Google and Amazon have ambitions to operate at global level. It is a stated ambition for Amazon, for example to be recognized as the "Earth's most customer-centric company."

Of his decision to start *Virgin Atlantic Airlines*, iconic entrepreneur Richard Branson wrote in his autobiography, "My interest in life comes from setting myself huge, apparently unachievable challenges and trying to rise above them... from the perspective of wanting to live life to the full, I felt that I had to attempt it." Branson's attitude is typical of the level of ambition we have found in successful entrepreneurs: the desire to *rise above seemingly unattainable challenges in order to live life to the full*.

Such ambitions are clearly not necessarily at odds with our visions or missions. In fact, when aligned, ambition brings an important level of extra motivation. In addition to a sense of vision and mission, the most successful entrepreneurs also want to achieve something, prove themselves to others, be recognized for their accomplishments and leave an enduring legacy. This combination frequently provides the fuel for a tremendous amount of personal effort.

At a certain point between 2007 and 2010, for example, all three of Elon Musk's companies (Tesla Motors, SolarCity and SpaceX) seemed to be collapsing. Musk had to lay off almost 1/3 of his staff and close Tesla's branch in Detroit. SolarCity began staggering and the bank that had backed its leases pulled out of the deal. Some entrepreneurs and leaders from other companies were even eager to see Musk's companies fail because they were seen as attacks on mainstream businesses and traditional ways of doing things. Poll votes and TV hosts belittled Tesla cars claiming that they weren't worth buying.

In addition to his vision and sense of mission, Musk's drive to achieve, prove himself and disprove the "naysayers" pushed him through the crisis. With only a week's worth of cash in the bank, Musk put $40 million of his own money to keep his ventures going and worked tirelessly to make them succeed. As he advises aspiring entrepreneurs:

> *Work like hell. I mean you just have to put in 80 to 100 hour weeks every week. [This] improves the odds of success. If other people are putting in 40 hour work weeks and you're putting in 100 hour work weeks, then even if you're doing the same thing you know that... you will achieve in 4 months what it takes them a year to achieve.*

Our ambitions are frequently connected to our "idealized self." An *idealized self* is who we have learned we need to be in order to be loved, accepted or recognized by our families, friends, society, etc. Our idealized self evolves to help us survive in the world, find our place and to function with as much stability and security as possible. In Elon Musk's words, "Constantly think about how you could be doing things better and keep questioning yourself."

If our idealized self consumes too much of our focus, however, it can create a type of "mirage" of success. We think we are successful, but ultimately end up realizing that it is not what we really wanted. It is not uncommon for people to reach a certain age and suddenly realize that they have not been living their "own life," but rather the life that others told them they were supposed to live. My earlier account of the young CEO who had achieved material and social "success" but no longer had "a sparkle" in his eye is an example of this.

Another consequence of the idealized self has to do with the fact that it also naturally defines certain things that we cannot be or do or be because we fear we will not be loved, accepted or recognized. Those aspects of ourselves that do not conform to the idealized self can become excluded from our desired identity and become "shadows." The "shadow" of either an individual or a group is made up of the emotions, thoughts, behaviors, etc., that have been deemed to be unacceptable.

Our ambition is usually connected to our "idealized self" – i.e., who we have learned we need to be in order to be loved recognized and accepted. This can be a powerful drive, but also create a type of "mirage." It can also cast a "shadow" made up of the emotions, thoughts, behaviors, etc. that are perceived as unacceptable.

When our ambition is in the service of a bigger vision, our sense of recognition and achievement come from our contribution to something beyond ourselves.

Ambition that is disconnected from vision can become a type of imbalanced compensation strategy that leads to an insatiable desire for for power, dominance and possessions

If according to my idealized self, for example, I should "always be positive and resourceful," then the times that I am "negative," "stuck" or "unresourceful" can become shadows. If my idealized self has to be "confident and decisive," then the opposite side of those qualities, "doubt, vulnerability and confusion," can become shadows.

On the other hand, when there is space to hold both sides, they form "generative complementarities." Wisdom, for example, comes from having enough confidence to acknowledge doubt. Generative complementarities can be a powerful source of energy, creativity and motivation for entrepreneurs.

The problem comes when we do not accept these "shadow" parts of ourselves or give them a place. In that case, they never get the chance to become integrated with the rest of the system of ourselves or the group. This keeps them out of relationship with the rest of parts of the system and creates a perpetual conflict.

Interestingly, some people are afraid to express their ambitions, or even admit that they have them, because they are afraid to appear "egoistic" or "selfish." The fact is, this is just as much a product of an idealized self as being a driven, high achiever.

One other important source of ambition is our need for compensation. *Compensation* is the process of offsetting a difficulty or deficiency on one area of one's life by developing excellence or achieving results in another area. The term "compensation" comes from the Latin *compensare* which literally means to "weigh against." Thus, it implies something that counterbalances or makes up for an undesirable or unwelcome state of affairs in order to attempt to bring balance.

In psychology, *compensation* is the term used for the process through which a person "covers up, consciously or unconsciously, weaknesses, frustrations, desires, feelings of inadequacy or incompetence in one life area through the gratification or (drive towards) excellence in another area." Compensation can cover up either real or imagined deficiencies and personal or physical inferiority or inadequacy.

Appropriate compensations help people to overcome difficulties and can often function as a positive motivation in their lives and become a resource in the lives of others. Captain Sullenberger, who piloted the airliner in the Miracle on the Hudson incident, indicated that a good deal of the motivation for his heroic actions came as a type of compensation relating to his father's suicide. As he put it, "I'm willing to work very hard to protect people's lives, to be a good Samaritan, and to not be a bystander, in part, because I couldn't save my father."

If one's compensation strategy does not truly address the source of the feelings of deficiency or inferiority, however, it can result in a reinforced feeling of inferiority and create an escalating cycle of *overcompensation*. Overcompensation, characterized by a need for superiority, leads to striving for power, dominance and possessions. Excessive materialism is an example of overcompensation that can affect entrepreneurs.

The key to developing a healthy ambition is the awareness of the dynamics that underlie it and the ability to align and balance it with our vision and mission. We have found this fundamental alignment of ego and soul and the integration of vision, mission and ambition to be the foundation for a whole new generation of leaders and entrepreneurs. You will have a chance to explore each of these dimensions more fully in the coming chapters of this book (in such exercises as the *Identity Matrix*), as well as to see how they operate as success factors in a number of different entrepreneurial cases.

One analogy I like to use for the differences and relationship between mission and ambition is that of a sailboat versus a motorboat. A sailboat is a holon, carried by the energy of the wind coming from the system around it. The wind is like the inspiration that comes to us when we share a common vision with those in the larger systems of which we are a part. A motorboat is more of an independent whole. The energy that powers a motorboat comes from its own internal engine (ego) powered by the fuel of ambition.

We could say that a successful entrepreneur has a vessel equipped with both sails and a motor (in case of emergencies). When the timing is right—and our mission is supported by the wind of a strong, shared vision—we sail almost effortlessly, carried by the alignment of our mission with that vision. As Elon Musk points out, "Putting in long hours for a corporation is hard. Putting in long hours for a cause is easy." There are other situations, however (as in the case of Musk's period of crisis with his three companies), when the wind dies down, or it is blowing in a direction different from the mission we have chosen. Then, we need to use the motor of our ego and fuel of our ambition to drive us on until we can catch the next empowering breeze.

MOTORBOAT
POWERED BY ITS OWN
INTERNAL ENGINE (EGO)
AND THE FUEL OF AMBITION

SAILBOAT
CARRIED BY THE ENERGY OF THE WIND
COMING FROM THE SYSTEM AROUND IT

Role

A particular role provides the link between a person as a separate whole and as a holon. A role is defined in the dictionary as "the function assumed or part played by a person in a particular situation." That is, it is how we, as individuals, fit into a larger context. More specifically, the dictionary defines role as "a set of connected behaviors, rights and obligations" characterized by the "appropriate and permitted forms of behavior, guided by social norms, which are commonly known and hence determine the expectations for appropriate behavior in these roles." Again, this speaks of the interaction between the competences and actions of an individual and how they fit within a larger social system.

In organizations, roles are related to both personal competency and also position or status. On one hand, a role reflects personal skills, abilities, and effort. It is related to what a person does (or is expected to do). On the other hand, it reflects "status"; i.e., who the person is in relation to others. In other words, it is related to both the position a person occupies with respect to others, and the expected capabilities and behaviors attached to that position. Similar to the notion of mission, it is not meaningful to think of a role in terms of one person alone. Rather than service to the vision, however, role focuses more on the ways in which a person complements, co-operates and competes with others with respect to his or her ambitions. Some common roles in business teams are: coordinator/chairperson, shaper, innovator, resource investigator, monitor/evaluator, implementer, team-worker, completer/finisher, and specialist. Role has to do with questions such as:

- *What type of person do you need to be in order to create the life you want?*
- *What type of position and status would support you to succeed in your ambition? Mission? Vision?*
- *What are the core competences necessary to be the type of person you need to be in order to achieve and remain in the necessary position or status?*

People are most successful in roles that are "compatible with their personal characteristics and skills." Thus, finding your role can be greatly enhanced by identifying your "area of excellence." The notion of one's area of excellence was created by Joel Guillon. An entertaining analogy for a person's "area of excellence" is the notion of SuperPowers. We all know about Super Heroes from Comic books and movies. Super Heroes have "SuperPowers" that give them special abilities. Each super hero has a different SuperPower. For instance, the Pixar animated movie "The Incredibles" tells the story of a family of Super Heroes: the father is very strong, the mother can stretch her

Role is related to both the position a person occupies with respect to others, and the expected capabilities and behaviors attached to that position.

The most effective roles are those that support us to simultaneously achieve our ambitions as well as our vision and mission.

People are most successful in roles that are "compatible with their personal characteristics and skills."

We perform best when our role is connected with our "area of excellence."

limbs indefinitely, the daughter can emit a force field and become invisible, and the son can run very fast. While each one excels in their own area, they are unable to perform each others' SuperPowers. In the areas where they can't use their SuperPowers, or where their own SuperPower is not relevant, they are "Mere Mortals" with normal capacities.

One's area of excellence is like his or her SuperPower. Each individual has a SuperPower that makes him or her able to perform far above the norm in a particular field. These SuperPowers are unique to each individual and different from one person to another. When people are outside of their "SuperPower Reach" — i.e., when they are in a situation where they can't use their SuperPowers or where these powers don't apply — they just perform the same as any "Mere Mortal."

These SuperPowers are subject to a number of paradoxes. One key paradox is that we are frequently not aware of our own SuperPower. In contrast to those of Super Heroes, our SuperPowers are not necessarily visible from the outside. For instance, our SuperPower may only be visible when we express an opinion on a situation that startles other because of the unexpected accuracy or out judgment. From our point of view, we believe everybody sees the same as we do. It takes somebody to ask: "How did you know that?" or "How did you do that?" to realize the SuperPower that we possess.

Within our "SuperPower Reach" — i.e., in situations where we are within our area of excellence and we can use our SuperPower — everything is easy and effortless. We do not have any hesitation as to what to do: even if the situation is new, we know where to go, what to do. We have the strong feeling that we will get to the right results no matter what. We are extremely efficient, compared to others in similar situations.

Another paradox is the feeling of "humble authority" that fills us when we are within "SuperPower Reach." Our self-assurance of being able to get the right results gives us a natural authority towards customers, team members and partners. At the same time, we feel humble because we do not have any impression of doing anything extraordinary. For us, we just happen to see something that is obvious. Nothing special.

"My area of excellence is organization and logistics. That's why I take care of the operations of my company."

"My area of excellence is communicating with people. That's why I take care of the Public Relations of my company."

Our "area of excellence" can be likened to the superpower of a superhero. It comes naturally to us and brings us a sense of "humble authority."

When we are within "SuperPower Reach," we are not afraid of competition. We feel invulnerable in the sense that we know that nobody can steal our expertise. As a consequence, we are not afraid of others who are potential competitors. We are able to acknowledge their areas of excellence and create win-win partnerships.

In contrast, when we are in "Mere Mortal Territory" -- i.e., outside of our area of excellence and unable use our SuperPower -- everything appears difficult, tedious, boring. We perform worse than others who are within their "SuperPower Reach" and we become afraid of competing with them.

To begin to explore your role, reflect on your own area of excellence.

- *What awareness do you have about your own area of excellence or "SuperPower"? Where do you have a feeling of "effortless excellence" and "humble authority."*
- *What do others (especially those who know you well) tell you that you do as well or better than anyone else?*
- *In contrast, what are the situations or activities where you struggle to perform; i.e., more like a "mere mortal"?*
- *What can you do in order to identify and engage the support of others who have the complementary capabilities (or SuperPowers) that would support or supplement yours?*
- *How well does your role support your ambition? Your mission? Your vision?*

Being an entrepreneur involves taking on many roles. It is also important to identify others that have complementary areas of excellence in order to build successful teams and partnerships.

Being an "entrepreneur" itself, of course, is a type of role; and there are additional more specific roles that accompany it. Engineer, chief executive, salesperson, marketing manager, technology specialist, coach, financial officer, designer, human resource director, etc., are all roles that an entrepreneur may find himself or herself taking on at certain times. Some of them will be within our "SuperPower Reach" and others will not. This is why, as we will see, one of the keys to successful entrepreneurship is building the right team.

Of course, sometimes we have multiple roles that support different ambitions and mission. Role conflicts can take place when a person has different and seemingly incompatible roles at the same time. For example, a person may find conflict between his or her role as a parent and his or her role as a manager or entrepreneur when his or her child's demands for time and attention distract him or her from the needs of the business or team.

Exploring Your Own Vision, Mission, Ambition and Role

An important starting place for achieving success is reflecting on your own personal sense of vision, mission, ambition and role. The following worksheets can help you to begin to explore and define these key success factors for yourself as an individual. In my coaching work with both individuals and organizations, this is always where I begin. It sets the stage and provides the framework for everything else to be done.

It is not necessary for you to have a clear or final answer at this point. In fact, areas of uncertainty, confusion or conflict will be useful feedback. In the further chapters of this book, you will be given other exercises and case examples that will help to clarify and align these important foundations for success, and use them as the underpinnings from which to build a successful venture.

For now, just consider the questions and take notes on your answers in the space provided on the worksheet. Don't worry about being specific. In fact, it is more appropriate to not become too detailed at this stage. Think big and let your imagination go free.

I usually encourage people to use as few words as possible to start with. Keep your answers to no more than ten key words. Elon Musk, for instance, stated his vision as "increase the scope and scale of human consciousness ." Disney described his vision for the future as simply "big and glittering." Captain Sullenberger's statement of his mission was to "protect people's lives," and "to be a good Samaritan." The purpose of this exercise is to help you see the "big picture" — i.e., to focus on the "forest" more than the "trees."

A vision, for example, could be expressed as "more empowered and creative people" or something as simple as "people helping people." A mission could be verbalized as "creating connection between people" or "helping others in need." An ambition could be something like "to be internationally known and respected" or "to live comfortably and do what I love." A role could be "a creator of new tools" or "a coach and teacher."

You may find it easier to use symbolic or metaphoric language to capture and express your answers. For example, you could express your role as "a pioneer" and your mission as "making paths for others into new territories." I frequently invite people to use a metaphorical description as well as a literal one for each question.

Exploring and defining your own vision, mission, ambition and role is an essential starting point for living your dreams and creating a better world through your business.

Ego and Soul Worksheet for Individuals

SOUL	EGO
Vision What do you want to create in the world through you that is beyond you? What do you want to see more of and less of in the world? What is the world to which you want to belong?	**Ambition** What type of life do you want to create for yourself? What type of status and performance do you want to achieve with respect to yourself and others? What would like to be able to add to your resume or bio?
Mission What will be your unique contribution to making your vision happen? What are the special gifts, resources, capabilities and actions that you will enact to help reach the vision?	**Role** What type of person do you need to be in order to create the life you want? What are the core competences necessary to be this type of person?

Reflections and Conclusion

Reflect on your answers.

- Which ones are clear for you?
- Are there questions you find difficult to answer at this point?
- How well are your vision and ambition aligned?
- How about your role and your mission?
- What could you do to bring them even more into alignment?

We have found this fundamental alignment of ego and soul and the integration of vision, mission, ambition and role to be the foundation for a whole new generation of leaders and entrepreneurs.

You will have a chance to explore each of these dimensions more fully in the coming chapters of this book, as well as to see how they operate as success factors in a number of different entrepreneurial cases.

In the next chapter we will explore some of the principles and skills necessary to be able to manifest the vision, mission, ambition and role in a way that form the foundation for a new venture.

References and Further Readings

- *When Elephants Weep: the emotional lives of animals*,
  Jeffrey Moussaieff Masson & Susan McCarthy
  Delacorte Press, New York, 1995.

- *Maternal behavior in the rat*,
  Weisner BP,
  Sheard NM, Oliver & Boyd, Edinburgh, 1933;121–122.

- *Highest Duty: My Search for What Really Matters*
  Chesley Sullenberger
  William Morrow, New York, 2009

02
Next Generation Entrepreneurship
and the SFM Circle of Success™

People have the notion of saving the world by shifting things around, changing the rules, and who's on top, and so forth. No, no! Any world is a valid world if it's alive. The thing to do is to bring life to it, and the only way to do that is to find in your own case where the life is and become alive yourself.

Joseph Campbell

Antonio Meza

The Silicon Valley Phenomenon

Perhaps no area has characterized the developments associated with our evolving society and economy and spawned the new generation of entrepreneurs more than Silicon Valley in San Francisco's Bay Area. In addition to the well-known industry leaders that have been established there—such as Apple Inc., Cisco Systems, Intel, Hewlett-Packard, Sun Microsystems and Oracle—thousands of smaller companies have prospered in its unique business culture. In the late 1990s, stories of the spectacular success of Silicon Valley start-ups made headlines around the world, sending other countries scrambling to replicate the Silicon Valley phenomenon in their own homelands.

Innovations in business models, business practices and organizational structure in Silicon Valley created a business context which was able to sustain an unprecedented period of growth and prosperity. Innovative investment strategies (characterized by the emergence of the "angel" investor) created a highly incentivized climate in which people were willing to take greater risks because the potential rewards were tremendous.

Still today, the Silicon Valley culture is optimistic, possibility-focused and oriented toward the future. New industry leaders such as Google, Facebook, Pixar, LinkedIn and Yahoo have their roots and their headquarters there. The Silicon Valley environment is one that embraces diversity of all types. Silicon Valley companies are highly customer-oriented and quick to adjust, taking a "hands on" approach and emphasizing the "bottom line." They are primarily focused on creating value, not only through technology developments, but also by establishing and leveraging relationships and alliances.

This culture has encouraged a proliferation of start-up companies, which while inherently "risky," also have many benefits. In addition to possibilities of a big payoff, start-ups offer dynamic opportunities and a diversity of activities—people get to wear "different hats." Start-ups have a more casual culture than traditional organizations that is less restrictive, less stratified, and emphasizes ideas more than position or authority. Generally, there is a high degree of mutual respect between team members, regardless of their roles; and they have greater responsibility, autonomy and ownership (everyone has a "chunk" of the company). This leads to a greater sense of self-fulfillment and achievement (proving yourself to yourself and others), and of having personal impact (i.e., by believing what you are doing makes a difference).

Many of the success factors applied by Silicon Valley technology start-ups can also be applied to increase the chances of success for other entrepreneurs, and to encourage effective entrepreneurship in established organizations. There are many goals and activities that are common to both start-ups and traditional companies, such as:

- Defining and Communicating a Clear Vision for the Organization
- Innovating New Technologies and Updating Business Models
- Recruiting Expertise/Enhancing Competency
- Motivating and Incentivizing Team Members
- Creating Value and Satisfying Customers
- Establishing Clear Identity and Brand
- Securing Sponsorship (Attracting Investors)
- Achieving Benchmarks and Communicating Progress to Shareholders
- Staying Ahead of Competition
- Becoming/Remaining Profitable—Maintaining Cash Flow
- Returning Value to Shareholders (Defining an "Exit Strategy")

Successful Silicon Valley start-ups provide a unique road map for how to accomplish these goals in new and innovative ways. Just as the Italian Renaissance brought Europe from the Dark Ages into a new era of innovation and opportunity on many different levels, the Silicon Valley phenomenon has ushered in a new era of creative thinking that is continuing to transform the world of business and technology.

The entrepreneurial spirit and skill of the successful founders of Silicon Valley start-ups provide important principles and guidelines for success in today's challenging business environment. In the coming chapters, we will see how the innovations and developments modeled from progressive leaders in today's complex and changing world overlap with and complement time-tested skills and principles of business and leadership from well-established companies to form a powerful new paradigm for success in the evolving economy.

ATTITUDES
BELIEFS
VALUES
SKILLS
PRACTICES
BUSINESS MODELS

 Many Hats   Casual Style Focused on Ideas Respect of Peers Sense of Ownership   Risk Taking   and more...

ATTITUDES
BELIEFS
VALUES
SKILLS
PRACTICES
BUSINESS MODELS

CRITICAL SUCCESS FACTORS

SUCCESSFUL
SILLICON VALLEY
TECHNOLOGY START-UPS

START-UPS AND
ENTREPRENEURS
IN OTHER AREAS

TRADITIONAL
ORGANIZATIONS

The success factors applied by Silicon Valley technology start-ups can be applied to increase the chances of success for other entrepreneurs and to encourage effective entrepreneurship in traditional organizations.

Entrepreneurship

Jeff Bezos
Founder and CEO Amazon

An *entrepreneur* is generally defined as "a person who organizes and manages an enterprise or venture and assumes significant accountability for the inherent risks and the outcome." The term comes from the French *entreprendre* which means "to undertake." The name is most frequently applied to a person who is willing to take on a new venture, project or enterprise, creating value by offering a product or service, and accepting full responsibility for the outcome.

Successful entrepreneurship involves the linking of opportunities with people well-positioned to take advantage of them. Entrepreneurs typically perceive themselves as being uniquely suited to be able to solve a problem or fill a need. Therefore, vision is essential to successful entrepreneurship. The vision of highly successful entrepreneurs is able to spot major opportunities that are potentially "game changing."

Jeff Bezos, founder of the Internet e-commerce giant Amazon, for example, claims he left his "well-paying job" at a New York City hedge fund when he "learned about the rapid growth in Internet use" in the United States. He comments that his realization of this trend coincided with a "then-new U.S. Supreme Court ruling [that] online retailers [would not] have to collect sales taxes in states where they lack a physical presence." He saw this combination as a major opportunity for people to have easier access to products (initially books) and pay less because they would not have to pay taxes on their purchases, provided they lived in a different state than the one in which the business was located. He decided to start the company in the state of Washington because its relatively small population meant fewer of his future customers would have to pay sales tax. He launched Amazon.com in 1994 after making the cross-country drive from New York to Seattle, writing up the Amazon business plan on the way. Like other budding entrepreneurs, he initially set up and operated the company from his garage. By 2014, Amazon had become the world's largest on-line retailer.

As we saw in the example of Elon Musk in the previous chapter, entrepreneurs must also be willing to accept a high level of personal, professional or financial risk to pursue opportunity. Thus, entrepreneurs need strong beliefs about a market opportunity and the contribution that they are making, and to have the capacity to organize their resources effectively to accomplish their goals.

Mastering entrepreneurship involves developing skills for acquiring and managing a number of key resources relating to:

• Environment (perceiving opportunities and constraints, and managing property and other natural resources)
• Labor (human input into production and services)
• Technology (equipment used in production or services)
• Know-how (intelligence, knowledge, and creativity)
• Financing (acquiring the money necessary to fund the critical activities of the venture)
• Marketing (effectively promoting and creating demand for a product or service)

Environment
(perceiving opportunities and constraints, managing property and
other natural resources, etc.)

Labor
(human input into production and
services)

Technology
(equipment used in production or
services)

Know-how
(intelligence, knowledge, and
creativity)

Financing
(acquiring the money necessary to
fund the activities of the venture)

Marketing
(promoting and creating demand
for a product or service)

In addition to these skills, leadership, management ability, creative thinking and team-building are essential skills for an entrepreneur. Poise, presence, persistence, passion and the capacity to communicate and inspire others are frequently key success factors in a next generation entrepreneur's ability to bring his or her vision into reality.

In this chapter, we will begin to explore how to develop and bring these skills together in order to transform vision, mission and ambition into a successful venture.

A New Generation of Entrepreneurs

Muhammed Yunus
Founder Grameen Bank

As I mentioned in the previous chapter, there is a new generation entrepreneurs emerging who are not only focused on financial gain, but on living their dreams and making a better world. Principles of entrepreneurship are effective and essential for all types of growth, innovation and change. *Social entrepreneurs'* principal objectives, for instance, include the creation of a social and/or environmental benefit as well as financial revenue. An iconic example of social entrepreneurism is Bangladeshi Muhammed Yunus. Yunus is the founder of Grameen Bank which pioneered the concept of microcredit for supporting innovators in developing countries in Asia, Africa and Latin America.

Yunus' vision emerged when he discovered that very small loans could make a huge difference for people who had scarce economic resources. In his native country of Bangladesh, for instance, Yunus observed that village women who made bamboo furniture struggled to keep their small businesses going and were often taken advantage of when they tried to borrow money. Traditional banks did not want to make loans to poor people due to what they perceived as the high risk of default. Yunus, however, was convinced that, given the chance, the women would be more than willing to repay the money and a reasonable amount of interest. Yunus lent $27 of his own money to 42 women in the village and made a small but significant profit on every loan. This validated his vision and reinforced his belief that microcredit was a viable business model that could positively transform the lives of people living in poverty.

In December 1976, Yunus secured a loan from the government bank of Bangladesh to lend to the poor in the local village of Jobra. To ensure repayment, Yunus developed a system of "solidarity groups." These small informal groups apply together for loans and its members act as co-guarantors of repayment and support one another's efforts at economic self-advancement.

The venture was successful and continued to expand, securing loans from other banks for its projects. By 1982, it had 28,000 members. On 1 October 1983, the pilot project began operation as a full-fledged bank for poor Bangladeshis and was renamed Grameen Bank ("Village Bank").

Like any entrepreneurial endeavor, however, the path was not always easy. Yunus and his colleagues encountered everything from violent radical leftists to conservative clergy who told women that they would be denied a Muslim burial if they borrowed money from the Grameen Bank. In spite of these obstacles, Yunus and his team persisted with their vision, and by July 2007 Grameen had issued $6.38 billion to 7.4 million borrowers.

In 2006, Yunus and Grameen Bank received the Nobel Peace Prize for these efforts, the success of which has inspired similar programs throughout the world.

The Ashoka Network (http://www.ashoka.org/) is a group that promotes and supports social entrepreneurs and their projects around the world.

The Grameen Bank makes micro-credit loans to individuals; lending is based entirely on trust.

These individuals use their credit to support their own small business.

And they start producing value.

They can start selling their products and begin making profit.

They are happy to pay back the loan, with interest. And the cycle starts again.

MUHAMMAD YUNNUS AND THE GRAMEEN BANK

ANTONIO MEZA

Zentrepreneurs are individuals who have made a conscious decision to become more passionate, purposeful and creative through their ventures.

Zentrepreneurism is another emerging form of entrepreneurship that combines traditional Western thought with an Eastern philosophy of seeking answers to the daily challenges of business and life. It resonates with people who are experiencing a new direction and purpose in their lives and have made a conscious decision to become a more passionate, purposeful and creative person. Many of you reading this book may be exactly this type of person.

Blake Mycoskie, creator of TOMS shoes, is a good example of this new generation of entrepreneurs. Already the founder of several successful small ventures, Mycoskie's vision for TOMS emerged in 2006 while he was on vacation in Argentina. While there, he met an American woman who was part of a volunteer organization that provided shoes for children in need. Mycoskie spent several days traveling from village to village with the group, as well as on his own, and was struck by the degree of poverty he saw. In his words:

> *"(I witnessed) the intense pockets of poverty just outside the bustling capital. It dramatically heightened my awareness. Yes, I knew somewhere in the back of my mind that poor children around the world often went barefoot, but now, for the first time, I saw the real effects of being shoeless: the blisters, the sores, the infections."*

Mycoskie returned to the United States with the inspiration for a new venture: *Shoes for A Better Tomorrow*, later shortened to TOMS. Designed as a for-profit business, Mycoskie set up the "One for One" business model in which the company could donate a new pair of shoes to disadvantaged children for every pair of shoes sold. TOMS shoes were designed to appeal to a worldwide audience in order to ensure sales that would both sustain the company's mission and generate profit. The shoes are sold globally in more than 1000 stores. Launched in 2006, by 2013 the company had donated more than 10,000,000 pairs of shoes to people in need!

In 2009, Mycoskie was honored by Hillary Clinton as the recipient of the Secretary of State's 2009 *Award of Corporate Excellence* (ACE). Established by the State Department in 1999, the award celebrates companies' commitment to corporate social responsibility, innovation and democratic values worldwide. In 2010, TOMS received the prestigious *Footwear News Brand of the Year Award*.

In 2011, TOMS expanded to include eyeglasses in its "One for One" offering — for every pair of sunglasses purchased, sight-saving medical treatment, prescription glasses or surgery is donated to a person in need.

Blake Mycoskie
Founder and CEO of TOMS

That same year, Mycoskie published the best-selling book *Start Something That Matters*. In it, he writes about the virtues of the new generation of entrepreneurship and the concept of businesses using their profits and company assets to contribute to making a better world. Mycoskie uses about his experience with TOMS to demonstrate both the intangible and real benefits and returns of such ventures. Not surprisingly, for every copy of *Start Something That Matters* sold, Mycoskie gives a children's book to a child in need. Fifty percent of royalties from the book were used to provide grants to up-and-coming next generation entrepreneurs. Mycoskie increased this to 100% in late 2012.

In 2014, Mycoskie announced the launch of TOMS Roasting Co., a company that offers coffee sourced through direct trade efforts in Rwanda, Honduras, Peru, Guatemala and Malawi. TOMS Roasting Co. will donate a week of water to people in need in its supplier countries for every bag of coffee sold.

Mycoskie recently announced that TOMS would launch an additional "One for One" product every year. A member of Virgin Group founder Richard Branson's "B Team," Mycoskie is looking for partnerships with Fortune 500 companies to help with the expansion of the TOMS concept to different categories.

Social business TOMS uses its policy "one for one" to help many children in the world to get shoes, eye-glasses, water and other benefits.

The "Three Jewels" of Zentrepreneurship

Social entrepreneurism and zentrepreneurism reflect a new entrepreneurial model that shifts from bottom line thinking to one that emphasizes a *"blended bottom line"* founded on the belief that organizations can and should produce social good and contribute to the sustainability of our planet's ecosystem while producing financial returns that reasonably reward the risk and commitment of stakeholders.

Interestingly, there is an even deeper connection between the notion of "Zen" and the new generation of entrepreneurs. The ancient tradition of Buddhism, for instance, is centered on three practices referred to as the "three jewels": Dharma, Buddha and Sangha.

- *Dharma* refers to discovering and pursuing one's purpose and place in the world. It is about authentically living your life path and fulfilling your purpose.
- *Buddha* symbolizes the commitment to the full development of one's highest potential.
- *Sangha* is a reference to one's community of peers, mentors, sponsors and collaborators who are using the same methods and working towards the same goals (i.e., of fulfilling your purpose and achieving your highest potential). Muhammed Yanus' "solidarity groups" are a good example of an entrepreneurial sangha.

Similarly, next generation entrepreneurs want to create both a successful *and* purposeful business or career; combining ambition with contribution and mission ("Dharma"), and the desire for personal growth and fulfillment ("Buddha"). They also desire to attract and collaborate with others who share the same vision, mission and ambition ("Sangha"). In other words, next generation entrepreneurship involves *creating a world to which people want to belong.*

Zentrepreneurship applies a "blended bottom line" integrating social good and contribution to the sustainability of the planet's ecosystem with producing financial returns that reasonably reward the risk and commitment of stakeholders

ZENTREPRENEUR
THE THREE JEWELS

DHARMA
CREATE A SUCCESSFUL AND PURPOSEFUL
BUSINESS / CAREER

BUDDHA
DESIRE FOR PERSONAL
GROWTH AND FULFILLMENT

SANGHA
ATTRACT AND COLLABORATE
WITH OTHERS WHO SHARE
THE SAME VISION MISSION
AND AMBITION

ANTONIO NEZA

Five Keys to Creating a World to Which People Want to Belong

As a result of our research, "creating a world to which people want to belong" slightly expands the "three jewels" of Buddhism to the following five key commitments:

- Growing personally and spiritually
- Contributing to society and the environment
- Building a successful and sustainable venture and career
- Supporting the emotional and physical well-being of oneself and others
- Sharing visions and resources with a community of peers, igniting new possibilities

These five keys can be summarized in the following diagram:

Example:

Growing personally and spiritually.

"I WANT TO GROW AS A BUSINESMAN AND AS A FATHER, AND CONTRIBUTE TO CREATE A HEALTHIER WORLD"

Contributing to society and the environment.

"THROUGH MY BUSINESS PEOPLE WILL HAVE ACCESS TO CARS POWERED WITH SUN-LIGHT. THE ENERGY NEEDED WILL BE CLEAN AND CHEAP"

Building a successful and sustainable venture and career.

"AS WE ARE PIONEERS THERE IS A BIG MARKET TO BUILD AND OPPORTUNITIES FOR LONG-TERM INNOVATION."

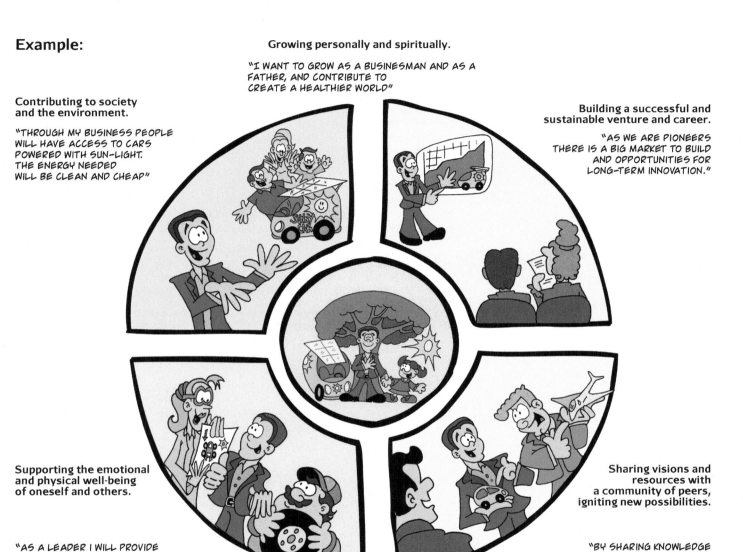

Supporting the emotional and physical well-being of oneself and others.

"AS A LEADER I WILL PROVIDE OPPORTUNITIES FOR GROWTH TO MY COLLABORATORS AND WILL ENCOURAGE THEIR CONTRIBUTIONS."

Sharing visions and resources with a community of peers, igniting new possibilities.

"BY SHARING KNOWLEDGE AND IDEAS WITH OTHERS, WE CAN MAKE A DIFFERENCE AND THRIVE TOGETHER."

Modeling Next Generation Entrepreneurs

The ideas, methods and tools in this book come from modeling the new breed of entrepreneurs, many from the Silicon Valley in California. Successful Silicon Valley entrepreneurs most represent this new class of leaders who live in a world of tremendous progress, contribution and risk. They are not simply CEOs who lead their organizations to make incremental improvements or to keep pace with competition. People like Apple's Steve Jobs and Tesla Motors' Elon Musk are good examples of this phenomenon.

Throughout history, the four driving criteria for success for all entrepreneurs have been *more, better, faster and cheaper.* In addition, the new generation of entrepreneurs are also constantly striving to "push the edge of the envelope," stretching existing possibilities in order to create something unique or produce a *"game-changing" breakthrough* that benefits many others and makes a better world.

As the failure of many new ventures also illustrates, however, entrepreneurial activities are highly risky. In spite of the risk, what makes entrepreneurial initiatives attractive is that they produce an exponential possibility of reward for oneself and others. The payoffs offset the risks and are tied directly to performance.

One of the first and primary applications of Success Factor Modeling™ has been to identify key skills and characteristics of successful entrepreneurs and zentrapreneurs. Many of these findings will be summarized in the coming chapters.

This book is the result of modeling successful representatives of the new generation of entrepreneurs who have produced "game changing" breakthroughs that benefit others and make a better world through creating a successful business that fulfills their dreams.

The information was gathered through observations and interviews that focused on the questions such as:

1. How important is vision to success in today's economy? What is your vision? What do you want to bring into the world and why?

2. How are you a "leader"? What role does leadership play in achieving success with respect to your vision, mission and ambition in today's economy?

3. What are the personal and company values that drive you and position you and your company for success in the current business environment?

4. It has been said that a key to Walt Disney's success was that he was able to be a "dreamer," a "realist" and a "critic" in equal parts. To what degree do each of these processes play a role in your strategy for your company?

5. What distinguishes you as a new generation entrepreneur most from a traditional organization? What advantages do you have that a traditional company does not have?

6. How have you adapted your business practices and models to address your vision and the changes brought about by the evolving economy and how does your business strategy take full advantage of the changing economy?

7. How have you prepared to deal with possible adversity? There is a lot of uncertainty and competition in today's business environment. What do you believe that convinces you that you will be a "game changing" breakthrough?

The process of Success Factor Modeling has been applied to identify a number of different characteristics, skills and "differences that make a difference" at all of the different levels of success factors identified in the previous chapter.

The SFM Circle of Success™

The answers we received to interview questions such as these and our study and observations of successful entrepreneurs and entrepreneurial leaders have led to the formulation of a model that we call the *SFM Circle of Success™.*

We observed that the founders of successful ventures divide their focus of attention evenly between five fundamental perspectives: 1) themselves and their sense of purpose and motivation for what they are doing, 2) their customers and their products or services, 3) their investors and stakeholders, 4) their team members or employees and 5) their strategic partners and alliances.

To survive and flourish in their ventures, effective entrepreneurs of all types need more than a good product or service that is attractive to potential customers. They must also be sufficiently supported by team members, investors, alliances and strategic relationships. In a way, an entrepreneur's Circle of Success is what the Buddhists would call his or her *Sangha*; the circle of supporters who help you to fulfill your purpose and achieve your highest potential. As one successful entrepreneur put it, "You have to work with everybody, everyday (your employees, your investors, your customers and your partners) to bring your vision together."

According to the Circle of Success, in order to be effective, entrepreneurs and business leaders need to balance their time between:

1. Connecting with *themselves* and their purpose and motivation for the venture.
2. Moving from vision to action in order to develop products and services for their *customers* and generate enough interest and revenue to support their enterprise — establishing both sufficient "mind share" and market share.
3. Growing a team of competent *team members* aligned with and committed to the mission of the venture and continuing to increase their competency as the business matures.
4. Raising funds and securing other essential resources needed to support the venture to reach its ambition, then continuing to develop the business strategy and infrastructure necessary to grow the venture and create value for *stakeholders*.
5. Building key strategic *partnerships* and win-win relationships in order to expand the venture's role in the marketplace by leveraging resources and increasing visibility.

As the name "circle of success" implies, we represent the relationship between these perspectives as a circle, with oneself and one's purpose and motivation in the center surrounded by four quadrants of customers/market, team members/employees, stakeholders/investors and partners/alliances.

While these five domains have been recognized as essential for creating a successful venture of any type for some time, the importance of a true balance of attention, as we shall see, is crucial. When we coach entrepreneurs and people who want to be more entrepreneurial, we use these five perspectives of the SFM Circle of Success™ as the primary building blocks for creating a successful venture.

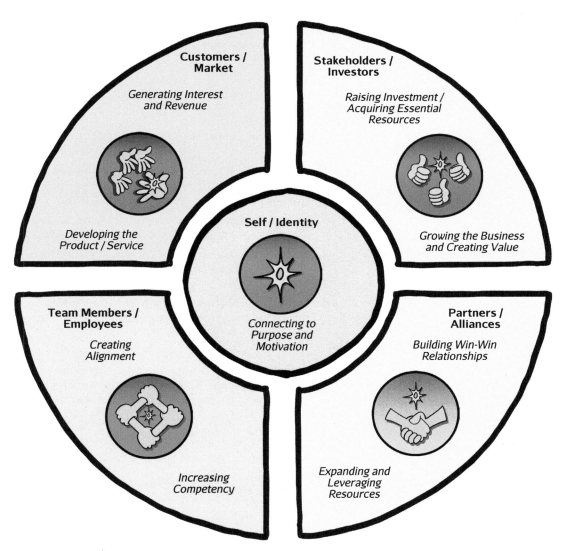

The SFM Circle of Success™

The SFM Circle of Success™ and the Five Keys to Creating a World to Which People Want to Belong

The five domains of the Circle of Success also have an important relationship to the Five Keys for Creating a World to which People Want to Belong mentioned earlier:

1. Connecting with oneself and one's passion is about growing personally and spiritually.

2. Developing and providing meaningful products and services for customers is the primary way one contributes to society and the environment.

3. Growing an aligned, committed and competent team requires supporting the emotional and physical well-being of oneself and others.

4. Acquiring resources, growing the business and creating value for stakeholders is how one builds a successful and sustainable venture and career.

5. Building partnerships and win-win relationships is a function of sharing visions and resources with a community of peers, igniting new possibilities.

Establishing a successful venture is a direct expression of "creating a world to which people want to belong." To become real, this world must touch all areas of the Circle of Success. One of the main goals of this book is to help entrepreneurs to create such a world.

The SFM Circle of Success identifies five fundamental areas of focus necessary for entrepreneurs to build a successful and sustainable venture through which they can live their dreams and make a better world:

- *Self / Identity*
- *Customers / Market*
- *Team Members / Employees*
- *Stakeholders / Investors*
- *Partners / Alliances*

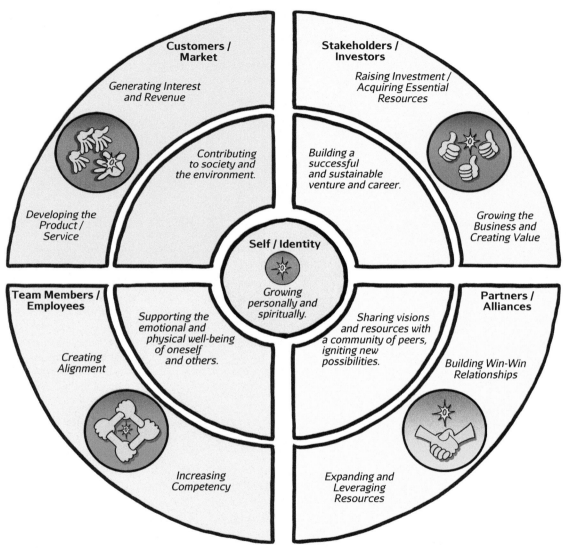

The SFM Circle of Success™ provides the context for the Five Keys to Creating World to which People Want to Belong

Integrating Passion, Vision, Mission, Ambition and Role with the SFM Circle of Success™

In fact, creating a world to which people want to belong is a result of the entrepreneur's capacity to share his or her passion, in the form of vision, mission, ambition and role, with the perspectives defined by the Circle of Success.

A successful entrepreneur's vision, mission, ambition and role begin to take shape when his or her personal passion is expressed outward towards the key perspectives defined by the SFM Circle of Success.

- The entrepreneur's *vision* is a function of their personal passion expressed outward toward *customers* and the *market* in order to make a contribution.

- The alignment of *team members* and *employees* working together to reach the vision is a result of the entrepreneur communicating and sharing his or her passion in the form of the *mission* of the venture and supporting their well-being.

- The entrepreneur's passion in the form of his or her *ambition* to build a successful and sustainable venture and create value is what motivates *stakeholders* and *investors* to offer the resources and take the risk to join the venture.

- The entrepreneur's passion for applying his or her area of excellence in the form of a *role* and building win-win relationships with peers that leverage resources is what forms the basis for effective *partnerships and alliances.*

As we will explore in the coming sections of this book, the alignment, synergy and chemistry between the five keys for creating a world to which people want to belong, the five building blocks of the Circle of Success and the entrepreneur's passion, vision mission, ambition and role are the essential ingredients in the recipe for entrepreneurial success.

For now, let's take a closer look at the various parts of the Circle of Success and how they combine to produce a successful venture.

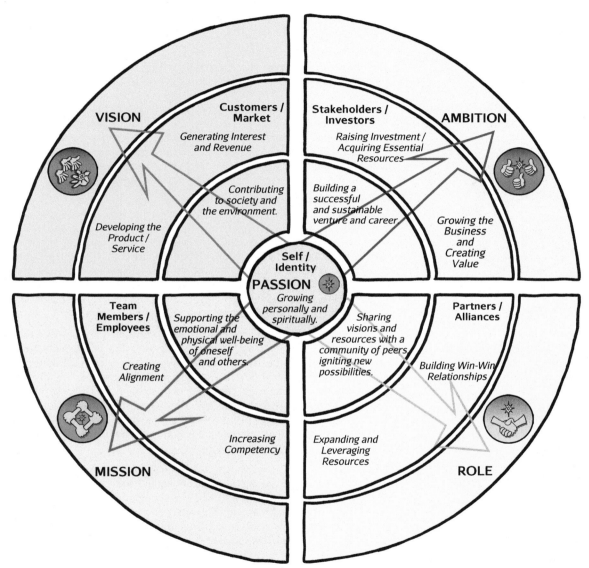

VISION

Customers / Market
Generating Interest and Revenue

Stakeholders / Investors
Raising Investment / Acquiring Essential Resources

AMBITION

Contributing to society and the environment.

Building a successful and sustainable venture and career.

Developing the Product / Service

Growing the Business and Creating Value

Self / Identity
PASSION
Growing personally and spiritually.

Team Members / Employees

Supporting the emotional and physical well-being of oneself and others.

Sharing visions and resources with a community of peers, igniting new possibilities.

Partners / Alliances

Creating Alignment

Building Win-Win Relationships

Increasing Competency

Expanding and Leveraging Resources

MISSION

ROLE

Vision, Mission, Ambition and Role, and the SFM Circle of Success™

Self and Identity

At the center of the SFM Circle of Success is the identity of the entrepreneur, his or her personal sense of passion and purpose, and his or her desire to create something new that makes a difference.

Identity / Self
*Connecting to
Purpose and Motivation*

Steig Westerberg
Founder and CEO
Stream Theory

The journey around the Circle of Success has a very distinct starting point: yourself, your sense of purpose, your personal passion and your intention to manifest that passion as a project or venture. The most effective entrepreneurs have an extremely focused understanding of who they are and how they are aligned with the purpose of their venture. Those who make up the new generation of entrepreneurs begin their quest to create a new product or service because they have a contribution they want to make; such as seeing a problem that they want to solve or having a dream of a better way of doing something. The most successful of these entrepreneurs have a passion and desire to create something new and different that is "revolutionary" and "game changing" in a positive way for the larger systems of which they are a part.

This passion serves to unite their "ego" with their "soul" to such a degree that their drive to succeed at fulfilling this passion and intention consumes them mentally, physically, emotionally and financially. As Richard Branson pointed out, it is an expression of "wanting to live life to the full." The venture becomes a very personal endeavor that is extremely close to the core of their identity. It becomes the vehicle through which they grow personally and spiritually. This sense of calling and personal passion is what drives entrepreneurs to take risks and stay focused in the face of the many challenges they confront. It is what pushes them beyond what they ever dreamed possible and causes them to grow their confidence and their skills to new heights.

A good example from the entrepreneurs we studied is Steig Westerberg. Steig was founder and CEO of *Stream Theory*, a Silicon Valley-based software company that enabled software to be streamed for real-time use over broadband networks. Steig conceived the idea for this venture while working as a computer consultant for a law firm. Steig had a passion for creating global solutions to common problems. He loved coming up with ideas that would provide the most effective solution to the greatest number of people. A large part of his job was to make sure that all of the computers in the law firm had current software loaded on their hard drives.

As he strove to solve this ongoing problem, Steig's passion for global solutions led him to a dream of a better way of distributing current software titles to the computers in large organizations. At that time, technologies had begun to exist to stream audio and video files on the Internet, but no one had thought of streaming software. Steig began to envision a plan for streaming software over the Internet from a central server where only the software on the server would need to be updated. The new, updated software would then be streamed to individual computers throughout an organization.

As he continued to dream, Steig's vision expanded to the possibility of creating the technology for streaming any kind of software over any broadband network to any computer anywhere in the world. A revolutionary idea at the time, Steig realized it would be a game changing innovation.

In the process of turning his vision into a viable venture, Steig would sell his house to finance his company, he would reach the brink of bankruptcy and he would face employee revolts over not being paid. Fueled by his passion for his dream, however, Steig persisted and ultimately struck a $10 million deal with Japan's Softbank, the most advanced broadband network in the world at the time.

Subsequently, Stream Theory's distribution platform (branded *StreamFlow*) was used by major service providers, such as Softbank, Chello and iCable as a games and application sales and rental platform. Additionally, it was licensed to enterprise customers such as Wyse, Citrix and Microsoft. Stream Theory was sold to Tadpole Technology in 2004, providing the Angel Investor group Keiretsu Forum with its largest return in the shortest time to that date.

Following the success of Stream Theory, Steig's continuing passion for global solutions drove him to co-found and become Chief Operating Officer of *StreamServ*, a company that brought cloud-based gaming and application streaming to the market. StreamServ was successfully sold to GameStreamer with Steig again taking the role of Chief Operating Officer. GameStreamer developed an enterprise class distribution platform operating as a cloud-based service delivering games, music and books.

Steig's technology has enabled software to be streamed to millions of people and it all started with his personal passion and commitment to creating revolutionary, global solutions.

Not all entrepreneurs have a happy ending in creating a new product or service for a variety of reasons. One common reason is that they are not personally aligned with their passion and the vision for their venture. This brings up the issue of truth and passion for what you do. There is a common saying that you should "strive to make your hobby or passion your profession." This saying easily describes what should be the goal of every entrepreneur: to find what it is that you care deeply about and for which you have talent and pursue it with all of your heart. In Steig Westerberg's words, *"The dream is something that can never die. The dream quite literally is part of me. It is something that I think about all the time. It is something that permeates everything that I do."*

Thus, a major success factor among effective entrepreneurs is that they have a very solid understanding of who they are and what they want in creating a new venture and the product or service it provides. Asserting the combination of passion and truth can have explosive results and serves as the genesis for the long-term success of most thriving companies.

An entrepreneur's passion can be highly infectious and is the foundation for all of the other parts of the Circle of Success. The reason for this is that the entrepreneur's primary activity is to inspire others to join him or her in pursuing the vision. Accomplishing this is a unique ability that every successful entrepreneur has acquired and mastered. It involves opening up his or her heart to share this passion and backing up the vision and plan for going forward with the firm belief deeply inside the entrepreneur that his or her vision is possible.

The more closely aligned your personal truth and passion for your vision, the more likely you are to persevere, to continue to innovate, improvise, to stare down failure against all odds.

It helps you to view obstacles not just as obstacles but as a springboard to adapt and find new ideas that may even be better than the initial idea. Elon Musk and the other founders of PayPal, for example, started by creating security software for the Palm Pilot, a precursor to today's smart phones. They quickly realized that the market was too small for their software to be "game changing." Their idea evolved and they tried many other business ideas before coming up with the idea of PayPal that we know today.

IDENTITY / PASSION EXAMPLE:
"I am a business woman and a mother passionate about watching my girl growing up. I am also passionate about music."

Applying personal passion to create a vision of a product or service that fulfills an important need for customers or a market is the primary way that successful entrepreneurs make a contribution and generate sufficient interest and revenue to build a sustainable business.

Another dynamic aspect relating to the self and identity portion of the Circle involves giving yourself permission; permission to take a risk, permission to succeed and permission to fail.

Once you have made the personal commitment to pursue your truth in a passionate manner, there is still the challenge of what that will mean to you and to those around you who rely on your ability to provide for them. More than any other challenge facing an entrepreneur, the obstacles involved in obtaining permission – from yourself, from your spouse or family, from your business partners or employers, etc. – are the most formidable.

At the end of the day, a solid and grounded understanding of one's self, knowledge of one's core identity and personal passion coupled with the intention to live that passion and transform it into something that will benefit others is the most important part of the Circle of Success.

In the coming chapters we will provide exercises and tools to help you develop a strong center for your own Circle of Success by discovering and deepening your passion and strengthening your intention to manifest that passion in the world around you.

Customers and Market

Fundamental to creating a successful venture is the application of the entrepreneur's passion and intention to the needs of customers and the marketplace to create a dream or vision of new possibilities. It is this process of transforming passion into vision that produces an idea for a product or service that provides a benefit to potential customers and creates a win-win relationship between them and the entrepreneur.

Knowing and understanding potential customers and creating a product or service that fulfills an important need for them is the classic "holy grail" of all business ventures. The customer and the marketplace provide the revenues to ultimately determine the success or failure of any venture. In Silicon Valley, there are countless examples of entrepreneurs who have invented a new technology that may serve a particular purpose or have considerable promise to solve a problem or create a new way of doing something. However, if no one will buy the product and it appeals only to the inventor, then there is no business to develop and the product should have remained in the lab or the imagination of the inventor. There is a great deal of gray area here and many products languish until they are simply marketed more properly, the timing for their release improves, or the design and usability improves. Creating a successful product or service comes from understanding the customer and results from getting customer feedback and developing a better awareness of the market demand.

Thus, the ability of an entrepreneur to deeply understand the market demand for his or her product or service is hugely important. It requires more than subjective intuition and vague estimates about the level of customer acceptance and overall market size. It requires extensive focus and research. This has taken many forms over the years: focus groups, customer interviews, competitive analysis and good old-fashioned trial and error. Sheer persistence comes into play for this latter endeavor. Sometimes, it is nearly impossible to predict market demand and there are many examples of corporate blunders where millions of dollars have been spent to create and market a product that no one wants. The attempt by the Coca Cola Company to introduce a "New Coke" in the mid 1980s, for example, was such a huge failure that for years every can of Coca-Cola had to say Coca Cola "Classic" in order to avoid association with the failed "new" recipe.

The most successful entrepreneurs are able to repeatedly focus on understanding their customers and address both their "felt" and "latent" (unexpressed or, as yet, unrecognized) needs. Consider the example of Ronald Burr and Marwan Zebian, founding partners of NetZero; a very successful large ISP (Internet Service Provider). The core idea for the company came to Zebian in 1998 while he was driving down the highway listening to an expensive Super Bowl advertisement. In those days, Internet service operators were like telephone companies. Users had to pay a fee in order to connect through a specific service provider. The experience of listening to the radio and the advertisement sparked in Zebian the idea that Internet access should be free to users, like the radio. Such a system would substantially increase the access and freedom of users. And, if there were enough users, the company could make money by selling advertising to large sponsors; similar to radio or television. This would be a "game changing" idea for how Internet services functioned.

Zebian shared his inspiration with Burr who saw the possibilities and felt it was a potentially revolutionary idea. Neither of them, however, knew anything about advertising, which was critical for making the venture successful.

According to Burr, he and his team began an "extreme planning" phase, involving intensive market research in which they immersed themselves into understanding the advertising business. Burr, a native of California and self-trained software engineer with no college degree, had no real experience in dealing with advertisers. "We didn't know anyone in that business, but we had friends who did. Somebody always knows someone, and we started pulling on our network," Burr explains. "Our founding team all had a strong entrepreneurial focus. We worked hard to get to know people in advertising. We thought through every aspect of the business. We did a great deal of research with advertisers who were our real customers. We spent weeks meeting with them on Madison Avenue, asking them if this is a model they would support."

Customers / Market

Generating Interest and Revenue

Developing the Product / Service

CUSTOMER / VISION EXAMPLE:
"I can see families using the power of social networks to support their kids to learn and enjoy all types of music."

Marwan Zebian
Co-Founder NetZero

Ronald Burr
Co-Founder NetZero

The NetZero founders then absorbed themselves with understanding the market demand and looked to related business models in the software industry to develop new ways to create revenue. According to Zebian's original vision, they offered free access to the Web as well as a discount pay service, using advertising to make money. Of course, other Internet service providers used advertising too. Unlike their competitors, however, they decided to charge fees for customer service. "That is an ISP's biggest expense. Customer-call centers have to be available 24/7 and that costs a lot of money, much more than telecom costs which have become cheaper over the years," says Burr. "So we followed the playbook of the software industry and charged for customer service."

NetZero's extreme planning and intensive market research plus its ingeniously borrowing business models from related industries (radio and software) spawned a new type of ISP, the likes of which the Internet had not seen before that time. The NetZero model quickly hit gold. The new ISP signed up more than a million subscribers in just the first nine months. By the early 2000s the company had reached 2.5 million users. "We had first-mover advantage," explains Burr. The basic business model created by Burr and his team still survives today and provides NetZero with a key competitive advantage in the ISP marketplace.

One key to the NetZero founder's success was understanding their potential customers' interests and needs (both end users and advertisers) and realizing that these customers were ready for a new type of Internet service model that offered them significant benefits and advantages. Like the other successful entrepreneurial ventures we have mentioned so far – Elon Musk's Tesla Motors, Richard Branson's Virgin Express, Jeff Bezos' Amazon, Muhammed Yunus' micro credit and Blake Mycoskie's TOMs – the combination of deep customer understanding with a vision that provides them with significant new benefits produces a game changing result.

Team Members and Employees

The importance of the ability to attract and inspire team members and employees cannot be underestimated. This is especially true for founders of a new start-up ventures who have no choice but to wear numerous hats until the company is up and running. A major challenge for start-ups is that most entrepreneurs don't have the resources to hire on all of the people they need. As a result, the company founder has to rely on his or her own efforts and often has to entice key employees to work for little or no money. Perhaps they will receive some ownership in the company in the form of stock options, a common practice in Silicon Valley. However, the stock often has little or no value at the start up of a new enterprise and the founder must rely on the ability to articulate his or her dream and create excitement and confidence in the minds and hearts of much-needed employees and team members.

The ultimate success of new ventures relies heavily on the capacity to create high performing teams. High performing teams demonstrate the characteristic of *collective intelligence*. Intelligence, in general, is defined as: *The ability to interact successfully with one's world, especially in the face of challenge or change.* Collective intelligence, then, can be viewed as: *A shared or group intelligence that emerges from the collaboration and communication between individuals in groups and other collective living systems* – e.g., synergies and resilience of ecosystems; high performing teams; "wisdom of crowds."

In businesses and organizations, collective intelligence relates to the ability of people in a team, group or organization to think and act in an aligned and coordinated fashion, sharing a common mission and vision. Similar to the way that hydrogen and oxygen combine to form the third entity of water, collective intelligence transforms separate individuals into a cohesive group and creates a team in which the whole is truly greater than the sum of its parts.

The fruit of effective collective intelligence is what is known as *generative collaboration*. Generative collaboration involves people working together to create or generate something new, surprising and beyond the capacities of any of the group members individually. Through generative collaboration, individual team members are able to utilize their abilities to the fullest and discover and apply resources that they did not yet realize that they had. They draw new ideas and resources out of each other. Thus, the performance or output of the group as a whole is much greater than it would be if the individuals were working by themselves.

The success of new ventures relies heavily on the capacity to build high performing teams capable of genertive collaboration.

Team Members / Employees
Creating Alignment
Increasing Competency

TEAM / MISSION EXAMPLE:
"My vision will attract and inspire a team to produce and sell the tools that will teach music to kids in a fun and collaborative way."

To create collective intelligence and generative collaboration, it is crucial to fully understand and appreciate what motivates people. In the end, it is not just money or a heightened job title. The most powerful motivator is to be part of something important and to achieve a common dream that relies on that person's full use of their talents and abilities in order to be successful. This represents "empowerment" in its highest form – inspiring individuals in a team to draw from their own experience and skills to create something that everyone in the team agrees is worth pursuing passionately.

Developing a high performing team is the part of the Circle of Success that most directly requires the entrepreneur's leadership skills in order to effectively tap the collective abilities of a team and provide the necessary inspiration to achieve a desired outcome. Based on hundreds of interviews with successful managers we have found certain distinctive leadership actions and qualities that are focused on achieving organizational outcomes, a balance of which is required for success.

Emotional intelligence is one of the entrepreneur's key leadership skills. By putting himself or herself into the shoes of the team members or employees, understanding their needs and desires, their motivations and their abilities, the entrepreneur becomes a true leader. He or she inspires as well as coaches, stretches, shares and ultimately empowers the team to tap their abilities to achieve a common goal. All of these leadership activities require the entrepreneur to have a clear understanding of the team members' perspectives and inspire and align them toward a common mission and vision. This capacity is another one of the key success factors for new ventures and projects.

The failure to do so can have significant negative consequences. Consider the example of the large well-known multinational telecommunications company who learned this lesson the hard way. The company was struggling to stay competitive and knew it needed to develop a product for a very important segment of its market. It would also need to do this quickly in order to have "first mover" advantage. The project was so critical to the company's success that its top management assembled a team of 1000 people to develop the new product as quickly as possible. It turned out, to their surprise and embarrassment however, that one of their competitors was able to create a better product in a shorter time that cost much less—completely outperforming them in the marketplace—and they did it with a team of just 20 people!

Of course, the burning question for the large telecommunications company was, "How is it possible that 20 people could so completely outperform 1000?!" The difference that made the difference is what we are referring to as the capacity for collective intelligence and "generative collaboration." Applying the filters of Success Factor Modeling to help the company reflect upon how their team of 1000 people had worked together, it became obvious that the team members had operated in "silos," largely isolated from one another. The various team members simply worked to carry out the task that they had been assigned by the project leader, who viewed people as essentially parts of a machine or computer software program – what we call "brain and pencil" leadership in SFM. At best, this creates a type of "collected" intelligence; where $1 + 1 = 2$.

The group of 20 people, on the other hand, were led by a person who was passionate about the vision for the project. This leader operated much more like an orchestra conductor, infusing the team members with a sense of common purpose and mission. Team members were encouraged to be in constant communication and interaction (like musicians in an orchestra); challenging, stimulating and supporting each other to be and give the best of themselves, think "outside of the box" and reach for excellence in everything they did.

They were able to achieve a high level of generative collaboration, stimulating and supporting one another to move forward in new ways and create something unprecedented; i.e., $1 + 1 = 3$. This required that the group members share vision, incorporate multiple perspectives and create a strong "team spirit" based on trust and mutual respect.

Stakeholders and Investors

A *stakeholder* can be any individual or group related to a project or venture who:

1. has resources or skills which can significantly effect the quality of results
2. affects decisions
3. is affected—positively or negatively—by the consequences of decisions and the intended results
4. can either hinder or facilitate reaching the expected results

The term comes from the old practice of placing a series of (wooden) stakes to delineate the boundary of a property, claiming it for the "holders" of the stakes. It has evolved to indicate a person or group owning a significant percentage of a company's shares, or a person or group not owning shares in an enterprise but affected by or having an interest in its operations. Typically, stakeholders are individuals or groups who hold the key to essential resources that the company needs in order to succeed.

Investors are a particular form of stakeholder who commit money to a venture in order to earn a financial return. An investor in a technology start-up is typically someone who has a surplus of money, which he or she wants to make use of to get a longer-term payoff. In existing organizations that do not need start-up capital, the investors or stakeholder are literally the stockholders or at times people in top management from whom one is seeking sponsorship.

For most entrepreneurs, the pursuit of financing and acquisition of key resources occupies the bulk of their time and focus. For the most effective entrepreneurs, this is still true, however, they use their skill in inspiring others around their Circle of Success to gain momentum in achieving the funding and resources they need. The more an entrepreneur is able to demonstrate interest and support from potential customers, team members and partners, the more attractive they become to potential investors and stakeholders.

The process starts with taking an honest look at what the company has to offer the investor by assuming the perspective of someone investing money or some other essential resource and hoping to get some type of return on their investment. In order to do this correctly, the entrepreneur has to first consider the specific attributes of that particular investor. What kind of investor is it? A venture investor that is making an investment of institutional funds has a far different view of the deal than an angel investor that is putting in personal dollars.

Stakeholders are individuals or groups who hold the key to essential resources that the company needs in order to succeed.

Stakeholders/ Investors
*Raising Investment /
Acquiring Essential Resources
Growing the Business and
Creating Value*

STAKEHOLDERS / AMBITION EXAMPLE:
"With additional capital, our product can be sold around the world. The tools can be expanded to different instruments and different skills than music."

The entrepreneur's passion, in the form of his or her ambition to achieve success and grow his or her venture, is what is most attractive to potential stakeholders.

To be successful, an entrepreneur needs investors and stakeholders that are not just interested in financeal gain, but are also passionate about what the entrepreneur has created and who are willing to provide other resources and relationships that ensure the success of the venture.

Angel investors are a new breed of investors willing to take a high level of risk and become intimately involved in ensuring a new venture's success.

An entrepreneur has to understand the values of his or her investors: is the investor simply looking for a financial return or are they also passionate about what the entrepreneur has created and they are willing to invest not only capital but other resources and relationships to assist the company in succeeding? The latter perspective is typical of many angel investors who enjoy "dabbling" in the speculative world of early stage private equity financings.

Angel investors got their name from none other than Broadway's theater district in New York City. Struggling theater productions would seek alternative financing when banks and other financial institutions would not lend them money. Instead an individual "angel" investor would seem to come down from heaven and bestow the necessary funds to get the production started.

The term "angel" made its way out to California in the early days of Hollywood where angels took the form of financial backers in the movie business. Eventually the term made its way up to Silicon Valley where it applies today to wealthy individuals who can afford to invest relatively small amounts of money in early stage companies with the hope that they will see an exponential return on their investment. They often become intimately involved with the company as an advisor or board member. The rewards for that involvement often far exceeds the mere financial return as the experience, relationships and ideas of the angel can be extremely beneficial to entrepreneurs. Savvy founders of start ups prefer angel investors, because they are more likely to get more involved with helping the entrepreneur and give him or her access to their network and resources.

There are fairly distinct attributes that an investor wants to hear in any entrepreneur's "pitch" of their company vision and especially its ambition. Obviously, how the investor will make money or receive concrete value from the venture is an important point that the investor will want to know. It is generally the achievement of the venture's ambition that will create the value necessary to repay the investor. The presentation of the company's ambition involves not only a concise description of the company's product or service, but also the size of the market and the company's plan for capturing sufficient market share. Of course, investors will also want a description of the company's management team and an explanation for why they are specially qualified and capable to achieve the venture's ambitions.

The primary success factor in pursuing investment is therefore to understand the perspective of the investors, their needs and desires, their values and interests as well as the fears and concerns they may have in risking their hard-earned money or other resources on a fledgling company.

Once the entrepreneur understands the viewpoint of the investors, then the next success factor becomes paramount: persistence. Ron Burr, the former CEO of NetZero, mentioned earlier, serves as a good example of the importance of persistence. As you will recall, co-founder Marwan Zebian came up with the idea for a free ISP service while he was driving down the freeway listening to a high-priced Super Bowl ad. The idea was that Internet access should be free to users, much like drivers listening to their car radios on the open freeway, and that, with enough users, the company could make money by selling advertising to large sponsors.

In retrospect, this business model was not so successful for many companies founded during the Internet boom. Many had unrealstic expectations, anticipating very large numbers of users of their Internet software. For most companies in this space, the large number of users never materialized. As a result, this advertising model has been widely discredited as not viable; though some companies, like Google, Yahoo and Facebook have primarily advertising driven businesses.

Nevertheless, Ron and his team persisted and were turned down by no less than 37 investors, until finally a single investor came forward and put the first two million dollars into the company.

NetZero swiftly built up its user base to millions of users and ultimately went public at the height of the Internet boom after acquiring seven other companies along the way. By 2005, NetZero's market cap was in the billions of dollars and the four founders, including Ron, have long since retired following years of hard work.

A primary success factor in securing resources from potential stakeholders is to understand their perspective, their needs and desires and their values and interests, as well as their fears and concerns.

Partners and Alliances

In the dynamic and uncertain world of emerging growth companies, establishing key alliances and partnerships is another important success factor. In fact, who you know and who you have connections with is frequently as important for the valuation of your company as is your technology or revenue. Partnerships and alliances are win-win relationships that allow an entrepreneur to expand or leverage resources or to increase visibility. Partners are different from team members and stakeholders in that their relationship with the venture is more "arm's length"; i.e., the success of their venture is not dependent on the success of their partner. Thus, the degree of dependency and risk is small compared with the possible benefits. The most successful partnerships and alliances are those in which the roles of potential partners complement each other, creating an effective synergy between their resources.

Partnerships and alliances are often an unexplored part of the Circle of Success that can make a huge difference. By finding ways to bring together complementary roles to create win-win relationships, entrepreneurs can greatly leverage and expand their resources.

Partners /
Alliances

Building Win-Win Relationships

*Expanding and
Leveraging Resources*

PARTNERS / ROLE EXAMPLE:
*"I have made a deal with a significant toystore
chain to feature my product in their advertizing
as an example of how toys can enhance learning."*

Strategic alliances, for instance, are formal (and sometimes informal) relationships between organizations through which they coordinate technical and business activities and share resources in order to reach goals more quickly, less expensively and/or more easily, and to create a competitive advantage. Strategic alliances also help companies to achieve what is known as "open innovation." *Open innovation* is essentially defined as "innovating with partners by sharing risk and sharing reward."

According to Henry Chesbrough, "Open innovation is a paradigm that assumes that firms can and should use external ideas as well as internal ideas, and internal and external paths to market, as the firms look to advance their technology." The central idea behind open innovation is that in a world of widely distributed knowledge, companies cannot succeed by relying entirely on their own research. The knowledge and resources necessary for innovation resides in employees, suppliers, customers, competitors and universities. Thus, in order to accelerate innovation and leverage resources, companies need to create win-win partnerships and alliances with other organizations and entities.

New companies also build partnerships and alliances by establishing an *advisory board*—a group of individuals who provide advice and other resources to start-up companies. These individuals usually have expertise or experience in some area that is essential to the success of the start-up. In fact, one guiding principle for establishing a successful advisory board is to make sure you have representatives from each of the four quadrants of the SFM Circle of Success (investor, customer, team and partner).

Companies, new and old, also benefit from having relationships with others with whom they can share "best practices." Best practice comparisons involve the process of sharing, discussing and comparing business practices or behavioral action steps, and searching for those that produce the best results. *Best practice groups and networks* compare the approaches that they have taken with respect to shared problems and goals in order to identify practices that will improve the overall operations of the members. In fact, when combined with benchmarking, the sharing of best practices becomes a powerful form of Success Factor Modeling and an effective source of synergies and new ideas.

When establishing best practice groups and networks, however, it is important to involve individuals and organizations from outside of your own industry. If the sharing of best practices is applied within the same industry, it tends to validate what each other is already doing and is therefore not particularly innovative. Sharing best practices within a particular industry will only serve to help avoid mistakes. As the example of NetZero's adopting a model of free service supported by advertising from the radio industry and the idea of charging for customer service from the software industry, sharing best practices from other trades can be an excellent method to "borrow an idea from another industry."

It should be noted that interfacing with a partner can also be one of the more challenging areas of the Circle of Success to manage. This is true, not because partnering is hard but because starting partnerships can often be too easy.

One of the most common mistakes entrepreneurs make is to partner too soon with the wrong people. Once a partnership is in place, it can often be very difficult and time consuming to try to undo.

The reason that entrepreneurs are susceptible to partnering too quickly with the wrong alliance is that once they begin telling their story, it can be comforting to find a willing audience. The problem is, how is the partnership really going to work and what happens if the partnership begins to hold you back?

A common pitfall arises when an entrepreneur of an early stage company attracts the attention of a larger strategic corporate partner. The acknowledgment by the larger and more credible entity can be intoxicating, especially when there is an offer of funding attached to that interests. However, the down side arises when there are significant strings attached to accepting investment from a strategic partner too soon.

In the best-case scenario when this occurs, the strategic partner would provide a market channel for the entrepreneur's product or service and otherwise completely leave the business management decisions to the entrepreneur. In the worst case scenario, the larger strategic partner has significant conditions attached to providing their strategic investment and expects the company to alter or limit its focus only to those areas of business that serve the strategic partner's own financial agenda.

The best partnerships arise where both parties have complementary roles and derive a clear and obvious benefit from their collaboration. They both come away with something greater than if the partnership did not exist. They are able to create a "win-win" relationship versus a "win-lose" or worse yet, a "lose-lose" relationship (e.g. both parties are worse off because of the wasted time and money spent on the collaboration).

As we established in the previous chapter, roles are most effective and satisfying when they are based upon one's "area of excellence." Companies and organizations will also have their areas of excellence. The best partnerships are those where one individual or organization's area of excellence is complemented and enhanced by a different area of excellence of their partner.

"Open innovation," advisory boards and best practice networks are examples of possible types of partnerships.

The best partnerships are those in which both parties have complementary roles and derive a clear and obvious benefit from their collaboration, coming away with something greater than if the partnership did not exist.

Ed Hogan
Founder and CEO
Pleasant Hawaiian Holidays

"Vacation package" pioneer Ed Hogan applied his passion for travel to exotic places to create win-win partnerships that grew into a more than half-billion dollar a year business.

Like many other successful entrepreneurs, Ed also developed a desire to "give back" to his community and society as a whole as a gesture of gratitude for the success he enjoyed in his life. In 1998, Ed and his wife Lynn established The Hogan Family Foundation; a non-profit organization dedicated to promoting the entrepreneurial spirit through the creation and operation of educational, civic-minded, and humanitarian programs designed to encourage a more productive and contributory society. Since it's founding, the Foundation has invested approximately $67 million in its educational and charitable programs.

Humanitarian programs include the Hogan Angel Flight Program, assisting with travel arrangements for needy medical patients with a contribution of a quarter million dollars annually.

When facing a limited market opportunity, a cooperative vision with a trusted partner or ally can develop new territory that is more robust and promising than your current market outlook. One example is this win-win scenario is the experience of Ed Hogan, CEO of Pleasant Hawaiian Holidays, a company founded in the post-World War II era by this former GI in Pleasant, New Jersey. Ed began his travel agency with very little money in his pocket, but with a strong passion to travel to exotic places. As a result of his own travels and input from customers of his travel agency, Ed realized that Hawaii was fast becoming a popular tourist destination. He rounded up enough funds to buy a retired airplane that he refurbished. Ed then began making flights to Hawaii where he dropped off tourists who vacationed at various hotels. He soon realized that he could not easily compete with the larger airlines that had more volume of business and could charge lower fees. In other words, providing the actual travel was not his "area of excellence."

This led Ed to develop a vision and ambition that involved a way to compete better on price while capturing a larger market share. He realized that in order to scale his business, he needed the help of an ally with complementary business goals and expertise to increase revenue from Hawaiian tourists. As a result, he partnered with selected hotels and negotiated blocks of rooms in order to receive a volume discount. It was a win-win for both sides. Even though their respective margins were lower, they each expanded their revenue exponentially by increasing their volume of customers overall. Ed would sell the travel packages that included both the flight and hotel fees at a reduced package price. The partnership catapulted his company into a profitable business. He eventually bought several hotels from his partners, absorbing them into his growing travel empire.

Ed gained international notoriety as a pioneer of the "vacation package" within the tourist industry. His business enterprise grew dramatically over the next four decades, as he expanded to destinations around the world, generating over $500 million a year in sales. He sold Pleasant Hawaiian Holidays to the Southern California Automobile Association of America, a leading American travel agency, for several hundred million dollars.

Still connected to his passion, Ed continues to be a well-known figure in the travel industry, as the companies he founded attain growth and success in an ever-changing world. He serves as Chairman of the non-profit Hogan Family Foundation, Pleasant Travel Service, Pleasant Aircraft Leasing, Royal Lahaina Development Company, and Royal Lahaina and Royal Kona resorts.

If Ed had not learned the art of partnering, he may have simply given in to his competitors years ago or never had the opportunity to scale his business.

EXAMPLE OF THE SFM CIRCLE OF SUCCESS

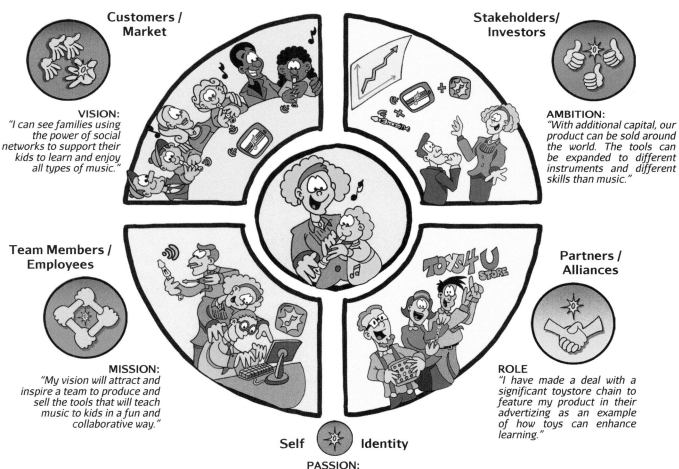

Customers / Market

VISION:
"I can see families using the power of social networks to support their kids to learn and enjoy all types of music."

Stakeholders/ Investors

AMBITION:
"With additional capital, our product can be sold around the world. The tools can be expanded to different instruments and different skills than music."

Team Members / Employees

MISSION:
"My vision will attract and inspire a team to produce and sell the tools that will teach music to kids in a fun and collaborative way."

Partners / Alliances

ROLE
"I have made a deal with a significant toystore chain to feature my product in their advertizing as an example of how toys can enhance learning."

Self   Identity

PASSION:
"I am a business woman and a mother passionate about watching my girl growing up. I am also passionate about music."

The Influence of Context and the "Field of Innovation" on the Circle of Success

The examples of Ed Hogan and Pleasant Hawaiian Holidays, Marwan Zebian and Ron Burr and NetZero, Steig Westerberg and Stream Theory bring up another key factor relating to the Circle of Success; which is reflected in the success of all of the entrepreneurs and their ventures that we have mentioned so far – Elon Musk and Tesla Motors, Walt Disney and his entertainment empire, Richard Branson and Virgin Express, Jeff Bezos and Amazon, Muhammed Yunus and micro credit, and Blake Mycoskie and TOMs. This has to do with the larger social and cultural "field" or "zeitgeist" in which it the entrepreneur and his or her venture are operating.

Like everything else, the success of new ventures is largely determined by their fit into the larger systems of which they are a part. The evolving state of these bigger systems defines the context in which the entrepreneur's passion and intention takes shape with respect to the different parts of the Circle of Success. The state of these larger systems can be viewed as a type of field that is a function of the evolving socio-economic dynamics as well as technical developments. Such a field is composed of not just the existing needs, attitudes and opinions of the individuals making up the Circle of Success but also their latent or developing needs and attitudes.

It is the state of this larger field of possibilities that determines whether an entrepreneur's idea is perceived as feasible and desirable. Those ventures that are most successful are the ones that produce something that is truly a breakthrough and "game changing." This happens when they are able to catch the "crest of the wave" of an emerging trend in the surrounding field.

The capacity to understand and track key developments in the larger field of interests and possibilities is a major success factor for aspiring entrepreneurs. This has to do with understanding the forces that are shaping the field and applying what could be called "weak signal detection" to tune into upcoming trends. The ability of Amazon founder Jeff Bezos to recognize the vast potential opened by the rapid growth in Internet use combined with the ruling that online retailers in the US would not have to collect out-of-state sales taxes is a good example of this.

New possibilities and game changing potentials are constantly emerging. A key success factor for entrepreneurs is having a way to sense and predict where and when these game changing developments will next arise.

The success of new ventures is a consequence of how well they serve and are received into the larger socio-economic system within which they are launched.

Evolving technical developments and shifts in people's needs and attitudes make up a type of "field of innovation" that determines the feasibility, desirability and acceptability of new products and ideas.

In order to be successful, entrepreneurs need to be able to sense and take advantage of emerging trends and opportunities within the dynamic "field of innovation."

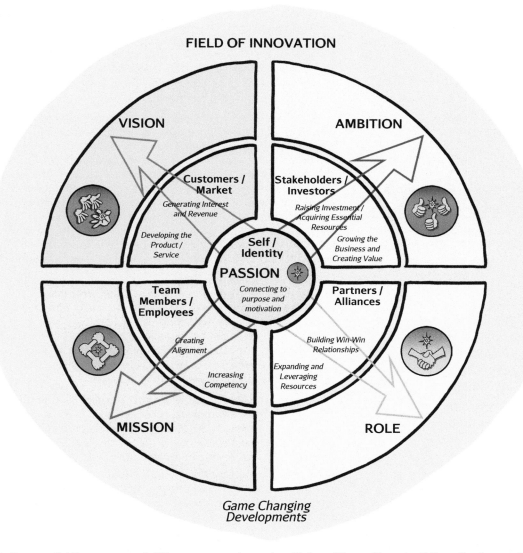

FIELD OF INNOVATION

VISION

AMBITION

Customers / Market

Generating Interest and Revenue

Developing the Product / Service

Stakeholders / Investors

Raising Investment / Acquiring Essential Resources

Growing the Business and Creating Value

Self / Identity

PASSION

Connecting to purpose and motivation

Team Members / Employees

Creating Alignment

Increasing Competency

Partners / Alliances

Building Win-Win Relationships

Expanding and Leveraging Resources

MISSION

ROLE

Game Changing Developments

The Most Successful Entrepreneurial Ventures are those that Make a "Game Changing" Contribution to the Larger Socio-Economic Context or "Field of Innovation" in which they exist

**Abraham Maslow's
Hierarchy of Needs Pyramid**

According to Maslow's Hierarchy of Needs, there are basic human needs which must be satisfied before more sophisticated, higher level needs can be considered. This ordering of needs is a key influence on the direction of development within the "field of innovation." Newer developments tend toward the satisfaction of higher level needs.

In his prophetic article *Forces Shaping the New Information Paradigm* (1985) Glenn C. Bacon, a senior technology manager at IBM, proposes psychologist *Abraham Maslow's Hierarchy of Needs* as one of the fundamental forces influencing the direction of social and economic developments. As Bacon explains, Maslow's theory states that there are basic human needs which must be satisfied at some level in order for more sophisticated, higher level needs to be considered. This hierarchy of needs determines the direction and speed of technical developments.

For example, our basic need for *physiological survival* must be satisfied before we can do anything else. To survive, individuals and organizations must have a proper functioning of the fundamental mechanisms that support their existence. Once survival can be assured, there is a need for *security and safety*. That is, not only is one alive, but is also in a social environment which is secure and not overly hostile. At the next level, once one is satisfied with the safety of the environment, concerns turn toward social connection and a focus upon achieving a sense of *belonging*. At the level above is the need to move beyond the group and obtain a unique and more autonomous position and sense of personal *self-esteem*. Bacon writes, "the top level of Maslow's hierarchy is that of *self-actualization*. Here a person is self-sufficient and highly autonomous. He cooperates with his community but acts with his own style and priorities."

In his later versions of the model, Maslow added a seventh level that he called *self-transcendence* — to experience, unite with and serve that which is beyond the individual self. This emerges from the desire to go beyond our ordinary human level of consciousness and experience oneness with the greater whole, the higher truth, whatever that may be. It is also connected with the desire to help others to self-actualize. This description fits that of what referred to in the last chapter as a being a "holon," where ego and soul are in harmony – a person perceives him or herself as simultaneously an independent whole and part of something larger than him or herself.

According to Bacon, the development of technologies, and the accompanying products and services that go with them, have been and are continuing to provide solutions that steadily move up Maslow's hierarchy of needs. Anticipating such developments as smart phones, tablets and social media, Bacon claimed 30 years ago that the technology developments and new ventures that are able to support this momentum to the top parts of Maslow's hierarchy will be the future "winners."* Bacon's implication is that ventures that create an increasing experience of belonging, esteem, self-actualization and ultimately self-transcendence for their founders, customers, employees, stakeholders and partners will be increasingly successful.

It seems clear that this is where what we are calling "next generation entrepreneurs" are putting their focus. The notion of "zentrapreneurism" and the five keys for creating a world to which people want to belong that we identified at the beginning of this chapter largely center around what Maslow would call "self-actualization" and "self-transcendence."

Richard Branson's statement that his interest in life comes from setting "huge, apparently unachievable challenges and trying to rise above them... from the perspective of wanting to live life to the full" is a clear expression of a desire for self-actualization.

Tesla Motors founder Elon Musk's stated aspiration to "increase the scope and scale of human consciousness in order to better understand what questions to ask" and "strive for greater collective enlightenment" is a clear expression of this trend. Musk's daring decision to open all of the patents held by his company to other organizations is a concrete example of a type of self-transcendence. As Musk put it, "Tesla Motors was created to accelerate the advent of sustainable transport. If we clear a path to the creation of compelling electric vehicles, but then lay intellectual property landmines behind us to inhibit others, we are acting in a manner contrary to that goal."

Muhammed Yunus' development of micro credit, and Blake Mycoskie's "One-For-One" business model for TOMs are other examples of an entrepreneurial trend toward self-transcendence and the desire to help others to self-actualize by supporting them to move beyond the lower levels of needs. In fact, the "One-For-One" approach fulfills esteem needs for one group of customers in order to satisfy physical needs for others.

The trend to support others to self-actualize is not only limited to customers. Starbuck's Coffee Company, for instance, has initiated a program in which they pay for their employees to finish college, with no obligation for the employee to continue working for the company after graduation.

Angel investors who want to grow and give back by helping entrepreneurs succeed, supporting the venture's team members and providing meaningful benefits to customers are another example of this trend.

When ventures, team members, stakeholders, partners and customers all support each other toward self-actualization, it creates a powerful field of innovation. As we shall see in the coming sections of this book, the Silicon Valley in California has developed a particularly strong field of innovation in this regard.

---

* In a recent article titled *As IT's Industrial Age Ends the Humanist Era Begins*, the author confirms Bacon's prediction. The article points out that IT (Information Technology) "was once a function that tamed the semiconductor and brought order to a bunch of ones and zeroes so that transactions could be efficiently and accurately tabulated." The earliest developments of IT were to serve basic survival and safety needs; i.e., record keeping, databases, system coordination functions, etc. According to the article, "IT must become a competency that does more than crunch numbers, process journal entries and print reports... The new IT problems involve people, emotions, and other less-than-static, logical or perfect resources." The article asserts that, rather than technical skills, technology developers will need an intimate knowledge of how the human mind works, feels and thinks. It claims that entrepreneurs of this new era require (1) Design skills (e.g., how color, emotion, etc., drive behavior), (2) Social/Human skills (social Insights, human behavior knowledge) and (3) Translation and Transition skills. This coincides quite well with what we have discovered through our studies with Success Factor Modeling.

The Law of Requisite Variety and the Field of Innovation

Another major shaping force on development of the field that Bacon brings up in his article is that of "exploding variety". According to system theorist Ross Ashby's *Law of Requisite Variety*, in order to successfully adapt, achieve or survive, a member of any system requires a minimum amount of flexibility. That amount of flexibility has to be proportional to the variety that member must contend with in the rest of the system. When the context is simple and stable, you don't need much variety or flexibility to get by. When things become dynamic and complex, a great deal of flexibility and variety is necessary.

One of the implications of the Law of Requisite Variety is that, if you want to consistently get to a particular goal or outcome (whether in business, athletics, health or any other area of life), you have to increase the number of options available for reaching that goal in proportion to the degree of potential variability in the system. If the environment changes, we cannot keep doing the same things and expect the same results.

In fact, in his book *Designing Freedom* (1974), organizational consultant and systems theorist Stafford Beer treats the Law of Requisite Variety as a "law of nature", calling it *the dominant law of societary systems*. Pointing out that our deep desire for freedom is a manifestation of the Law of Requisite Variety, Beer says we must face the fact that one of the challenges of our modern world is how to address an ever increasing amount of diversity of all types; cultural, technical, organizational and social.

According to the law of requisite variety, technologies, products, services and business models that provide more flexibility, choice and freedom for business owners, customers, team members, stakeholders and partners will become potential game changers and naturally evolve into the dominant position.

A good illustration of this is that of Brian Chesky and Airbnb, an Internet service that helps connect people looking for a temporary place to stay with people who have rooms or other types of housing temporarily available. The vision for Airbnb arose in 2008 when Chesky and Airbnb co-founder Joe Gebbia were roommates together in San Francisco. The two had moved there after graduating from college in Rhode Island and were looking for work in the area of industrial design. They soon found themselves unemployed and in need of money. The idea for Airbnb first emerged when there was an Industrial Design conference coming up in the city and many hotels were overbooked. The pair believed they could make some money by renting space in their place out to people struggling to find a hotel. They purchased three airbeds and marketed this idea by creating a website called "Air Bed and Breakfast" (thus Airbnb).

This particular time period happened to be the beginning of a boom in what is called the "sharing economy." Following the lead of companies like EBay and Craig's List, services began to emerge where bicycles, cars even dogs could be rented online on a temporary basis. Chesky and his partners believed this trend would continue to expand. They thought why not use the Internet to rent a bed, an apartment or even a castle in Ireland? They took the risk and began to extend the range of listings they provided on the website. The company had a difficult time at first because the concept behind their venture was new and untested in that domain of sharing services. Chesky and his team believed that it was an idea whose time had come, however, and persevered in their mission.

Today, with more than more than 600,000 listings, Airbnb provides significantly more flexibility, choice and freedom for people looking for a place to stay than standard hotel services do. It provides the same freedom and variety for those looking to rent out space on a temporary basis. It also fulfills multiple levels of Maslow's hierarchy of needs. In addition to providing for physical needs in the form of a place to stay, Airbnb allows people much greater autonomy in which they are able to "cooperate with their community but act with their own style and priorities." Airbnb also takes the level of the need for safety very seriously, implementing insurance policies and has over 100 employees devoted exclusively to trust and safety.

Touted as a "disruptive" innovation for the hotel and travel industries, Airbnb was valued at $10 billion dollars as of 2014 and had rental listings in 192 countries. On average, each day there are about 50,000 to 60,000 people using Airbnb. Chesky's personal stake in the company made him, at age 32, one of the world's youngest billionaires. Passionate about his own vision and service, Chesky still continues to use Airbnb himself and has not owned a home since 2010.

In conclusion, we can say that innovations that support the upper levels of Maslow's hierarchy and that allow us greater flexibility, variety and freedom to be both independent wholes and holons will continue to be the "game changers."

Of course, any individual, group or industry will be at different stages of Maslow's hierarchy and have different requirements relating to the degree of flexibility, choice and freedom needed in order to consistently and successfully reach desired outcomes. This will be true for each part of the Circle of Success as well; customers, team members, stakeholders and partners. At the same time their needs will be evolving as the larger field of innovation continues to evolve. The better you can anticipate their needs and the needs that the evolving field of the larger system imposes, the more chance of game changing and lasting success you will have.

As we go through the coming sections of this book it will be important for you to continually reflect on the questions, "How can you incorporate progressively higher levels of the Maslow hierarchy to your vision, mission, ambition and role?" "How is your idea or venture contributing to greater flexibility, choice and freedom for your customers, team members, stakeholders and partners?"

My system to support kids to learn music is flexible. It can work with different instruments. It supports kids' belonging needs because it helps them to learn in community, and it supports their esteem needs as they achieve mastery in different levels of skill.

Barney Pell
Founder and CEO Powerset
Co-Founder Moon Express, LocoMobi
Assoc. Founder, Singularity University

PASSION
Identity / Self

Barney Pell's lifelong passion for learning is at the center of his Circle of Success.

Success Factor Case Example:
Powerset's Barney Pell

"Change the world and make a fortune at the same time."

Barney Pell is an iconic example of the new generation of entrepreneurs that we have been studying in this book. His case provides a clear example of how to build a powerful and effective Circle of Success as well as the challenges that can go with it.

Barney grew up in Los Angeles, California, the son of a single mother who embodied many of the attitudes of the cultural revolution of the 1960s. "I was born when my mom was 20," Barney recounts, "She was an independent spirit and chose to have me on her own." Barney's mother was an only child of Eastern European Jews who had escaped to the US. He spent a lot of time with his grandparents who instilled in him a "super positive attitude—a true belief that thoughts create reality—and that you can achieve anything that you set your mind to." Barney showed himself to be very gifted as a kid and was told to use his gifts "for good." From early in his life, he felt he had a major role to play in the world, "But I didn't know what it was," he says. As result he decided, "I will develop all of my capabilities so that when I figure out what it is going to be then I am ready."

"I really loved learning," Barney explains. "We didn't have much materially, but I knew I was loved. I felt so grateful and felt I couldn't lose anything. That is why I became a risk taker. I was not materialistic. I felt I had health, friends, etc., and there was always something to learn."

Barney loved playing all types of games. For instance, he began playing chess at an early age and became a competitive tournament player as a youth. This led him to a fascination with the optimization of learning ability. Later, he became intensely interested in science fiction and artificial intelligence. "I reflected on the concept of what is intelligence, where does it come from, what are the ways that we think and how can we get better and better at that," he asserts.

Because his mother was a spiritual seeker, Barney also explored many spiritual traditions at a young age: Jewish, Born Again Christian, guru Maharaj Ji, lord Krishna, Synanon, etc. "You can't go through all that and think there is only one truth out there," he claims. Rather, it gave him a further sense of being part of something bigger than himself to which he would one day contribute.

At 13, Barney read the *Silva Mind Control Method* and learned about clearly visualizing outcomes. "I developed my own process," he explains. "Go into a relaxed state, get calm, visualize where I am now and the outcome that was most important to me in all sensory modalities (sight, hearing, feeling, etc.). I would then do the same with my family, the community and then the world." Barney credits this habit of visualizing his goals and desired outcomes as the foundation for an ongoing pattern of life success.

"From early on, I had a long-term success strategy," Barney points out. "I developed a stepping-stone strategy. I realized that success is built on a series of steps." He applied this strategy first to his own education. "I would go look at the possible awards in the awards case at school and choose the ones I wanted to get," he says. In high school, a girl came to talk to the class who had gotten into Stanford University. "No one in my family had even gone to college," explains Barney. "I asked what I needed to do and she said, 'Get 4.0 grade point average, become student body president, have tons of extra curricular activities, and do a lot of volunteering, etc.' So I did." Barney was accepted into Stanford University and went on from there to Cambridge University getting a PhD in Artificial Intelligence focusing in the area of games, strategy and learning.

Barney's work on games and learning strategies opened up a whole new area of artificial intelligence for general game playing. He developed a program that could begin to learn and master any game without having any previous information about the game. Through this research, "I got to make a gift to humanity and understand how the brain works," says Barney.

After getting his PhD, Barney began working at NASA Ames Research Center in the San Francisco Bay Area. He quickly distinguished himself through his capacity for vision, seeing the big picture and applying system level thinking. Even though he was the youngest person in the entire center, he ended up managing an 85-person advanced technology research organization at NASA, developing the technology for autonomous flight control for deep space exploration. His accomplishments there included flying the first AI system in deep space (on the Deep Space One mission), the first spoken dialog system in space, and supporting the Mars Exploration Rovers mission

Barney's research successes made him quite well known in the field of artificial intelligence. He was invited to keynote international conferences and submit articles to leading journals. Normally that would be the ultimate aspiration of a researcher, and Barney realized that he could continue to follow that path and be perceived as very successful without much risk or effort. "But it was not going to grow me," he points out. Furthermore, Barney had recognized that "the power of an idea can move the whole world."

Barney's practice of entering a calm and relaxed state and then visualizing outcomes for himself, his family, his community and the world is an example of developing a type of COACH state and bringing awareness to his position as a "holon."

At NASA, Barney discovered an "area of excellence" in his capacity to see the big picture and apply system level thinking.

Barney's desire for growth and his ambition to make a difference motivated him to leave NASA and explore starting a business in which he could impact the world and also generate financial success for himself and his friends.

VISION
Customers Market

Fueled by his passion for learning and artificial intelligence, Barney began to look for ways he could create something that would benefit others.

"Most people's minds are limited. They only think the world will be the same or a little bit different. So that means that all of these possibilities are opening up that even the big companies won't see coming because they are stuck in today's reality. I could see many possibilities."

Barney liked the idea of starting a company that could impact the world and also generate financial success for himself and his friends. But he didn't feel ready. "I had the idea for e-Bay before e-Bay," he explains as an example of his many business ideas. "But I kept thinking some other bigger company is in a better position to do it than me. As a chess player, you always assume your opponent will make the best move."

Also, while he was clearly strong on technology, Barney didn't have business experience. He felt that if he started a company with partners, he'd need to find a "business guy" to be CEO, "and that put a lot of risk in the mix." So instead, Barney decided to become the "business guy" himself. Given his interests in strategy, it seemed a natural next step. Barney decided to put his research career at NASA on hold and learn something about business to prepare himself to one day start his own company.

Barney left NASA to join his friend's early-stage startup, StockMaster.com, as VP of Strategy and Business Development. "A wonderful thing about startups is that people can jump in and learn by doing," he points out. For Barney, this was like an on-the-job MBA. The venture was successful, growing the company from 5 to 50 people in 2 years and ultimately selling the company in March, 2000.

Still not ready to start his own company, Barney joined another startup company, WhizBang! Labs, developing advanced natural language and search engine technology. WhizBang got caught in the dot bomb and 9/11 market crash. Coming out of this in 2002, Barney wanted to start a company and had learned a lot more, but now the obstacle was a disastrous market environment. Thus, Barney decided to go back to NASA, this time leading a larger organization and working on skills and networking that would be helpful for him when the economy rebounded.

In 2004 the economy and technology market was improving and Barney went to work in a Venture Capital firm as "entrepreneur in residence" in order to "learn how the world looks from an investor perspective." However, he also committed to give his own ideas a chance if he could start something based on his own thoughts.

His passion for learning and artificial intelligence was still very much alive inside of him and Barney looked for ways to apply that passion to create something that would benefit others. As he explored the field of possibilities, he realized that, "according to Moore's Law, computers would double every 18 months and, if you project that forward, there would be 100 times the current computing power in ten years." According to Barney, "Most people's minds are limited. They only think the world will be the same or a little bit different. So that means that all of these possibilities are opening up that even the big companies won't see coming because they are stuck in today's reality. I could see many possibilities."

Barney started envisioning a natural language search engine that could be "potentially the next Google." The idea was to create a search engine that "could match the person at their own level of semantics and meaning." In other words, you could ask questions to in everyday language, just as you would ask a teacher or librarian or shopkeeper, etc. Barney had worked on a prototype in college and decided the technology was not sufficiently advanced at the time and had made a decision to leave it and come back in 20 years when technology was more developed. Now he had an intuition that the time was right for this type of development. He had a more difficult time convincing potential stakeholders to support him however.

He found an interesting company that had developed some innovative applications of natural language processing systems with computers. He tried to get the venture capital firm he was working for to invest, but they wouldn't. After a few other disappointing attempts, it became clear that the venture was not going anywhere. Barney thought he had "lost the opportunity" and was facing a lot of disappointment because he had really worked hard trying to get the project off the ground. It was at this point that Barney started thinking that maybe he could do it himself and start his own company. Drawing on his experience in college, Barney made a prototype that worked to recognize natural language. He realized he could turn the setback into opportunity and develop his own ideas into a game changing search engine that would usher in an era of "conversational computing."

This led to a further insight that his vision and ambition had to be even bigger. From working in the VC firm, he realized that "Venture Capitalists want to invest in billion dollar projects." Therefore, "Ideas have to be absolutely massive," he says. "They are willing to take big risks if the idea is really big." Taking this perspective back to his position as an entrepreneur, Barney thought, "Really what I should be doing is creating massive opportunities for investors. They may be highly risky but are game changers in which you can change the world and make a fortune at the same time." He also realized that "the VCs will want the same percentage of equity, regardless of the amount of money they put in, so I might as well ask for more." Creating a "natural language Google" seemed to fit very well into that recipe. It suddenly seemed like all of his history and identity had led up to that opportunity.

Applying what he had learned from his study of decision theory and artificial intelligence, Barney started by making "a list of all the reasons not to do it." "I ended up with a list of 10 reasons not to do this company," he says, "and started going down and checking them off." One item, for example, was the fact that Barney was a solo entrepreneur that had never started his own company before and it was going to take

VISION
Customers / Markets

Barney started envisioning a natural language search engine that could "could match the person at their own level of semantics and meaning."

AMBITION
Stakeholders/ Investors

Barney realized he could develop his own vision and ideas into a game changing search engine that would usher in an era of "conversational computing" and potentially become "the next Google".

AMBITION
Stakeholders/ Investors

Barney realized that he could apply his vision and ambition to create "massive opportunities for investors" which could be highly risky but are "game changers in which you can change the world and make a fortune at the same time."

"I had a super clear vision, connected to my own personal identity that would positively impact the world. I could go out and recruit the best team in the world because this opportunity was so meaningful and I could go out to investors with exactly the opportunity that I knew everyone was looking for. From my personal passion, I could be building one of the greatest companies of all time. And even if it took twenty-five years it wouldn't matter to me because I would be doing what I loved doing."

a lot of money. "But then I figured I am an expert on artificial intelligence and have certainly participated in starting up companies, so this is the completion of my journey." Another reason on the list was, What if Google does this? "This was the fear I had experienced before," Barney realized; the fear that some other bigger company would be in a better position to carry out his idea than himself. So he thought, "Let me confront that fear. I started supposing 'what if they did?' Then it validates my idea. I have 'moved the giants.' The world is a better place and that is what is most important to me." In fact, "If it is not you, it is all the better," he thought to himself, "Its about the power of the idea to make a better world." Besides that, there would be other big companies competing for search technologies and "in a fierce battle, others will be desperate for what I have."

Ultimately, Barney concluded that "there was an unlimited upside and almost no downside," "In the worst case," he reasoned, "we would have assembled an awesome team and technology that would probably be acquired for more than was put into it."

This realization led to a "wonderful feeling of alignment." He had finally come upon something he believed he was here to do. Everything was perfectly aligned. "I had a super clear vision, connected to my own personal identity that would positively impact the world. I could go out and recruit the best team in the world because this opportunity was so meaningful and I could go out to investors with exactly the opportunity that I knew everyone was looking for. From my personal passion, I could be building one of the greatest companies of all time. And even if it took twenty-five years it wouldn't matter to me because I would be doing what I loved doing."

Barney named the company *Powerset* and decided to begin by seeking out others who had already succeeded in developing advanced natural language software algorithms so that he could "get the biggest head start." He went to speak with people at the Stanford Research Institute and Xerox PARC, two of the most famous research centers in the world. He found that at Xerox PARC they had been working on something similar for 30 years but didn't quite know how to put it all together. Barney proposed that they license him the technology they had been working on for 30 years for his venture. "I was one man with no other resources," he laughs. "They asked, 'Why should we give this to you?' Barney was so aligned with his sense of his mission and vision that he answered, "Because you have to be me in order to do this thing. You have to have my history, which brings together all the right elements. Otherwise it just won't happen."

"I needed exclusive license from them because there was too much risk without it," explains Barney, "but it was too much risk for them to give me exclusive license. It was a chicken and egg situation." Because of his passion and congruence, Barney was able to negotiate an option for 6 months in order to get the investment. If he could raise the right amount of money in that time period, they would agree to the terms he was offering. In the end, it took 18 months to finalize the agreement. "By then I had raised $12 million and had a team of 25 people," he says.

Once he had secured the option, Barney "started hiring people just for stock." He told his potential team members, "If I get the agreement (with PARC), it will be awesome. But my contingency plans will also be awesome." He explained to them, "This is not a question of IF, it is a question of WHO and WHEN. The idea is inevitable. Why not US and why not NOW?" Barney used the metaphor of Stone Soup, pointing out that each new person made the chances stronger. "It has the chance of being one of the greatest companies in history," he said confidently to his potential team members. "Shoot for the stars. Even if you fall short, you may hit the moon." Barney set high standards and created a culture of excellence. He got the people who joined with him to be constantly searching for, "What do we need?" "Who is the best?" He told his team, "Whoever we hire has to be as good at what they do as you are at what you do."

With the option for the algorithms from PARC and a team in place, Barney was able to get angel investment. Even though there was no agreement signed yet with PARC for their technology, Barney had already assembled a great team of people. And even if the PARC agreement never materialized, it was evident that the venture would be valuable. "It was clear we would still do great things," says Barney. "The possibilities with the Xerox PARC technology were awesome, but my contingency plans were also good."

By now, Barney had angel investment secured, his team in place, and a prototype with Xerox PARC who was clearly very committed. The future was starting to evolve as he thought it would. Barney worked on getting a message out to the world about what he and his team were doing. He developed a strategy he called "semi-stealth". Normally, a venture at such an early stage would be in a type of "stealth" mode, not saying anything about what they are doing out of the worry that someone else might steal the idea. But Barney felt that putting his vision out to the world and letting people know he was doing something great was the only way he would be able to attract all of the talent, resources and partnerships that he needed. He let people know that he was doing something on using artificial intelligence and search engines, but did not specify anything about using natural language.

MISSION
Team members / Employees

Barney started hiring people "just for stock," using the metaphor of Stone Soup and pointing out that each new person made the chances stronger.

MISSION
Team members / Employees

Barney set high standards and created a culture of excellence, constantly asking "What do we need?" "Who is the best?" He told his team, "Whoever we hire has be as good at what they do as you are at what you do."

ROLE
Partners / Alliences

Barney was able to use Powerset's role as
a provider of an infrastructure that would
enhance many applications to establish key
partnerships.

ROLE
Partners / Alliences

He said to a start-up PR firm, "We want
you to work with us for free for six months.
What we are doing is so big it will make your
company." He was right!

Within a year, Barney was eventually able to get Ron Kaplan, the lead scientist at PARC, on board and to join as Chief Scientist. Barney recruited other key people – such as the lead search engine architect from Yahoo – and assembled a team of "the best and the brightest" in all of the areas relevant to the venture. He also developed key partnerships and alliances to gain access to key resources. "For example," explains Barney, "we needed a PR firm. We went to a firm that was also just starting up and said, 'We want you to work with us for free for six months. What we are doing is so big it will make your company.'" They agreed and, in fact, their partnership with Powerset was responsible for launching them as a successful PR firm.

Another partnership was with the open source project HADOOP who had developed a scalable data infrastructure that would be critical for a natural language search function. Barney and Powerset also partnered with Jeff Bezos and Amazon, and became the "poster child" for their developments with Cloud computing and their "crowd source" platform.

All of this allowed Barney to secure a $12 million first round of venture capital funding and build an incredible amount of momentum in the venture. The challenge was, as Barney points out, "It also attracted an equally incredible amount of hype. And hype can come back and bite you."

"I tried to be humble," says Barney, "and focus on what I was doing to help the world. At the same time, it is also easy to get caught up in the greatness of what you are doing. You have to believe strongly in what you are doing, but sometimes passion can come through as arrogance." Barney was always very careful not to publicly assert that Powerset would "be the next Google." Rather, he claimed that what they were working on "would be the future of Internet search," which he believed very strongly. In January of 2007, however, the *New York Times* came out with an article on the front page of their business section titled *In Search of the Next Google* with a photo of Barney and the other founders of Powerset as part of the cover story. "This created quite a backlash," explains Barney, "especially from people we knew at Google."

The strategy of "reaching for the stars" also produced a high amount of pressure. "What we were trying to do was really quite complicated," comments Barney, "and there was still a question about whether we actually had all the capabilities to deliver." All the while, the venture was now "burning" $1 million per month in salaries and expenses. Furthermore, while Barney had put together an awesome team and found lots of ways to apply natural language algorithms better than anyone else had so far, he still had no live product. As he put it, "We had never actually shown it would work successfully for a user, even in a test case."

As the pressure built, so did the doubts. This created a new leadership challenge for Barney; "How do we keep that passion and belief going when it is taking longer than we had expected and people are saying it is going too slow or won't work?" "Even though I was very positive, I had to consider that maybe we were just being unrealistic and not hearing all of the *no's*." With the hype and pressure increasing, some of the team members were wanting to retreat back to doing something less ambitious.

The hype and pressure also created challenges for Barney and his stakeholders. One of Powerset's key board members maintained that Barney should raise as much money as possible before the "market meltdown" that he perceived was coming in 2008. A similar situation had happened with the burst of the Internet bubble in the late 1990s. As a result, Barney tried to raise an additional $25 million just two months after completing the $12 million venture capital round. It was a big challenge and Barney found himself away from the team and spending all of his time with investors.

In addition, Barney's co-founder of Powerset, who was also the chief operating officer, was not supportive of raising so much more funding and asking for a higher valuation of the company. There started to be increasing tension between Barney and his co-founder, which created reverberations through the team. "Problems happen when you start questioning the vision," says Barney. "If you believe what you are doing is going to work, the venture is incredibly valuable. If you don't, it isn't worth anything."

Furthermore, Barney was tired, not sleeping well due to all the pressure and his intense focus on raising additional investment. He himself began to experience a greater and greater degree of tension and insecurity. He even began to think about "getting a new CEO and replacing myself."

When Barney went back to the investors and shared what he was considering, however, they said, "We invested in you, not some other CEO." They began to feel that perhaps Barney was going to back out. "In the eyes of investors, the need to get a new CEO meant the venture was worth nothing," explains Barney. To his investors, Barney had expressed a dangerous lack of confidence in himself.

Barney stepped back from the idea of getting a new CEO, replaced his co-founder, and immediately shifted his mindset to focus on options. Barney had already had previous conversations with Microsoft about them potentially acquiring Powerset, and he felt this was now a good option to take the company, and his vision, to their next stage. "I told them, 'We need 100 days before you can valuate us so we can show you what we have,'" he says. Barney shifted his focus onto what he termed "the 100-day march."

The hype and pressure generated by Barney's early successes created a leadership challenge for him: "How do we keep that passion and belief going when it is taking longer than we had expected and people are saying it is going too slow or won't work?"

Barney's efforts to raise investment for growth also began to keep him away from the team.

Conflicts with his co-founder created a leadership crisis. "Problems happen when you start questioning the vision," says Barney. "If you believe what you are doing is going to work, the venture is incredibly valuable. If you don't, it isn't worth anything."

Barney shifted his focus to a potential acquisition by Microsoft as the best option to take the company and his vision to their next stage.

Barney shifted the team's mission from creating "the best possible natural language search" to "a superior user experience compared to Google."

Barney adopted what he called a "Zen warrior" approach. This involved dropping his attachment to any particular result and living in the moment – being and giving the best of himself.

A first step was to rearrange the priorities of his team. "I realized I had been measuring things wrong, which gave a false sense of confidence. We needed a truly more user-centered test." Barney shifted the team's mission from creating "the best possible natural language search" to "a superior user experience compared to Google." He told the team to focus on searching an online knowledge source like Wikipedia and "do better than Google." The test would be that, if the user entered a certain sentence, the search would return pages with the same sentence, not just key words.

Google used a keyword search format, forcing people into an artificial way of thinking when trying to find something on the Internet. Barney coined the term "keywordese" do describe the phenomenon. To communicate the difference between using key words and natural language, Barney used the metaphor of a phrasebook when visiting a foreign country. For example, if you go to Japan and use a phrasebook it creates a type of limited filter. If this is all you have access to you may begin to think, "Well, all people want/need to know when they go to Japan is how to say 'hello', 'goodbye', 'thank you' and 'where is the bathroom'." If you develop access to the full range of the language, however, your experience becomes much richer.

Barney also knew that sometimes keywords are the best thing to use in order to initiate a search. So the new solution needed to be able to work as well as Google if you used key words, but give a much better result if the user wanted ask a question as if speaking to another human.

To reduce the level of stress that all of the hype and pressure had brought on earlier, and which had interfered with his level of confidence, efficiency and clarity, Barney adopted what he called a "Zen warrior" approach. This involved dropping his attachment to any particular result and living in the moment – being and giving the best of himself.

In the end, Barney's "100-day march" was successful and he ended up selling Powerset to Microsoft for in excess of $100 million after less than three years since starting the company. As Barney puts it, "Even though we 'missed the opportunity to own the future' there were really good returns and everyone did well." Barney himself became a multi-millionaire. Parts of the technology and the framework were integrated into the Bing search engine used by Microsoft and Yahoo and also were adopted by Google. Powerset's developments significantly changed users' experience in a number of key areas and had a wide impact on the industry. For example, the Google Search Team is now called the "Knowledge Team." Powerset's technology also became the basis for Apple's Siri voice guidance system used on the iPhone and iPad.

Barney stayed on with Microsoft for a couple of years as search strategist and evangelist for Microsoft's Bing web search engine and later became the architect and development manager for Bing's Local/Mobile Search. Today he continues to be an active entrepreneur as well as angel investor and a technology and product strategist. "I enjoy helping bring advanced technology and big ideas into real applications and markets that change people's lives," he states.

Barney is currently co-Founder, Chairman & Chief Strategy Officer at LocoMobi, a mobile parking commerce startup that is bringing the major trends of digital innovation to the parking industry. He is also co-founder, Vice Chairman and Chief Strategy Officer at Moon Express (MoonEx), a privately funded lunar transportation and data services company building autonomous robotic lunar landers. "We want to be the first private company to land on the moon and help establish new avenues for commercial space activities beyond Earth orbit," Barney explains. He is an associate founder and serves on the board of trustees for Singularity University, an institution dedicated to "educating present and future leaders in the areas of exponentially accelerating technologies." In addition to these ventures, Barney is on the board of advisors to a number of companies, including the online business networking site LinkedIn.

Barney's refocusing of the team's mission was successful and he ended up selling Powerset to Microsoft for in excess of $100 million after less than three years since starting the company.

Barney Pell's Circle of Success

Barney Pell's journey with Powerset provides a classic example of a zentrapreneur building an effective Circle of Success. It also illustrates some of the challenges and pitfalls that a next generation entrepreneur can face.

Barney's story clearly centers around what we referred to earlier as the three jewels of zentrapreneurship:

1. pursuing his purpose and place in the world (dharma)
2. committing to the full development of his highest potential (Buddha)
3. engaging a community of peers, mentors, sponsors and collaborators who are aligned toward the same purpose (sangha)

It is also a good example of the Five Keys for creating a world to which people want to belong—Barney's desire to grow personally and spiritually and to contribute something to the world were the foundation for building a successful venture. This involved sharing visions and resources with a community of peers. Barney's experience also highlights the importance of working to maintain emotional and physical well-being in oneself and others.

VISION
Customers / Market

Internet search capability using natural language

Conversational computing

AMBITION
Stakeholders / Investors

Become the next generation Google

Move the giants
Change the world and make a fortune

In reflecting on Barney's Circle of Success, at the core was his passion for learning and artificial intelligence and his belief that he had a role to play in the world. Later, this was supported by his ability to adopt the identity of "Zen warrior," dropping his attachment to any particular result, living in the moment and being and giving the best of himself.

Barney turned his passion into a *vision* when he saw that the "field of innovation" had evolved enough to support the game changing possibility of "conversational computing." Focusing on the expanding world of Internet users and the exponential increase of computing power, Barney began to envision a natural language Internet search capability that would allow users to interact with their computers as if speaking with another person.

Barney realized that a vision that big had to be balanced by big enough *ambition* in order to attract investors and other stakeholders. Barney figured that achieving the vision could make Powerset "potentially the next Google." Such an idea could "change the world and make a fortune at the same time." Minimally, it would "move the giants" and would spawn an "awesome technology."

With a sufficiently large vision and ambition, Barney could begin to go out and seek investors and other stakeholders. One of those stakeholders was Xerox PARC, who had already developed much of the software technology that Barney needed in order to realize his vision and ambition. The clarity of his vision and his personal passion and congruence made it possible for him to negotiate the option for an exclusive license, an essential resource that allowed him to go out and seek funding from investors.

It also gave him leverage to go out and begin to assemble an exceptional team, even though he had no money and no product. Again, Barney used the clarity of his vision and his personal passion and congruence to attract the talent that he needed to implement the vision and to encourage them to "shoot for the stars." He worked to create a culture of excellence by constantly encourage the team to search for "What do we need?" "Who is the best?" and to be sure that each new team member "be as good at what they do as you are at what you do."

In their moment of crisis, during the "100-day march," Barney managed to successfully realign the team's *mission* by temporarily narrowing the scope of the mission from "the best possible natural language search on the web" to "the best possible natural language search on Wikipedia"

Barney was also able to use Powerset's *role* as a provider of natural language capabilities to establish key partnerships and alliances, such as those with the PR firm, HADOOP and Amazon, to leverage resources such as public relations, scalable data infrastructure and cloud computing.

Barney's experience also shows some of the challenges of effectively managing the Circle of Success. *Passion* for instance, can have the potential shadow of *arrogance*. *Ambition* attracts the shadow of *hype*. *"Reaching for the stars"* can bring with it *pressure and doubt*. It takes strong beliefs, special skills and other personal resources to confront these naturally offsetting forces and keep them in equilibrium. This is one of the reasons that alignment with a deep sense of purpose is so important. As Barney discovered, "Problems happen when you start questioning the vision."

Barney's journey with Powerset also demonstrates for entrepreneurs the importance of *giving balanced attention* to each part of the circle over time. One of Barney's biggest times of crisis came because he found himself away from the team and spending all his time with investors trying to secure more financing. Maintaining balance is an ongoing challenge for all entrepreneurs.

Another lesson of Barney's story is the significance of *maintaining physical and emotional stability*. Some of his most difficult times came because he was "tired and not sleeping well." Taking care of oneself and one's team is especially important when pressure and doubt begin to build up.

Barney's example also highlights the importance of confidence in oneself and one's vision. When Barney told his investors that he was thinking of replacing himself as CEO for the good of the venture, they clearly pointed out, "We invested in you, not some other CEO."

As we shall see, the paths to success for effective next generation entrepreneurs have a lot in common with Barney's. His experience provides a good template to build upon. In the coming sections of this book we will be providing practices and exercises that will help you to establish your own Circle of Success and manage the challenges that come with it.

**MISSION
Team Members /
Employees**

Produce a superior user experience by replacing "keywordese" with natural language.

Culture of excellence: "What do we need?" "Who is the best?"

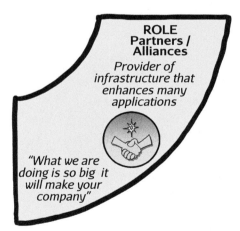

**ROLE
Partners /
Alliances**

Provider of infrastructure that enhances many applications

"What we are doing is so big it will make your company"

Barney Pell's Circle of Success

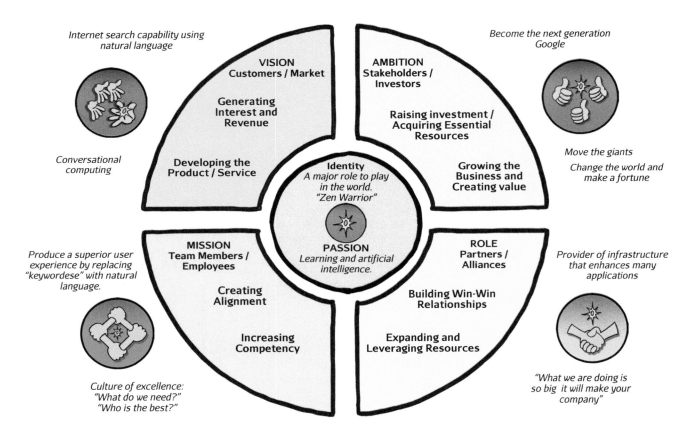

Internet search capability using natural language

Conversational computing

VISION
Customers / Market

Generating Interest and Revenue

Developing the Product / Service

AMBITION
Stakeholders / Investors

Raising investment / Acquiring Essential Resources

Growing the Business and Creating value

Become the next generation Google

Move the giants

Change the world and make a fortune

Identity
A major role to play in the world. "Zen Warrior"

PASSION
Learning and artificial intelligence.

Produce a superior user experience by replacing "keywordese" with natural language.

Culture of excellence: "What do we need?" "Who is the best?"

MISSION
Team Members / Employees

Creating Alignment

Increasing Competency

ROLE
Partners / Alliances

Building Win-Win Relationships

Expanding and Leveraging Resources

Provider of infrastructure that enhances many applications

"What we are doing is so big it will make your company"

BARNEY PELL'S CIRCLE OF SUCCESS

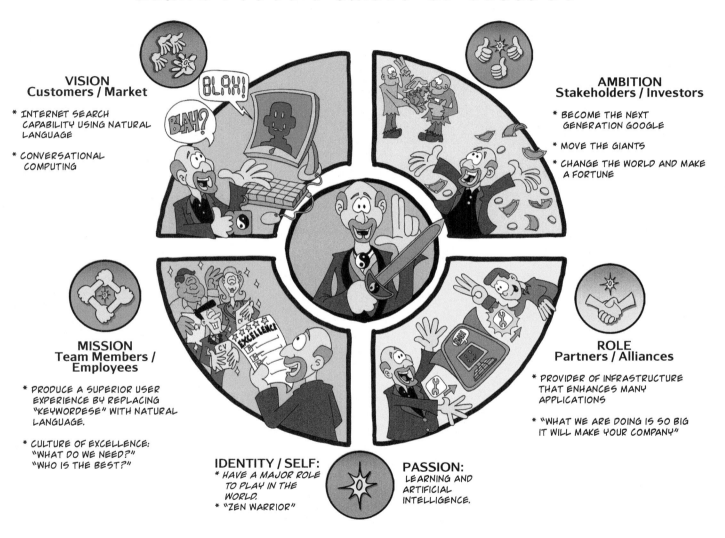

VISION
Customers / Market

* INTERNET SEARCH CAPABILITY USING NATURAL LANGUAGE

* CONVERSATIONAL COMPUTING

AMBITION
Stakeholders / Investors

* BECOME THE NEXT GENERATION GOOGLE

* MOVE THE GIANTS

* CHANGE THE WORLD AND MAKE A FORTUNE

MISSION
Team Members / Employees

* PRODUCE A SUPERIOR USER EXPERIENCE BY REPLACING "KEYWORDESE" WITH NATURAL LANGUAGE.

* CULTURE OF EXCELLENCE: "WHAT DO WE NEED?" "WHO IS THE BEST?"

ROLE
Partners / Alliances

* PROVIDER OF INFRASTRUCTURE THAT ENHANCES MANY APPLICATIONS

* "WHAT WE ARE DOING IS SO BIG IT WILL MAKE YOUR COMPANY"

IDENTITY / SELF:
* HAVE A MAJOR ROLE TO PLAY IN THE WORLD.
* "ZEN WARRIOR"

PASSION:
LEARNING AND ARTIFICIAL INTELLIGENCE.

Samuel Palmisano
Chairman and CEO of IBM 2002-2012

VISION – Customers
Why would someone spend their money with you – what is unique about you?

MISSION – Team Members
Why would someone work for you?

AMBITION – Stakeholders
Why would somebody invest their money with you?

ROLE – Partners
Why would a social group allow you to operate in their defined geography – their country?

Success Factor Case Example
IBM's Samuel J. Palmisano

"Leave it in better shape than you find it."

The SFM Circle of Success applies equally well to entrepreneurial activities in large companies as it does to start-ups. In 2002 Samuel J. Palmisano succeeded legendary leader Lou Gerstner as head of IBM. Gerstner had taken over the company in 1993 and managed to save it from being broken up and get it back on a viable course. When Palmisano retired as Chairman and CEO of IBM at the beginning of 2012, the company was posting a phenomenal 21% annual growth in earnings per share and its market capitalization had increased to $218 billion.

The story behind this remarkable growth is another great illustration of the application of the SFM Circle of Success.

According to Palmisano, his guiding framework boiled down to four questions:

- *Why would someone spend their money with you – what is unique about you?*
- *Why would somebody work for you?*
- *Why would somebody invest their money with you?*
- *Why would a social group allow you to operate in their defined geography – their country?*

It is easy to see how these questions connect to each quadrant of the SFM Circle of Success. The first question relates to *customers and the market*; the second question addresses the *team members and employees*; the third touches upon *partnering and alliances* and the fourth is clearly about *stakeholders and investors*.

To Palmisano, these four questions were a way to focus thinking, stimulate the company beyond its comfort zone and to make IBM a world-class company again. "You've got to answer all four and work at answering all four to really execute with excellence," claims Palmisano.

Before taking the helm as CEO, Palmisano had immersed himself in the center of IBMs Circle of Success, exploring its roots and legacy. He combed corporate archives, reading speeches and memos from the founder, Thomas Watson Sr. and had lunch on a regular basis with Thomas J. Watson Jr., a former chairman. He discovered that the Watsons had always defined IBM as a company that did more than sell computers. They believed that it had an important role to play in solving social challenges. Palmisano found this belief to be deeply inspirational.

With this knowledge of the deeper identity of the company and the four questions as a guide, a new vision for the company began to emerge for Palmisano. He saw its unique strength as offering complete solutions tailored to customers' needs in a way that no other company could match.

In this new vision, the emphasis moved from selling customers computers and software to helping them use technology to solve business challenges in marketing, procurement and manufacturing. The focus of innovation would shift to services and software, primarily delivered over the Internet from data centers, connecting to all kinds of devices, including PCs; the precursor to what today is called "cloud computing."

Palmisano began what he called the "Smarter Planet initiative," combining research, specialized skills and sophisticated technology, increasing IBM's research and development budget by 20 percent to about $6 billion a year. The idea, Palmisano explained, is to "go to a space where you're uniquely positioned and use the value of IBM's integration." The Smarter Planet initiative grew to more than 2,000 projects worldwide, applying computer intelligence to create more efficient systems for utility grids, traffic management, food distribution, water conservation and health care.

In order to concentrate on customer solutions as the company's primary mission, Palmisano realized the company would have to drop its traditional sales of personal computers and disk drives. Instead of focusing on consumer products, IBM acquired the business consulting firm PricewaterhouseCoopers Consulting for its expertise in specific industries.

Letting go of consumer products marked a launching point for a new identity for the company. It meant that IBM was no longer the world's largest information technology company.

It also meant transforming IBM's existing organizational structure, in which product silos and geographic entities operated independently, frequently in a way that was more competitive than collaborative. Palmisano realized that, in order to reach its new vision, IBM would need to be transformed into a "globally integrated enterprise" focused on worldwide collaboration. It would need to become a "client-centric, agile structure able to customize delivery of IBM's software assets, hardware assets, and intellectual property."

VISION – Customers
"Offering complete solutions tailored to customers' needs in a way that no other company could match."

ROLE – Partners / Alliances
"Smarter Planet Initiative."

MISSION – Team Members / Employees
"You can change the world, and you can compete for a Nobel Prize."

AMBITION – Stakeholders / Investors
"Leave the enterprise in better shape than you found it."

Palmisano also recognized that IBM's existing command-and-control culture would no longer work to support the company's new vision and mission. With 440,000 employees in 170 countries, Palmisano realized that IBM couldn't be run top-down, Instead, it needed a culture of leadership, with thousands of leaders operating collaboratively around the globe to fulfill its customers' diverse needs. He understood that shared values rather than command would need to provide the motivation and direction for people's actions.

Palmisano proceeded to shut down IBM's corporate executive committee and presented his four-question framework to the company's top 300 managers at a company-wide event. He then launched a massive, online, interactive "values jam" involving all employees for 72 hours to determine what IBM's values should be in order to reach its new vision and mission.

Three core principles emerged from the collective collaboration:

- *Dedication to every client's success*
- *Innovation that matters, for our company and for the world*
- *Trust and personal responsibility in all relationships*

Since then, these values have served to guide decision-making throughout the organization and have supported the creation of a unique collaborative organizational structure, leveraging the potential for greater collective intelligence. They have also resonated with young people and potential new employees. Eighty-seven percent of the candidates who were offered jobs by IBM Research in 2011, for instance, joined the company. As Palmisano points out, "You can change the world, and you can compete for a Nobel prize" (referring to IBM's five Nobel winners).

Perhaps one of the most important success factors of Palmisano's leadership ability is his dedication to a mission to something larger than himself. As he once said, "The CEO is not the brand! It is not about you. You are a temporary steward of a wonderful enterprise, so leave it in better shape than you find it." That is exactly what Palmisano did, by engaging all of the dimensions of the Circle of Success and aligning all the levels of success factors: vision, mission, identity, values, beliefs, capabilities and behaviors with the evolving environment of his customers and their needs.

We can map out Palmisano's Circle of Success in the following way:

At the center was Palmisano's *identity* as a *"temporary steward of a wonderful enterprise"* and his alignment with the deeper IBM legacy of passion for "solving social challenges."

When this aspiration was directed outward toward customers and the market through the question, "Why would someone spend their money with you – what is unique about you?" the new *vision* of *complete, custom tailored solutions*, using technology to solve business challenges in marketing, procurement and manufacturing, emerged.

With respect to his *team and employees*, his question "Why would somebody work for you?" led to Palmisano's quip that "you can change the world and compete for a Nobel prize." This captured key elements of the company's mission that were also reflected in the results of his "Values Jam": the dedication to every client's success, trust and personal responsibility, and especially *"innovation that matters for the company and for the world*. He restructured the company to support this mission.

Palmisano's question "Why would a social group allow you to operate in their defined geography — their country?" led to the "Smarter Planet Initiative" and IBM's *role* to *combine research, specialized skills and sophisticated technology*. Palmisano established *partnerships and alliances* to create more efficient systems for utility grids, traffic management, food distribution, water conservation and health care.

With respect to investors and stakeholders and the question "Why would somebody invest their money with you? Palmisano's *ambition* and commitment to *leave the enterprise "in better shape than you found it"* was no doubt very attractive. And one that he accomplished.

PASSION – **Identity / Self**
"A temporary steward of a wonderful enterprise."

Samuel Palmisano's Circle of Success

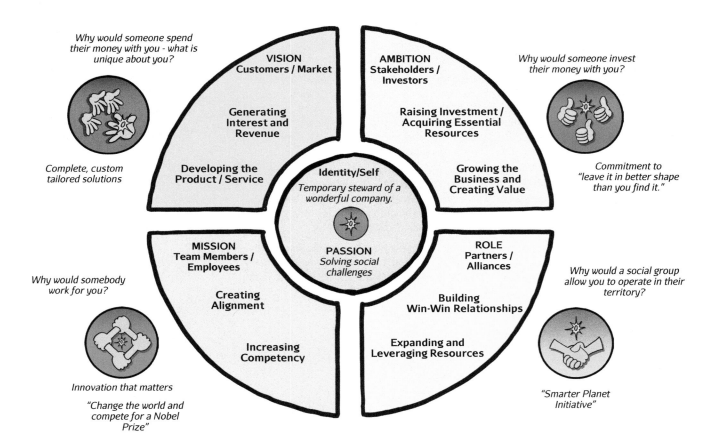

Why would someone spend their money with you - what is unique about you?

Complete, custom tailored solutions

VISION
Customers / Market

Generating Interest and Revenue

Developing the Product / Service

AMBITION
Stakeholders / Investors

Raising Investment / Acquiring Essential Resources

Growing the Business and Creating Value

Why would someone invest their money with you?

Commitment to "leave it in better shape than you find it."

Identity/Self
Temporary steward of a wonderful company.

PASSION
Solving social challenges

MISSION
Team Members / Employees

Creating Alignment

Increasing Competency

ROLE
Partners / Alliances

Building Win-Win Relationships

Expanding and Leveraging Resources

Why would somebody work for you?

Innovation that matters

"Change the world and compete for a Nobel Prize"

Why would a social group allow you to operate in their territory?

"Smarter Planet Initiative"

SAMUEL PALMISANO'S CIRCLE OF SUCCESS

VISION
Customers / Market

WHY WOULD SOMEONE SPEND THEIR MONEY WITH YOU? WHAT IS UNIQUE ABOUT YOU?

* *COMPLETE, CUSTOM TAILORED SOLUTIONS.*

MISSION
Team Members / Employees

WHY WOULD SOMEBODY WORK FOR YOU?

* *INNOVATION THAT MATTERS*
* *CHANGE THE WORLD AND COMPETE FOR THE NOBEL PRZE.*

IDENTITY / SELF
TEMPORARY STEWARD OF A WONDERFUL COMPANY.

PASSION
SOLVING SOCIAL CHALLENGES.

AMBITION
Stakeholders / Investors

WHY WOULD SOMEONE INVEST THEIR MONEY WITH YOU?

* *COMMITMENT TO "LEAVE IT IN BETTER SHAPE THAN YOU FIND IT".*

ROLE
Partners / Alliances

WHY WOULD A SOCIAL GROUP ALLOW YOU TO OPERATE IN THEIR TERRITORY?

* *"SMARTER PLANET INITIATIVE"*

Conclusion: Starting Your Own Circle of Success

The SFM Circle of Success lays out the basic perspectives which any entrepreneur or business leader must master in order to effectively grow a company or venture. Each of the perspectives are equally important, however understanding and aligning one's self with the vision and mission of the venture provides the engine that drives entrepreneurs to persist, learn, grow and develop. Once that engine is at full steam and set on its course, there can be no stopping the march around the Circle on the path to success.

In the coming chapters and volumes we will provide a variety of principles, exercises and practices to show how applying the Circle of Success can be used to Become a Success, Create the Future, Make the Pie Bigger, Do the Impossible and Make Something Out of Nothing.

To create a first draft your own Circle of Success, first review and reflect upon your *Ego and Soul Worksheet* from the previous chapter.

- Who are you and what are you passionate about? If you were truly living your dreams and creating a better world, what types of things would you be doing?

- What is your vision and who are the possible customers/clients who would benefit from it? What types of people would be most interested in the products or services that express your vision?

- What is your mission? Who are (or could be) your team members and co-workers on this project? Who else will you need to join you in order to fulfill your mission and support the vision?

- What is your ambition? Who are (or could be) interested in investing in your venture? Who do you need to provide funding or key resources in order for you to succeed? Who has a "stake" (i.e., could be effected positively or negatively) by your reaching your ambition?

- Who are (or could be) your partners? What is your role and with whom could you make potential alliances? Who could help to increase the value or benefits of your venture, products or services by linking it with their own?

Use the diagram on the following page to begin mapping out your own Circle of Success. Make a preliminary list of the key individuals and roles that you need to involve in order to successfully manifest your vision, mission, ambition and role?

It is then a valuable exercise to start considering Palmisano's guiding questions:

- "Why would someone spend their money with you — what is unique about you?"
- "Why would somebody work for you?"
- "Why would an individual or group want to partner or create an alliance with you?"
- "Why would somebody invest their money or other resources with you?"

We will be exploring these questions in greater depth and building on this fundamental model and map throughout the rest of this book. In the next chapter, however, we will focus on the center of the circle – *you* – and what it means to *become a success.*

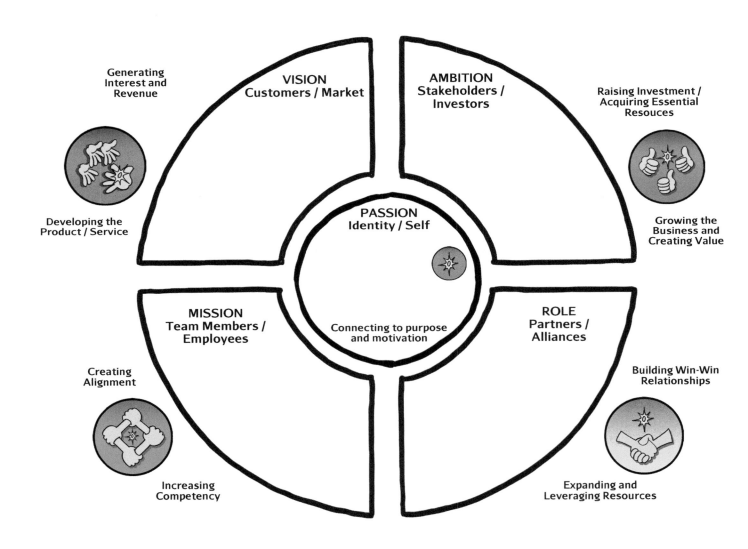

References and Further Reading

- *Forces Shaping the New Information Paradigm*, Glenn C. Bacon, 1985.
- *As IT's Industrial Age Ends the Humanist Era Begins*, Brian Sommer, Software & Services Safari, May 23, 2014.
- *Designing Freedom*, Stafford Beer, CBC Publications, Toronto, Ontario, 1974.
- *Even a Giant Can Learn to Run*, Steve Lohr, New York Times, December 31, 2011

03
Becoming a Success

Our deepest fear is not that we are inadequate. Our fear is that we are powerful beyond measure. It is our light, not our darkness, that frightens us. We ask ourselves, "Who am I to be brilliant, gorgeous, talented, fabulous?" Actually, who are you not to be? You are a child of god. Your playing small does not serve the world. There is nothing enlightened about shrinking, so that other people won't feel insecure around you.
We are all meant to shine, as children do.
We are born to make manifest the glory of god that is within us.
It is not in some of us; it is in everyone.
As we make our own light shine, we unconsciouly give others permission to do the same.
As we are liberated from our fear, our presence automatically liberates others.
Marianne Williamson

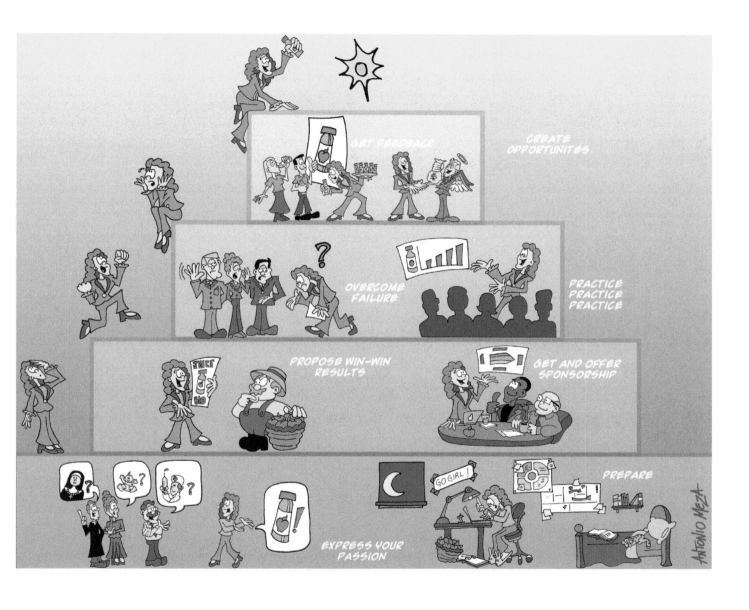

What Is Success?

"Success" has to do with your ability to reach your desired outcomes, whatever they may be.

A key theme in this book is the notion of "success." Success Factor Modeling™ and the SFM Circle of Success are clearly focused on the concept of achieving success. The title of this chapter is Becoming a Success. With such an intensive concentration on the topic, it is natural to want to ask the question, "What exactly is success and what does it mean to be a success?"

Linguistically, the word "success" comes from the Latin succedere which means to "go up" or "follow after." The term is a combination of the Latin roots sub ("under," "near" or "close to") and cedere ("to go"). The implication is that "success" is about going near to something you want. Merriam-Webster's dictionary defines success as meaning "to turn out well" or "to attain a desired object or end."

"Becoming a success" has to do with developing the motivation, skills and resources necessary to achieve your desired goals.

Viewed from this perspective, there is no single objective measure of success. It has to do with your ability to reach your desired outcomes, whatever they may be. You do not have to be a billionaire in order to feel or be "successful" or "a success." Essentially, "becoming a success" has to do with developing the motivation, skills and resources necessary to reach your desired goals.

Goals can be expressed on a number of different levels.

Similar to the various levels of success factors we identified in Chapter 1, goals may be centered on any one of a number of levels:

- **Environmental:** Producing something in the world or possessing material objects (e.g., building a bridge, owning a large house)

It is possible to be successful at one level but not another or to be successful on several levels simultaneously.

- **Behavioral:** Doing something you want to do or meeting a physical challenge (e.g., traveling, climbing Mount Everest

- **Capacities:** Developing or applying a particular skill (e.g., playing music, being creative)

Entrepreneurial success encompasses a number of these levels.

- **Beliefs and Values:** Acting or living in accordance with one's principles and philosophy (e.g., establishing a lifestyle, standing up for a certain ethical position)

- **Identity:** Becoming a certain type of person or fulfilling one's calling (e.g., becoming "a leader" or "an entrepreneur")

- **Vision and Purpose:** Making a contribution or "creating a world to which people want to belong" (e.g., spearheading or revolutionizing a particular service, technology or business model)

Thus, it is possible for someone to be successful at one level but not another or, alternatively, to be successful on several levels simultaneously. Entrepreneurial success, for instance, frequently encompasses a number of these levels, especially the levels of mission, vision and purpose.

It is significant to note that two of the most monetarily successful people of our times, Microsoft founder Bill Gates and Warren Buffett (widely considered the most successful investor of the 20th century), decided to give the vast majority of their fortunes to charitable causes. Gates has pledged to eventually give 95% of his wealth to charity and Warren Buffett has committed 99% of his fortune to go to philanthropic pursuits during his lifetime or at his death. Together, they have also formed the Giving Pledge, an initiative that has inspired more than 81 of the world's most financially successful people to pledge at least half of their wealth to humanitarian efforts. Some of the others having made the pledge include business magnate Larry Ellison, movie producer George Lucas, CNN founder Ted Turner and social media mogul Mark Zuckerberg.

Such examples reflect the ultimate importance of "soul" success in comparison with "ego" success. There is only so much happiness and gratification that can come from amassing wealth and possessions and spending money on oneself. It is interesting to note that the percentages – "at least half," or 95% and 99% in the case of Gates and Buffet respectively – are a good indication of the proportion of value placed on activities related to the "soul"; i.e., contribution, service, compassion, etc.

Of course, it is not necessary to wait until one has become a billionaire before opening one's heart, listening to one's soul or living one's dreams. I have seen some of my clients fall into the trap of thinking, "After I make my money, then I will live my life."

It is equally unnecessary to think that making money means to be closed hearted, selfish and ungenerous. TOMS founder Blake Mycoskie is good example of a class of entrepreneurs driven by compassion for others. In fact, the key to success for the new generation of entrepreneurs is to keep an ongoing balance between ego and soul.

The stereotypic definition of "success" for a Silicon Valley entrepreneur would be to raise a large sum of money from investors, develop his or her idea into a hit product, build a thriving business and ultimately reach a successful "exit" (either through "going public" on the stock market or being acquired) that makes the entrepreneur into a multi-millionaire or billionaire. Such clichés, of course, often reflect only part of the story. In this chapter we will be looking more deeply into some of the other aspects of entrepreneurial success.

Microsoft founder Bill Gates has pledged to eventually give 95% of his wealth to charity

Win-Win Results

From the Success Factor Modeling™ perspective, entrepreneurial success must produce "win-win" results, as opposed to a "zero sum" result. A zero sum outcome is one in which one person or party in the interaction wins (+1) at the expense of the other person or party who must give up or lose something (-1). The results cancel each other out to make zero (0).

Win-win outcomes produce a mutual benefit for all of the parties involved in the situation. For entrepreneurial success, this means creating mutually beneficial results between oneself and the other individuals or entities which make up the SFM Circle of Success.

Entrepreneurial "success" is the result of creating mutually beneficial results between youself and the other parties that make up your Circle of Success.

Big successes are usually made up of a series of smaller successes. Raising money in and of itself can be considered a key success for an early stage company. Similarly, so could generating significant revenue from sales, securing key team members, establishing a significant partnership or bringing a dream to fruition. Becoming a success as an entrepreneur involves achieving a series of interconnected win-win results related to each quadrant of the SFM Circle of Success.

An entrepreneur who raises a large sum of money from investors and proceeds to spend it, without producing any return for the investor, would be an example of a zero sum result. Similarly, an entrepreneur who succeeds in creating a huge sum of money for himself or herself, but whose team members do not benefit from their efforts in helping to generate that revenue would also be a zero-sum win.

The same could be said for any combination of elements in the Circle of success. If the entrepreneur and investors win, but customers lose, due to poor product quality or lack of support, this would be a zero sum result. Greg Smith, a senior analyst at the investment giant Goldman Sachs, created waves in the Spring of 2012, for example, when he quit the company because, as he put it, "not one single minute is spent asking questions about how we can help clients. It's purely about how we can make the most possible money off of them." Some people have speculated that it is this type of attitude that led to the global economic crises of the late 2000s and early 2010s.

A zero sum outcome is one in which one person or party in the interaction wins (+1) at the expense of the other person or party who must give up or lose something (-1). The results cancel each other out to make zero (0).

All of the individuals we modeled for our study were able to produce clear win-win successes with respect to the various parts of the circle of success.

With respect to investors and stakeholders, the win for the entrepreneur is to get the funding necessary to have a viable venture and grow the business. The win for the investor comes from the entrepreneur's ability to increase the value of the venture and achieve a profitable "exit" for the investor (a way for investors to recover their investment and get some margin of profit).

With respect to customers and the market, the win for the entrepreneur is achieving revenue and market share. The win for the customer is a beneficial product or service.

With respect to team members and employees, the win for the entrepreneur is getting the dedication and support of others who apply their skills to fulfill the mission of the organization or project and make a viable venture. The win for team members is developing increased competency and a sense of contribution to a winning endeavor. Team members, of course, also receive monetary compensation, although this can be little to none in some start-ups.

With respect to partners and alliances, the wins for the entrepreneur and the partners are essentially the same, the ability to leverage resources in a way that is mutually beneficial.

Thus, entrepreneurial "success" is the result of creating mutual beneficial results between oneself and the other parties that make up one's Circle of Success, and also between the different groups in the Circle of Success. As we saw in the case of Barney Pell and Powerset, this is not always so easy. There can be conflicts with respect to what is in the best interests of customers and shareholders, for instance, or between shareholders and team members, etc.

Win-win outcomes produce a mutual benefit for all of the parties involved in the situation.

Success and "Self"

The notions of "becoming a success" or "being a success" imply goals at an identity level. What makes someone perceive him/herself as successful or consider him/herself "a success?" This is a question that I have been pondering for some time since, in many ways, it is the ultimate quest of Success Factor Modeling™.

Clearly, money and possessions are not necessarily the main measure of inner success. In fact, I have found that successful people often see money as merely a means to an end rather than the end itself. One definition of "wealth," for instance, is access to resources. This is an important understanding in order to truly grasp the principles of Success Factor Modeling™. On a business level, sometimes a key partnership or committed team member can provide resources that "money can't buy." On a personal level, this definition links inner wealth to the development and expression of our personal resources.

"Wealth" can be defined as "access to resources" – both outer and inner.

As a result of our studies, one of our conclusions is that, at the level of self and identity, you are successful in any area of your life in which you have the inner experience of feeling both grateful and generous. Successful people are grateful for what they have and, at the same time, are able to generously share with others. Bill Gates and Warren Buffett's Giving Pledge initiative is great example of this principle.

Successful people are grateful for the wealth (in whatever form) that they have created or acquired and, at the same time, are able to generously share it with others.

There are many examples of people who have lots of money but who do not experience themselves as successful, either because they take what they have for granted, feel that they do not deserve what they have or constantly feel afraid that they will lose what they have at any minute. (As the old adage states, "You can't take it with you.")

Thus, gratitude is important because, even if you have enough to give away, if you don't feel grateful for what you have, you most likely do not perceive it as valuable. Or, to put it another way, if you do not value what you have, you won't feel grateful to have it and thus not feel successful.

Generosity is important because, if you feel grateful to have something, but believe you must hold onto every speck of it, then you will constantly worry about needing to have more of it, similar to an addiction. You will not feel that you have "enough." Successful people have enough of what they need and feel that they can give something back.

As a way to get a personal reference experience for this, take a moment and explore some areas of success in your life by considering the following two statements.

I feel *grateful* for the _____
I have.

I am able to be *generous* to others with my _____
because I have enough of it.

Be sure to consider different items at several levels such as "money," "time," "knowledge," "energy," "strength," "creativity," "support," "love," etc.

In many respects, whatever you are able to congruently fit into both of these statements is a key resource for the center of your Circle of Success. Whatever items you desire but cannot congruently place into both statements represent areas in which you can become more of a success.

The "Spirit" of Prosperity

In my seminars and coaching sessions, I find that people sometimes come up against deeply ingrained limiting thoughts and beliefs that hold them back from becoming successful. Many people have been brought up to believe, for instance, that having success and prosperity is essentially a selfish pursuit and at odds with developing a sense of purpose, meaning and the devotion of oneself to contribute to the lives of others. Yet, in many ways, it is the lack of healthy success and prosperity—which can take the form of poverty, greed, violence, scarcity, etc. — that is responsible for many of the darkest shadows that exist in our world today.

Considered from this perspective, win-win success and prosperity are not at odds with having a sense of vision and purpose. Rather, they are both a support for and a product of passionately pursuing one's sense of vision and purpose.

According to Webster's Dictionary, *prosperity* is "the condition of being successful or thriving; a state of good fortune; a state of vigorous and healthy growth." The term comes from the Latin *pro*, meaning "for," "toward" or "in favor of," and *spero*, which means "hope." Thus, prosperity means "in favor of hope."*

From the perspective of Success Factor Modeling™, environmental poverty is frequently a result of acting from an impoverished internal model of the world, molded by limiting beliefs and low self-esteem. This makes us fail to see or take advantage of opportunities that may be right before our eyes. Barney Pell's holding back from pursuing his earlier business ideas because he kept thinking "some other bigger company is in a better position to do it than me" is an example of this. When a person has an impoverished model of the world, he or she will feel impoverished even when surrounded by great material wealth and resources.

One of the missions of Success Factor Modeling™ is to provide people with the tools, skills and beliefs necessary to create a personal path to healthy prosperity, and to powerfully enrich their maps of the world. Our objective is to help you "become a success" by developing the ability to promote and sponsor prosperity in yourself and others, including:

Many people have been brought up to believe that having success and prosperity is essentially a selfish pursuit and at odds with developing a sense of purpose and a desire to contribute to the wellbeing of others

Success Factor Modeling™ views external poverty as frequently the result of an impoverished internal model of the world, molded by limiting beliefs and low self-esteem.

---

* It is interesting to note that the word "hope" come from the Old English hop meaning a fertile valley or basin surrounded by a wasteland (such as a swamp or marsh). This is the same root word for terms such as hype and hip. A woman's physical hip bone for instance, creates a hole through which a baby moves during the process of birth—a type of fertile basin surrounded by bone. This is a powerful metaphor for entrepreneurial success: to discover or create something fertile and valuable out of what appears to be barren or unproductive.

One of the missions of Success Factor Modeling™ is to provide you with the tools, skills and beliefs necessary to create a personal path to healthy prosperity, and to help you enrich your map of the world – i.e., to support you to "become a success" by developing the ability to promote and sponsor prosperity in yourself and others

1. Learning beliefs and values that create prosperity which have been modeled from successful people of all types.

2. Improving your ability to go beyond your current limitations by identifying and transforming limiting beliefs that hold you back from personal success and prosperity.

3. Eliminating fruitless and unnecessary efforts toward meaningless goals by learning how to identify your authentic goals and be decisive; i.e., to know what you feel and want.

4. Having the opportunity to discover your life-long mission, vision and purpose.

5. Becoming empowered to align all of your actions with your life's mission and freeing yourself to consciously and passionately act in the service of your purpose.

6. Acting from a framework of abundance instead of scarcity and create win-win interactions and relationships.

7. Increasing your self-esteem and understanding your value to others.

8. Evolving from confusion to the awareness which produces success, prosperity and abundance, and transforming "poverty consciousness" into the generative "spirit" of abundance and generative, win-win collaboration.

In this chapter, *Becoming a Success*, we will explore some formats and tools for how to clarify your personal goals, mission, vision and purpose, and discover some of the keys to achieving prosperity and satisfaction at many different levels.

1. Learning beliefs and values that create prosperity which have been modeled from successful people of all types.

2. Improving your ability to go beyond your current limitations by identifying and transforming limiting beliefs that hold you back from personal success and prosperity.

3. Eliminating fruitless and unnecessary efforts toward meaningless goals by learning how to identify your authentic goals and be decisive; i.e., to know what you feel and want.

4. Having the opportunity to discover your life-long mission, vision and purpose.

5. Becoming empowered to align all of your actions with your life's mission and freeing yourself to consciously and passionately act in the service of your purpose.

6. Acting from a framework of abundance instead of scarcity and create win-win interactions and relationships.

7. Increasing your self-esteem and understanding your value to others.

8. Evolving from confusion to the awareness which produces success, prosperity and abundance, and transforming "poverty consciousness" into the generative "spirit" of abundance and generative, win-win collaboration.

ANTONIO MEZA

Steps to "Becoming a Success"

Being True to Yourself and Your Dreams

The American movie, *The Rookie*, is based on a true story about an aging baseball player who had always dreamed of pitching in the major leagues. He was frustrated that he never got his chance. His dream had been snuffed out years earlier by his critical father who was a military man who moved the family around the country and treated the boy's intense interest in baseball as frivolous. When they finally laid roots in Texas, the player had an arm injury and quit the game before reaching his dream of joining a professional baseball team.

He became a high-school teacher and coach and promised his young baseball players he would try out for a major league team if they won the season championship. His throwing arm had long since healed and he was amazingly able to pitch the ball faster than ever. They won, and he tried out – with his three small kids in tow. He did well although he was much older than the other players. He was offered a spot on the minor league roster for a major baseball team. Taking the spot would mean quitting his stable job as a high school teacher and would also mean a reduction in salary since minor league players are not paid much until they are brought up to the major league. Most never get the chance.

He asked his father if he should go for his dream considering the compromises, and the father replied: "We can't always have what we want," and "You know the right answer," suggesting he should forget his dream and go back to his job at home. But the pitcher decided to believe in himself with the support of his wife despite their stressful financial situation. He began playing in the minor leagues but soon became frustrated with the low pay and not being called up to the majors. He missed his family terribly; the months apart took a heavy toll on him mentally and emotionally.

Nevertheless, his small son's belief in him and his dream of pitching in the major leagues kept him going until he was finally called up to play on a professional team. His first game was in his home state of Texas. All of his supporters from his hometown turned out for the game, including his former players. He came in as the relief pitcher and won the game in the last inning. His father unexpectedly showed up after the game to congratulate him. The player gave him the winning game ball and thanked him for finally taking an interest in his dream.

This story illustrates the importance of the center of the SFM Circle of Success™. Without a vision and a strong belief in yourself to sustain you through challenging times, it is difficult to take the risks necessary to be an entrepreneur. It is a clear vision and strong personal conviction that allows people to persist when they do not get support (such as the situation with the young ballplayer and his father) and to attract others (the man's high school team members, wife and son) who believe in you, share your passion for the vision and support you to help make the vision a reality.

It takes a clear vision and strong personal conviction to persist in difficult times and to attract others who believe in you, share your passion for the vision and support you to help make the vision a reality.

Taking Risks and Facing Failure

Becoming a success and being an effective entrepreneur requires the ability to step outside of familiar territory and take risks. It involves going into the unknown territory of the future; an activity that is inherently "risky" and involves the possibility of failure.

Like the "rookie" in the previous story, entrepreneurs do not always reach their goals right away. Don Pickens (former Vice President and General Manager of Connectix Corporation), whose team developed QuickCam, the first digital camera for computers, claims:

> If you get it wrong the first time, go back a second time, go back a third time. Lots of times, you won't get it right until the third time. There's nothing wrong with that. The problem is, when you screw up the first time, a lot of people are telling you, 'You got it wrong, you should do something else.' The hard part is understanding what part of it you got right, and what you learned about what you got wrong. [When we were developing the Connectix QuickCam] we were the only ones who were talking to our customers. Our next generation product was two generations ahead of everyone else.

As Pickens points out, success frequently involves learning from mistakes and persisting in spite of negative feedback. Consider the examples of Barney Pell, Steig Westerburg and Ron Burr mentioned in the previous chapter. To reach success, they required persistence in the face of, at times, seemingly overwhelming obstacles. It would have been easy to say to Ron Burr, after he had been turned down the 30th time, "Why don't you just give up? Isn't it obvious that this is not going to work? Admit that you have failed. You've been turned down 30 times for heaven's sake." Ron did not get the investment he needed until his 37th try. Had he given up after attempt number 36, he would have never achieved the fantastic success that he did.

Along these lines, it is interesting to note that some of the world's most accomplished people were not always initially successful, and were considered incompetent or "failures" at some point in their lives.

Don Pickens

CEO and Co-Founder of Urban Design Online, Inc., Don served as Vice President for Hardware at Connectix Corporation. There he was responsible for growing the QuickCam brand into a market leading $40M business, which was sold to Logitech, Inc. Prior to Connectix, Don was Group Product Manager for MS-Office at Microsoft Corporation, responsible for the $300M Macintosh applications business and PowerPoint.

Success frequently involves learning from our mistakes and persisting in spite of negative feedback.

Successful people do not always reach their goals right away. Some of the world's most accomplished people were not initially successful, and were considered incompetent or "failures" at some point in their lives.

Famous Failures

- *Albert Einstein*, considered the greatest genius of the twentieth century, did not distinguish himself in school (one of his teachers told him he "wouldn't amount to anything in life") and was 3 years old before he could speak. When he graduated from college, he had to get a job as a patent clerk instead of the teaching job he wanted because none of his former teachers would recommend him.

- The great scientist *Isaac Newton* also did poorly in grade school and was considered "unpromising."

- When the brilliant and prolific inventor *Thomas Edison* was a youngster, his teacher told him he was "too stupid to learn anything." He was counseled to go into a field where he might succeed by virtue of his "pleasant personality."

- *Beethoven*'s music teacher once said of him, "As a composer, he is hopeless."

- Well-known children's author *Theodore S. (Dr. Seuss) Geisel's* first book was rejected by 23 publishers. The 24th publisher sold 6 million copies.

- *Louisa May Alcott*'s family encouraged her to find work as a servant or seamstress rather than write. She wrote—and *Little Women* is still popular more than 125 years later.

- Popular actor *Harrison Ford* was fired by two studios before meeting George Lucas, with whom he made the classic films *American Graffiti*, *Star Wars* and *Raiders of the Lost Ark*.

- A newspaper editor fired entertainment giant *Walt Disney* because he "lacked imagination and had no good ideas." Disney went bankrupt three times before establishing his enduring entertainment empire.

- *F. W. Woolworth*, considered one of the fathers of the modern department store, got a job in a dry goods store when he was 21, but his employer would not permit him to wait on customers because he "didn't have enough sense to close a sale."

- *R.H. Macy* failed in retailing seven times before his store in New York became a success.

- Basketball superstar *Michael Jordan* was cut from his high school basketball team. Boston Celtics Hall of Fame basketball star Bob Cousy suffered the same fate.

- Baseball great *Babe Ruth*, one of the top home run hitters of all time, struck out 1,300 times.

- British prime minister *Winston Churchill*, whose leadership ability is considered one of the most important factors in the English victory against Hitler's army in World War II, failed the sixth grade and had to repeat it because he did not complete the tests that were required for promotion.

- *Abraham Lincoln* failed twice as a businessperson and was defeated in six states and national elections before being elected President of the United States.

- Talk show diva *Oprah Winfrey* was born into poverty in rural Mississippi to a teenage single mother and later raised in an inner-city Milwaukee neighborhood. She was raped at age nine and became pregnant at 14. When fired from her first broadcasting job, Winfrey was told that she "wasn't fit for T.V." Winfrey persisted and became a millionaire by age 32 and the first black woman billionaire in world history. As of 2014 Winfrey had a net worth in excess of 2.9 billion dollars.

- Harry Potter author *J. K. Rowling* was fired from the London office where she worked as a secretary for "daydreaming." Rowling had to go on welfare before publishing her first book. During this period Rowling was diagnosed with clinical depression and contemplated suicide. Harry Potter is now a global brand worth an estimated $15 billion, and the last four *Harry Potter* books have consecutively set records as the fastest-selling books in history.

What transformed these "failures" into successful people?

Based on our studies, we would conclude that it was their visions, their connection to something beyond themselves and the strong belief (or sense of "calling") in those visions and themselves that allowed them to persist in spite of opposition, transform inner blocks and "shadows" and learn from their apparent earlier failings.

It is our vision, our connection to something beyond ourselves and a strong belief in our vision and ourselves that allow us to persist in spite of opposition, transform inner blocks and "shadows" and learn from our apparent failings.

Perceiving "Failure" As Feedback

One of the core assumptions of successful entrepreneurship is that "there is no failure, there is only feedback." Another variation of this is the notion that "there are no mistakes, there are only outcomes." The implication of these statements is that the results of our attempts to reach our goals may be interpreted in different ways.

Depending upon the nature of a particular outcome, it may take more or less effort to accomplish. In many instances, our ultimate success is not a function of immediate results; it is a function of an ongoing feedback loop.

A humorous example of the power of feedback and flexibility is the story of the young entrepreneurial grocery clerk. He was very conscientious and hard-working and the boss had his eye on him as a good candidate for a promotion. One day, however, an elderly and extremely cantankerous customer approached the youth as he was in the produce department and rudely demanded that the youth sell him half a head of lettuce. After patiently trying to explain a number of times that the store did not sell lettuce in half heads, the youth became tired of the abuse he was receiving from the old man and said he would need to go ask his boss. Reaching the back of the store, the youth called back to his boss saying, "Hey, some jerk out here is demanding to buy a half a head of lettuce..." As soon as the words left his mouth, however, the youth suddenly noticed in his peripheral vision that the old man had followed him to the back of the store and just heard every word he had said. Intuitively applying the "feedback versus failure" principle, the youthful entrepreneur turned and with a gallant gesture continued, "... and this fine gentleman would like the other half."

After the old man had left, the boss congratulated the young man on his ability to turn a potentially disastrous situation around and said, "You know, I've had my eye on you for a long time. I was really impressed by the way you handled that incident today. How would you like to be the manager of the new store I'm opening up in Canada?" The youth thought for a moment and said, "I don't know if I'd like it in Canada. I hear all that's up there are whores and hockey players." Suddenly very indignant, the boss growled, "Well, my wife is from Canada!" With an innocent smile the young entrepreneur naturally asked, "Oh really ... What team did she play for?"

The point of the story is that entrepreneurs are able to use feedback as a way to quickly learn from mistakes and failures and transform them into something positive. This is known as the "ready, fire, aim" attitude or "in-course correction." It is sometimes necessary to do something that you know probably won't work in order to get the feedback necessary to progress.

Successful entrepreneurs are able to quickly learn from mistakes and failures and transform them into something positive.

Chester Carlson, inventor of Xerography, needed the feedback provided by failure in order to succeed.

A good illustration of this is the example of successful Silicon Valley inventor Lowell Noble (of QD Technology) who developed a very complex three-dimensional imaging device. It took him years to complete it, and he had made many versions that had not worked. In fact, he claimed that he had to run approximately 50,000 experiments to get the process right—that means 49,999 "failures" before he finally succeeded. During an interview with me sometime later (see *Tools for Dreamers*, 1991, pp. 166–185) I asked him, "How did you manage to keep going in spite of all of the failures you encountered along the way?" Initially he appeared confused by the question. Finally he said, "I guess I didn't consider them failures. I just figured they were a solution to a problem other than the one I was working on at the time." And, in fact, something that hadn't worked at one stage in the development of the device was often a useful solution at another stage.

Another example is that of the man who invented xerography, Chester Carlson. In an interview he said that at several points he had to make a prototype photocopy machine that he knew would *not* work in order to get the feedback he needed in order to know what to do next. You might say he had to make a "grander failure" than the previous version in order to eventually reach success.

The Allegory of the Twins

To illustrate our capacity to perceive the same thing as either "failure" or "feedback" I frequently use the allegory of the pessimistic and optimistic identical twins. Not only were they identical they were "Siamese twins," joined at the hip. As a result, they shared every life experience exactly the same, at least on the outside.

As one might imagine, their birth was not easy. After a difficult period initially, though, things got better. When they started to learn to walk, however, they entered another difficult stage. But eventually they figured it out and life got better again. Starting school, of course, was another challenge. They had to deal with strange looks and taunts from their classmates. Again, their situation eventually settled down and got better. More difficulties emerged when they became teenagers and struggled with a new phase of awkwardness.

The pessimistic twin complained, "See, I knew this would happen. It is the story of my life. Things started difficult and always end up going bad again. It was difficult when we were born. And even though things got better for a while, it just got worse again when we started to walk. It always ends up bad. It got a little better for a while after that, but it just got worse again when we went to school. That's the story of my life. Things always end up difficult. We were having a pretty good period recently, but I knew it wouldn't last. Our situation is bad again now just like I anticipated it would be. Things started bad and will end bad. That's the story of my life."

The optimistic twin, however, expressed a different view. "Things are bad now, but just you wait, they will become good again. The good always comes from the bad. That's been the story of my life. It was difficult when we were born, but it ended up getting better. Good always comes out of the bad. And even though we had a challenging time starting to walk, it all worked out and got better again. We had a tough time when we started school, but it turned out being just fine. It always ends up good. Things might seem tough now, but just you wait, it will end up okay. I am certain of that because that has been the story of my life. The good always comes from the bad."

Even though the two twins share the exact same "facts" of their life experiences, they have an opposite interpretation. An interesting question to ponder, then, is "Who is the liar?" They can't both be telling the truth can they? What they are saying is diametrically opposed.

Obviously, they are both telling their own truth. The same "facts" can be interpreted in different ways and given different meanings. This is one of the ways our belief systems work. They serve to "punctuate" our experiences. The pessimistic twin puts a "comma" after the good experiences and an "exclamation point" after the bad ones. The optimistic twin does the reverse, putting the "comma" after the bad experiences and an "exclamation point" after the good ones.

This is how we can create such different maps of the world. It also provides some important insight into how we can transform what seems to be "failure" into "feedback." Successful people have a strong belief in a positive future and are able to punctuate their experiences to emphasize and take advantage of opportunities and to effectively weather the challenging periods.

It has been said that a person may make mistakes, but isn't a failure until he or she starts blaming something or someone else when things go wrong. When we blame others and outer circumstances, we are admitting "failure" and giving away our power and accountability by making someone or something else responsible for a particular outcome. Certainly, we cannot control reality nor determine the behaviors of others, but we can choose to respond as resourcefully as possible to life's challenges.

To do this effectively and consistently, we must believe in ourselves, and somewhere along the way, we must meet someone who sees greatness in us, expects it from us, and lets us know it—that is, we must find a "sponsor." It is one of the golden keys to success.

Successful people have a strong belief in a positive future and are able to "punctuate" their experiences in a way that allows them to emphasize and take advantage of opportunities and to effectively weather the challenging periods.

Finding Support and Sponsorship

Sponsorship involves creating a space in which others can act, grow and excel. Sponsors provide a context, contacts and resources (including, but certainly not limited to, financial resources) that allow the group or individual being sponsored to focus on, develop and use their own abilities and skills to the fullest.

Sponsorship involves the commitment to promoting something that is already within a person or group, but is not being manifested to its fullest capacity. An organization that "sponsors" a particular program or research project, promotes that program or project by providing needed resources. A group that "sponsors" a seminar or workshop, provides the space and promotional effort necessary to create the context for the workshop leader to present his or her ideas and activities, and for others to receive the benefits of these ideas and activities. When top management "sponsors" a project or initiative, it is giving its recognition and "blessing" to that project or initiative as something that is important for the identity and mission of the company. From this perspective, sponsorship involves creating a context in which others can optimally perform, grow and excel.

As these examples imply, stakeholders are frequently also "sponsors." When Barney Pell's investors said to him, "We invested in you, not some other CEO," they were clearly stating that they had put their faith in him as an individual. Muhammed Yunus' "solidarity groups" are an example of mutual sponsorship where people believe in and support one another.

Though the notion of "sponsorship" today carries primarily a commercial connotation to many people, the term "sponsor" originally derives from the Latin *spondere* ("to promise") and was used to denote a person who had undertaken responsibility for the spiritual welfare of another (the word "spouse" shares the same root).

We can refer to the commercial form of sponsorship as small "s" sponsorship. "Sponsorship" at the identity level (what we might call "Sponsorship with a capital 'S'") is the process of recognizing and acknowledging ("seeing and blessing") the core characteristics of another person. This form of sponsorship involves seeking, supporting and safeguarding potentials within another person so that it can be fully expressed.

The sponsor of an individual believes in that person, makes him or her feel important and shows the person that he or she can make a difference. Thus, the process of sponsorship is primarily expressed through the communication (verbally and non-verbally) of several key messages. These messages have to do with the acknowledgment of the person in a very fundamental way:

Until a person has been seen and blessed by another person, he doesn't yet fully exist.

– Albert Camus

Our "sponsors" believe in us, make us feel important and show us that we can make a difference.

You exist. I see you.

You are valuable.

You are important/special/unique.

You have something important to contribute.

You are welcome here. You belong.

These fundamental identity messages are frequently accompanied by the following empowering beliefs:

It is possible for you to succeed.

You are able to succeed.

You deserve to succeed.

Clearly, the intention of these messages is to promote a person's sense of being unconditionally valued, feeling of belonging and desire to contribute and succeed. The impact of these messages is generally quite profound and lead to a number of positive and resourceful emotional responses.

When people feel that they are seen, for instance, there is a sense of safety and acknowledgment that comes with it; they no longer feel it is necessary to have to do something to get attention. The result is that they feel relieved and relaxed.

When people feel that they exist, are present in mind and body, and that their existence is not threatened, they experience a sense of being centered and at peace.

When people know that they have value and are valued, they feel a sense of satisfaction.

The knowledge that a person is unique leads to a natural desire and tendency to express that uniqueness which unleashes the person's natural creativity. It is important to keep in mind that being unique, important or special, does not mean that one is "better than" or superior to others. Uniqueness is the quality that gives a person his or her own special identity as distinct from all others.

People's recognition that they have something to contribute brings with it tremendous motivation and energy.

The belief that they are welcome makes people feel at home and engenders a sense of loyalty. Similarly, the feeling of belonging creates a sense of commitment and responsibility.

"YOU EXIST. I SEE YOU.
YOU ARE VALUABLE.
YOU ARE IMPORTANT/SPECIAL/UNIQUE.
YOU HAVE SOMETHING
IMPORTANT TO CONTRIBUTE.
YOU ARE WELCOME HERE. YOU BELONG."

*"IT IS POSSIBLE FOR YOU TO SUCCEED.
YOU ARE ABLE TO SUCCEED.
YOU DESERVE TO SUCCEED."*

"Angel investors" are frequently a type of sponsor for entrepreneurs wanting to start a new venture. They are "value-added" investors who believe in the entrepreneur and his or her vision and use their relationships and expertise to support the company to succeed.

Sponsorship is frequently ignored in organizational settings. It is obvious when you walk into a company where sponsorship is not practiced. It is as if no one there really exists. When people feel that they are not seen, not valued, don't really contribute (or their contributions are not recognized), can be easily replaced and don't really belong, their performance will reflect this sentiment. When people do feel sponsored, however, they feel present, motivated, loyal, creative and will perform beyond expectation.

For a start-up company in the Silicon Valley, sponsors frequently come in both a financial and personal form as "angel" investors. *Angel investors* are a new breed of investors that have emerged in Silicon Valley and in other technology centers around the world. Angel investors often fill the "funding gap" for investment in new companies where such early stage funding is preferable to venture capital investment. Business Angels often invest their own money in start-ups, making a relatively small but significant capital investment in return for an equity position in the company. Angel investors are often also "value-added" investors, in that they use their relationships and expertise to support the company to succeed. That is, they contribute something in addition to money to start-up, such as advice or a business relationship.

Gathering Your Allies

In the African nation of Togo, when a woman becomes pregnant all her friends go with her into the forest to find a song that will become the "song of that child". The women sit quietly together in the forest and slowly some mumbling begins to emerge. In an organic fashion and with a little time, a song emerges. As the song develops, it gets louder. When the child is born this song is sung to invite the child and to name him or her into the world. It is sung softly to the new baby, but as the child grows and becomes stronger and moves into adulthood it is sung with more force and strength. When the child or person gets into trouble, makes a mistake, steals or otherwise breaks a rule of the social structure the song is sung by the community to bring the person back home to himself or herself. Ultimately, when the person dies, the song is sung softly; softer and softer until the person's spirit and song leaves the body. And then that song is never sung again.

Our sponsors are like those who "sing our song." To find some of your own sponsors, take a moment and think of some of the people who have "sung your song" in your life. Bring to mind those who have supported your sense of self in a positive way, those who have reminded you of who you are, and/or brought you back home to yourself when you have forgotten yourself. Feel yourself surrounded by your "allies."

Choose or find a symbol, image or object that serves as a personal reminder or "anchor" for each of these allies or sponsors. Keep them with you or put them in your office or work environment where they are visible and can remind you of those who see you and bless you.

It is also possible to engage in one's own "self-sponsorship," in which one is able to learn to promote and safeguard core qualities within oneself.

In summary, it is important for an entrepreneur to believe in his or her vision, and work with others who believe in that vision as well. According to Don Pickens, "You have to identify and work with the people who are willing to move forward with you, because the rest will hold you back."

It is important to identify your sponsors and allies – i.e., those who believe in you and your vision and recognize your potential.

You can choose or find a symbol, image or object to remind you of your allies or sponsors. Keep them in your work environment to remind you of those who see you and bless you.

Dealing with Uncertainty and Getting "Lucky"

One of the challenges of trying to become a success in our dynamic world is that it is filled with uncertainty. This can either be a problem or an opportunity, depending on how it is perceived and approached. For example, entertainment mogul Walt Disney (a quintessential entrepreneur in his own right) once declared:

My business has been a thrilling adventure, an unending voyage of discovery and exploration in the realms of color, sound and motion.

That's what I like about this business, the certainty that there is always something bigger and more exciting just around the bend; and the uncertainty of everything else.

The visionary leaders of today's new ventures have a similar perspective. As long-time Silicon Valley entrepreneur Steve Artim put it:

Uncertainty is opportunity for us. Nobody knows how this is going to shake out. Nobody's got a lock on the technology that is going to drive the future. That's where small companies like us can benefit. We're leading the pack with the smartest and brightest people out there.

With all of the uncertainty and unpredictability surrounding new ventures, it is sometimes tempting to suggest that the ones that succeed do so largely on the basis of "luck." They were simply in the right place at the right time. No doubt, many successful entrepreneurs would agree with that assessment. If you ask successful for the main key to their success, you will frequently the response, "Well, the truth is I got lucky." Luck is indeed an undeniable success factor in starting a new venture.

The question is, are there things one can do in order to increase his or her chances of getting lucky?

It has been said that, "*Luck is the meeting of preparation and opportunity.*" Thomas Jefferson, for instance, claimed that he had been "a very lucky man"; but also noted how remarkable it was that the "harder he worked," the "luckier" he got. Similarly, the great golfer Arnold Palmer admitted that many of his tournament wins he owed to luck, adding, however, that the more he practiced, the luckier he got.

The implication of these comments is that you cannot necessarily "make" yourself be lucky, but you can put yourself in positions where you are more likely to take advantage of opportunities. Chesley Sullenberger, the pilot in the Miracle on the Hudson, for instance, claimed that it was his years of preparation and "regular deposits" in his "bank of experience, education and training" that was a key in making it possible for him to pull off the "miracle" landing.

The Importance of Preparation and Practice

The great Greek philosopher Aristotle maintained, "We are what we repeatedly do. Excellence then is not an act, but a habit." In his book *Outliers: The Story of Success* (2008), Malcolm Gladwell repeatedly mentions the "10,000-Hour Rule." Citing studies published by Anders Ericsson (2006), a psychologist who studies expertise and expert performance, Gladwell claims that the key to success in any field is, to a large extent, a matter of practicing for a total of around 10,000 hours.

"Outlier" is a scientific term to describe things or phenomena that lie outside normal experience. In his book Gladwell focuses on people who are *outliers*—exceptional men and women who have accomplished something quite outside of the ordinary. Gladwell claims that achieving such greatness requires an enormous investment of time in the form of practice. Drawing from examples as diverse as The Beatles, Bill Gates and Robert Oppenheimer, Gladwell shows how each met the "10,000-Hour Rule" as a prelude to their success.

The Beatles, for instance, performed live in Hamburg, Germany over 1,200 times from 1960 to 1964, amassing more than 10,000 hours of playing time, therefore meeting the 10,000-Hour Rule. Gladwell asserts that all of the time The Beatles spent performing shaped their talent, "so by the time they returned to England from Hamburg, Germany, 'they sounded like no one else. It was the making of them.'"

Bill Gates met the 10,000-Hour Rule when he gained access to a high school computer in 1968 at the age of 13, and spent 10,000 hours programming on it. In an interview for the book, Gates maintains that unique access to a computer at a time when they were not commonplace helped him succeed.

It seems clear that the foundation for excellence and high performance in any area begins with practice. And while 10,000 hours seems like a lot of time, it is a worthwhile investment when we truly seek to reach our vision, mission and ambition. It is important to keep in mind that practice and preparation of this type is not simply mindless, rote repetition. As Sullenberger pointed out, it is composed of "experience, education and training."

"Luck" is the meeting of preparation and opportunity.

"I owe all of my success to luck. The interesting thing is, the harder I work, the luckier I get."
– Thomas Jefferson

THE BEATLES!
PLAYING NOW FOR 8,545 HOURS...
...AND COUNTING!

Cultivating Your Luck Factor

As a complement to his assertion about the importance of preparation and practice, Gladwell also points out that the accomplishments and performance of remarkable and successful individuals are shaped by their environment and social context as much as they are by their skills and experience. Gladwell (2008) claims that success requires more than individual intelligence, ambition, hustle and hard work, concluding that "what we do as a community, as a society, for each other, matters as much as what we do for ourselves." This brings up the interface where preparation meets opportunity

While we undoubtedly all perceive practice and preparation as a matter of choice and something that is under our control, opportunity seems to be largely a matter of chance and something that is beyond our ability to influence. Yet, this is one of the areas that differentiates truly successful entrepreneur from the rest.

Because they are on the lookout for opportunities, entrepreneurs often find opportunities that others fail to see. This phenomenon is reflected in the old story about the two shoe salesmen. Both were sent to attempt to expand the shoe market in a rural area of a foreign country. Upon their arrival, both discovered that the inhabitants of their area primarily wore sandals. The first salesman sent a message back to the home office saying, "Bad luck. No one here wears shoes. I am afraid I am going to have to return empty handed." The other salesman (the natural entrepreneur of the two) wrote to the home office saying, "Good luck. Send as many shoes as you can. Nobody here has them." The implication of this story is that what we perceive as an opportunity has to do with the way we are viewing the situation.

There is a scene from the Jim Carey comedy film *Dumb and Dumber* that, although it is clearly adolescent humor, graphically illustrates how mindset an attitude influence our ability to recognize opportunities. Toward the end of the film the two protagonists, the "dumb" guy and his "dumber" partner, are walking along the side of the highway after they have blown all of their money and lost their car. One dejectedly says to the other, "I don't believe this. When are we ever going to catch a break?"

Suddenly a bus with the banner *Hawaii Bikini Tour* pulls over and a number of beautiful bikini clad girls come out of the bus. One of them says, "Hi guys. We are going on a national bikini tour and we are looking for two oil boys who can grease us up before each competition."

The two men look at each other incredulously. Finally the first guy says, "You're in luck. There is a town about three miles that way. I am sure you can find a couple of guys there." The girls are a bit surprised and disappointed that they have been sent on, but get back in their bus and it begins to drive off.

The "dumber" guy says to his friend, "Boy, there are a couple of lucky guys in that town." Suddenly, he has a revelation. "Wait a minute," he shouts. "Do you realize what you've done? How could you be so stupid?"

He chases after the bus, pounding on the door until it pulls over. The doors open and the beautiful girls come out again. "You'll have to excuse my friend," he says. "He is a little slow." With a triumphant grin he points in the opposite direction and says, "The town is back that way." The bemused girls reenter the bus and it heads off.

As the two men watch the bus drive down the road, one says to the other, "Wow! Two lucky guys are going to be driving around with those girls for the next couple of months." The other replies, "Someday we'll get our break too. We've just got to keep our eyes open."

While crude and intentionally humorously chauvinistic, the scene illustrates how limiting assumptions and expectations create perceptual filters that can blind us to opportunities that are right in front of our faces.

In his book *The Luck Factor* (2003) author Dr. Richard Wiseman makes the observation that successful people frequently consider their success a result of being "lucky" while people who struggle think of themselves as "unlucky." He decided to study the phenomenon of "luck," which he notes has a great deal to do with a person's outlook and attitude. For example, he set up interviews with people who considered themselves "lucky" and those who considered themselves "unlucky." Along with the interview he conducted an experiment. Along side the path on the way to his office, he tossed a £20 note to the side of the walkway. Revealingly, the majority of the people who considered themselves as "lucky" found the money. The majority of those who considered themselves "unlucky" did not notice it. The opportunity, in reality, was the same for both. The "unlucky" people missed the opportunity because of their perceptual filters.

Our "luck factor" has a great deal to do with our outlook and attitude.

Limiting assumptions and expectations create perceptual filters that can blind us to opportunities that are right in from of us.

As a conclusion of his research into "the luck factor," Wiseman provides the following four tips for improving your luck by creating opportunities:

There are several simple practices you can adopt in order to increase your "luck factor."

1. **Maximize Your Chances:** Create, notice and act upon opportunities. "Lucky" people are relaxed, open to new things, and maintain contact with a broad network of friends and associates. Dr. Wiseman recommends talking with people that you meet on the street and keeping up with old acquaintances as ways to create a *network of luck* – people who can support you and let you know about new opportunities.

2. **Listen to Your Instincts:** Intuition is something that everyone has had, but "lucky" people tend to rely on it more. They not only trust their intuition, they work to boost it. Intuition is frequently the result of subtle clues, or "weak signals," that you unconsciously observe and integrate.

3. **Expect to Be Lucky:** Expectations drive our actions. "Lucky" people persevere when things are tough, so they're more likely to succeed. They create better relationships by expecting good outcomes from those they interact with. Expecting positive results keeps you motivated to take risks. If you constantly tell yourself that you will never succeed, then you won't bother even trying.

4. **Look on the Bright Side/Turn Your Bad Luck Into Good:** A positive outlook helps you feel lucky no matter what. Bad things happen to lucky people, too. But they react by expecting, and working toward, a positive outcome. They don't dwell on the negative, but find something positive in any situation. If you tripped on the steps this morning, at least you didn't break your ankle. When you're not blaming all of the bad things that happen to you on bad luck, you're more likely to find ways to improve what you are doing. This is the principle of turning "failure into feedback."

INCREASING YOUR LUCK FACTOR

Maximize your chances by acting on opportunities and creating a "network of luck"

Expect to be lucky

Listen to your instincts

Turn your "bad luck" Into good by looking on the bright side and turning failure into feedback

ANTONIO MEZA

PITCH DAY!

"So many of our dreams seem impossible, then improbable, then inevitable."
— **Christopher Reeve**

"In the long run men hit only what they aim at."
— **Henry David Thoreau**

As a good illustration of these four principles, consider the case example that an acquaintance of mine from Germany shared with me some year ago. He had a friend who was an entrepreneur in Germany who very much admired former president Bill Clinton. This friend one day got the dream of having dinner with the former president. Of course, he had no idea how to go about contacting Clinton to ask him for dinner, but he knew that Clinton had lived at the White House in Washington D.C. So he called the White House. This was in the very early 2000s when George W. Bush had just begun his presidency. The operator at the White House essentially said, "Mr. Clinton doesn't live here anymore and did not leave a forwarding address. We don't know how to contact him and frankly we don't care."

The entrepreneur really wanted to fulfill his dream to have dinner with Clinton, so he realized he would have to find another route to contact the former president. He knew that Clinton was giving talks at various places around the world and figured that he would need to be interpreted. He also reckoned that the community of interpreters was not that big. He knew someone who had a friend that was an interpreter. This interpreter put him in touch with someone else who knew an interpreter who knew an interpreter that had translated a talk for Clinton. This person directed him to the group who had sponsored Clinton. The entrepreneur contacted this organization who then put him in touch with Clinton's booking agency.

The man called the booking agency and explained his dream to have dinner with Bill Clinton. The people at the agency said, "Well Bill Clinton doesn't have dinner with strangers. But if you want to sponsor him for a speech, it will cost $250,000. You have to guarantee the money, but we can't guarantee that Clinton will actually be able to show up."

The entrepreneur thought about his dream to have dinner with Clinton and decided it was worth the risk. He reasoned that if he sponsored Clinton, there was a good chance that he would be able to have dinner with him. The problem, of course, was that he didn't have a quarter of a million dollars and was not a conference promoter.

Following his heart and intuition, however, he agreed to sponsor the speech in Germany and then began to go out looking for partners. When he enthusiastically told people that he was putting on an event featuring former US president Bill Clinton, they became quite interested. He even got some people in his network to help put up the money for the guarantee.

As it turned out, hundreds of people signed up for the event. With that many people, Clinton couldn't refuse and happily made the trip to Germany. In the end, the entrepreneur actually made $50,000 profit and, of course, got to have a very enjoyable dinner with Bill Clinton.

As the story illustrates, when a person is active and optimistic he or she is able to create opportunities rather than passively wait for them to happen. The entrepreneur clearly put a "network of luck" in place, both to put on the event, but also to get in contact with Clinton to begin with. Getting his initial contact with the former US president demonstrates the principle known as "six degrees of separation." This principle states that anyone on our planet is only six relationships away from anyone else on the planet – i.e., they know someone who knows someone who knows someone who knows someone, etc. that knows any chosen individual. So that a chain of "a friend of a friend" statements can be made, on average, to connect any two people in six steps. Some people, of course, have many more connections than others. Increasing your number of connections, reduces your degree of separation.

The friend of my German colleague was following his heart and intuition in pursuing his dream of dinner with Bill Clinton. He took the risk in order to fulfill his dream, not just to make money. It is clear that this entrepreneur deeply trusted and believed in this dream, even though it was not rational.

This entrepreneur took a risk with the confidence that it would work out. You could say that the entrepreneur's successful conference was "luck" — he was the right person in the right place at the right time. But there never would have even been a chance for it to come about if he had not taken the risk and persisted. He had the belief that he would "find the way to make it happen."

Opportunities arise when you are in active communication with other people.

He clearly did not let dead ends or challenges phase him and transformed seeming "failure" into feedback. When one path did not work out, he tried another. New pathways and possibilities open up when you stay in action. Opportunities arise when you are in active communication with other people. Many entrepreneurs relate how one day they'll have a terrible meeting and feel like giving up. The next day they'll run into someone on the street who knows someone else who is exactly the person they needed in order to make all of their plans come together.

The following are some other Success Factor Case Examples that illustrate how some successful entrepreneurs have dealt with uncertainty, overcome obstacles, found unrecognized opportunities, transformed apparent failures into positive outcomes and, as a result, increased their luck and become successful.

Success Factor Case Example
Tidal Wave Technologies' Mark Fizpatrick

*"Take steps to improve yourself and
keep looking for opportunities."*

Mark Fizpatrick does not fit the typical stereotype people associate with a highly successful Silicon Valley Entrepreneur. He does not come off as driven, frenetic and all consumed with success. He is personable, soft-spoken and to some degree introverted. Yet, his story of success clearly illustrates the importance of the center of the SFM Circle of Success.

Mark began his career in the sales and marketing of client server hardware and software in Silicon Valley, working with well-known technology companies such as Data General Corporation and NeXT Computer, Inc. By the early 1990s, Mark was a sales executive at Sun Microsystems.

Mark had built his career by essentially following the footsteps of his father, who had also been a sales executive. Yet, while Mark did well at his job, he somehow felt dissatisfied. Like the man in the movie *The Rookie* mentioned earlier, he did not feel that he was following his passion or truly fulfilling his potential. He felt that somehow he had a calling to be more than a sales executive.

Unlike some other entrepreneurial success stories, however, Mark did not have a clear sense of a big vision for change (like a Steve Jobs, for example). His vision arose from the belief that there was something more or better out there and that he could make more of a contribution than being merely a salesperson. As he explains:

> I don't consider myself a born entrepreneur—someone that just constantly wants to change things and come up with a newer and better way. I just always think of myself as someone who just wants to refine things a little bit better, and instead of taking ten steps ahead of everybody, maybe taking one or two steps and seeing if it works. More of a heuristic approach to problems, as opposed to just saying, "Let's change the model."

Mark Fizpatrick
Founder Tidal Wave Technologies

PASSION
Identity / Self
Mark saw himself as "someone who just wants to refine things a little bit better."

Without really having a specific plan, Mark began to take classes to develop himself and cultivate the center of his Circle of Success. In his words:

You cannot make things follow a certain path, but if you stay active, you can do things to increase your chances of success. Your vision focuses you to be aware of opportunities and not filter them out. To succeed, you've got to take steps to improve yourself and keep looking for opportunities.

Mark's recommendations for the types of skills and resources people need to develop if they are thinking of becoming entrepreneurs include:

Setting yourself up so that you will be successful [in an entrepreneurial situation] if you ever decide to jump into that. Your command of the language, basic logic skills, communicating clearly with people. All of those kinds of skills that you are going to need if you are really going start your own entity. Clear communication, being able to detach yourself emotionally from situations.

Because he had constant customer contact, Mark was in touch with what they wanted and needed. One constant complaint, for instance, was about the loss of data when one of the computer systems failed. If the computer system in children's hospital, for instance, goes down, it can endanger lives of the patients. Customers such as these wished there was a way to have their essential files immediately and constantly backed up; what is known as "fail over" technology. The problem was that the existing solutions were expensive, complex and not entirely effective.

One day, after returning from a number of sales calls, Mark saw an engineer that he knew and mentioned the problem. The engineer claimed that he had been working on some innovative system software that would probably do the job. On the lookout for opportunities, Mark recognized the possibilities and immediately went to the top management with a proposal to develop the solution.

His proposal was rejected by the top management with the explanation that they had already tried to develop this type of solution before and it did not work. He was also admonished for not sticking to the job he was supposed to do.

VISION
Customers/Market
Mark's vision emerged from customers' wishes to have a way that their essential files could be immediately and constantly backed up.

As Mark explains it:

> In a traditional company you are given a job title and you have to stay within the boundaries of that job title. And if I were given the opportunity at a larger company to play marketeer and project lead on a product, I'd be able to do a lot more. I would be able to go out to the customers or talk to the sales folks, the engineers in the field, and get a real sense of what they could sell next quarter or two quarters or three quarters from now. If they only had "this" they could close this business and maybe follow-on business.
>
> But, because you are working at a company and your role is defined to be X, but to do all the things you really want to do you need to be X, Y and Z, your hands are tied, you are going to upset people in other parts inside the organization. You're going to upset your manager, because they are not paying you to be three people. They are paying you to be one person. They want you to focus on the one thing and get these milestones done.

Driven by his deep passion to continually "refine things," Mark did not give up. He encouraged the engineer to keep working on the program. As the software developed, Mark realized that they were onto something. Mark used his customer contacts to keep revising and improving the product, funding the endeavor with small loans and from his own pocket.

At a certain point, Mark realized that to move the project forward, he would have to make it a full time commitment. This was his "moment of truth." As he puts it:

> If you feel that something has a chance to be successful, you've got to jump on it, if you can. Maybe life doesn't allow you to do that because you have twelve kids or something. But maybe, even if you do have twelve kids, maybe it is OK. I don't know. But you will regret it more if you don't take the chance. You'll get back on your feet again. Age has something to do with this too. But if you've got a chance to go do it you have to go for it.

In addition to the other steps Mark had taken to develop himself and the center of his Circle of Success, he also needed to make an effort to develop and anchor himself spiritually. "For me a big thing was prayer," he says, "just to keep grounded and to keep it all in perspective." This became very important for him when he had to find the inner resources to face risks and deal with challenges. His larger spiritual focus helped him cope. "As bad as things may seem, they really aren't that bad," he maintains. "That's big."

AMBITION
Stakeholders / Investors
Mark felt that "if something has a chance to be successful, you've got to jump on it," He used his customer contacts to keep revising and improving the product, funding the venture with small loans and from his own pocket.

In 1993, Mark made the leap and co-founded Tidalwave Technologies together with the engineer in order to take their product, which was called FirstWatch, to the market. A key step was getting their first customer. Again, Mark used his customer knowledge and contacts to find a lead customer and begin generating revenue.

The visions of successful entrepreneurs frequently arise as a result of having first developed a strong understanding of customer needs through what we call "second position" with potential customers (the ability to put yourself into their shoes and understand their felt and latent needs). As Mark put it:

> *Our vision was centered on what our customer needs were, and we knew there was a need for a certain product. We then applied our vision to that need, and we used a lot of customer feedback to constantly adjust the vision, because we knew that without a captive audience, the product would be worthless and we would be wasting our time.*
>
> *I am sure that there are people brilliant enough to see beyond what the customer thinks that they need, but we certainly weren't that. We felt that working with the customer we could come up the best possible solution for them. They had problems today that they needed solved today, and we weren't really looking beyond today. We saw a need, the customer had a need, and we were just going to do our best job to fill that.*

Within a relatively short period of time, FirstWatch received global recognition and was able to maintain a leading market position. Ironically, their largest customer was, of course, Sun Microsystems.

In 1995, Tidalwave Technologies was acquired by VERITAS Software in a stock transaction with a value in excess of US$500 Million. Needless to say, Mark became an instant multi-millionaire.

Since then, Mark has remained in the Silicon Valley area, acting as an "angel investor" and technology advisor. He continues to fulfill his calling to "refine" things by "taking one or two steps" and seeing what works, and enjoys helping others to realize their visions. He is a co-founder of YOUnite, a patented data exchange company and CTO of BlueChip Exec, a startup targeting the career management space.

MISSION
Team Members / Employees
Mark and his team strove to create "the best possible solutions" for their customers.

ROLE – Partners / Alliances
Mark's commitment to "be on the lookout for opportunities" allowed him to leverage his contacts and create follow on business.

Mark Fizpatrick's Circle of Success

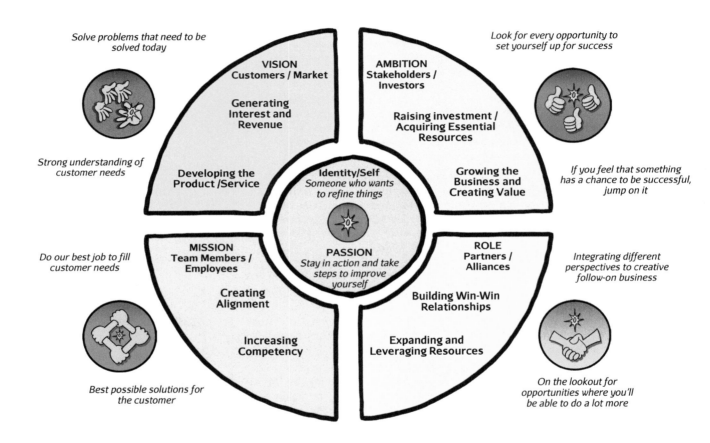

Solve problems that need to be solved today

Strong understanding of customer needs

Do our best job to fill customer needs

Best possible solutions for the customer

Look for every opportunity to set yourself up for success

If you feel that something has a chance to be successful, jump on it

Integrating different perspectives to creative follow-on business

On the lookout for opportunities where you'll be able to do a lot more

VISION Customers / Market

Generating Interest and Revenue

Developing the Product /Service

AMBITION Stakeholders / Investors

Raising investment / Acquiring Essential Resources

Growing the Business and Creating Value

Identity/Self *Someone who wants to refine things*

PASSION *Stay in action and take steps to improve yourself*

MISSION Team Members / Employees

Creating Alignment

Increasing Competency

ROLE Partners / Alliances

Building Win-Win Relationships

Expanding and Leveraging Resources

MARK FIZPATRICK'S CIRCLE OF SUCCESS

VISION
Customers / Market

* SOLVE PROBLEMS THEY NEEED SOLVED TODAY

* STRONG UNDERSTANDING OF CUSTOMER NEEDS

AMBITION
Stakeholders / Investors

* LOOK FOR EVERY OPPORTUNITY TO SET YOURSELF UP FOR SUCCESS

* IF YOU FEEL THAT SOMETHING HAS A CHANCE TO BE SUCCESSFUL, JUMP ON IT

MISSION
Team Members / Employees

* DO OUR BEST JOB TO FILL CUSTOMER NEEDS

* BEST POSSIBLE SOLUTIONS FOR THE CUSTOMER

ROLE
Partners / Alliances

* INTEGRATING DIFFERENT PERSPECTIVES TO CREATE FOLLOW-ON BUSINESS

* ON THE LOOKOUT FOR OPPORTUNITIES WHERE YOU'LL BE ABLE TO DO A LOT MORE

PASSION – Self / Identity

* STAY IN ACTION AND TAKE STEPS TO IMPROVE YOURSELF

* SOMEONE WHO WANTS TO REFINE THINGS

Mark Fizpatrick's story shows that, while it is not possible to guarantee success in the dynamic environment of entrepreneurial activity, there are critical inner and behavioral skills that can ensure that potential entrepreneurs will be prepared to take the best advantage of the opportunities which arise for them. As Mark contends:

> [If you did not get] what you wanted this time, at least you could have done what you can to set yourself up for success the next time something is going to come along. I think that just comes naturally when you put yourself in that spot where it is like, "I am leaving my comfort job. I've got this one chance now to maybe go make it in an entrepreneurial sort of sense." You look for every opportunity to set yourself up for success on the next round of whatever you are doing.

From this perspective, becoming a success is a bit like playing pool or billiards. Success is dependent on one's ability to position the cue ball for the next shot while making one's current shot. This comes from applying your vision to "be aware of opportunities and not filter them out" and taking steps to "improve yourself" and "keep looking for opportunities."

According to Mark Fizpatrick, in order to be a successful entrepreneur, it is important to "look for every opportunity to set yourself up for success on the next round of whatever you are doing."

Success Factor Case Example
Xindium Technologies' Cindana Turkatte

From Humble Beginnings...

Cindana Turkatte was born and raised on a farm. She grew up to run a number of successful start-up companies, raising tens of millions of dollars in investment money. While her pathway was quite different in many respects from Mark Fizpatrick's, her route to accomplishment also illustrates the implementation of the SFM Circle of Success and the principles of Success Factor Modeling™.

Cindana credits a major part of her success to coming from a strong family and getting a lot of support as an entrepreneur from her father and mother. Growing up on a farm in California, her first entrepreneurial project was selling flowers. "We had a little bit of land, so each child got a piece of land and you had to manage that land," she recalls. From the ages of 12 to 17 Cindana grew flowers on her piece of the family farm, first selling them to local florists and eventually to the San Francisco flower market.

A natural mathematician, Cindana also got support from her teachers. "I had great teachers in high school that encouraged me to push myself to the limit," she points out. Her entrepreneurial interests led her to a rich array of experiences. "I was a seamstress," Cindana recollects, "and to show off my clothes I would professionally model them." As she puts it, "I had a very broad background even from humble beginnings."

Distinguishing herself academically with her keen intelligence and the breadth of her knowledge, Cindana was accepted into Stanford University and West Point (the country's premier military academy). "I would have been the first woman going to West Point and I decided that would have been a shock to the system," Cindana says laughing. Besides, her dream since she had been 13 was to go to Stanford.

She attended Stanford, working 30 hours a week to help cover her room, board and books, and earned a Bachelor of Science in Chemical Engineering with Master's Research in Polymer Chemistry. While there, she was also elected President of the American Institute of Chemical Engineers.

Cindana Turkatte
Xindium Technologies.

Cindana Turkatte's belief that she could "do anything" led to a successive series of successes, from starting a dress shop to raising millions of dollars as President and CEO of a Silicon Valley technology company.

PASSION
Identity / Self
Cindana's belief in herself and her passion for creativity and "thinking outside the box" formed a solid center for her Circle of Success.

Cindana began her professional career working in sales for Westinghouse in Chicago. She moved up quickly and took her first million dollar order at the age of 23. When the plant where she was working closed down, Cindana switched to Texas Instruments in Chicago as a sales manager. As a result of her success there, Cindana was promoted to be in charge of creating a new product for TI. Cindana established a practice known as "Customer Councils," in which she drew in customers from the food industry and pharmaceutical industry in order to define the next generation product for Texas Instruments.

Cindana's life changed course when, at the age of 27, she married an Englishman and moved to the UK. "A lot of people told me that if I wanted to be a successful business woman I shouldn't get married," recalls Cindana. "But I said, 'Well I can do anything', and moved to England with my new husband."

Cindana wasted no time in returning to her entrepreneurial activities, running two companies in parallel: a dress shop and a high tech consulting company. "That's how I kind of got into the 'start-up craze'," she admits.

A year later, Cindana was hired by Sun Microsystems as a sales executive, running market development and setting up indirect sales channels for Sun Europe. As Cindana puts it, "That's when I really got involved in serious business."

By 1994 Cindana had "fallen in love" with telecommunications. She moved on to Nortel, becoming head of new business. Cindana managed many programs at Nortel, including the launch of the three "network rings" for Nortel Optoelectronics, which became a reference for the industry.

Cindana came back to the Silicon Valley in 1999 and became involved in the launch of a number of venture-backed technology start-ups, helping to position, launch, hire and raise funds for new ventures. She was eventually recruited by the venture capitalist firm KPCB to join the Seagate spin off *iolon* as vice president of Marketing and turn it into a leading supplier of tunable lasers for the long haul optical networking market. She successfully established the product niche positioning for the company, enabling the raising of $53 million in second round of financing and setting the stage for product portfolio expansion.

A Pattern of Success

Clearly, Cindana's accomplishments demonstrate a consistent and evolving pattern of success, not simply one or two "lucky breaks." It is more like an upward spiral in which the scope of Cindana's success increased with each loop. Cindana built this pattern by following Mark Fizpatrick's formula of following her passion and applying vision to "be aware of opportunities and not filter them out," and at the same time constantly "taking steps to improve."

Cindana's path of success also demonstrates a clear awareness and focus on the key elements in the SFM Circle of Success. Perhaps this is nowhere more evident than in one of Cindana's most challenging ventures.

In 2001 Cindana was brought in by a venture capital group to be President/CEO of one of their portfolio companies, Xindium Technologies, Inc., a compound semiconductor company started by four professors. The professors' vision was to create the next generation, high bit rate optical network.

Selected because of her background and IP knowledge, Cindana's mission was to move the venture from research and development to a business and produce a working product in order to secure a second round of venture funding. Key to managing this transition was the challenge of instilling a product and customer focus in the previously Research and Development driven organization.

Another huge and unexpected challenge, however, awaited Cindana. In 2001-2002, the optical network market died. This meant that she had to completely re-evaluate what the company was doing and move it into a viable market quickly.

At first, the founders were in denial. Cindana had to get them to accept that what they were best in the world at would not be valued for another 2-5 years. "You cannot be myopic," says Cindana, "You have to think outside the box."

Cindana saw the situation as an opportunity to work across disciplines. She needed an appreciation of engineering disciplines that was multifaceted, combining high end marketing, physics and chemistry, and computer science. "I knew I could do it," she says, adding, "Very few people could do that." To accomplish what was essentially a relaunch of the business, Cindana personally managed all customer, partner, supplier and marketing communications as well as legal and patent issues.

AMBITION
Stakeholders / Investors
Cindana was recruited as President and CEO of Xindium Technologies because of her ability to move into a viable market quickly and show a positive return on investment.

ROLE – Partners / Alliances
Cindana was able to establish and leverage partnerships to brainstorm new applications.

MISSION – Team Members / Employees
Cindana educated herself and her team on new requirements, and showed "respect and appreciation that the team can do it."

A first step was to find partners who helped think of other uses for the technology. A breakthrough came in the identification of the need for a new chip for the radio frequency side of mobile handsets. She rapidly shifted product direction to the wireless handset chip market from the faltering optical marketplace by educating herself and the team on the requirements for new chips sets for next generation mobile phones. She leveraged the technical expertise of the team to ensure engineering excellence in design and future manufacturability. According to Cindana, entrepreneurial leadership requires "respect and appreciation that the team can do it."

As a result of her creativity and teaming ability, she delivered an outstanding first product that met the aggressive customer program commitments. She completely switched the company around—a move respected by investors as a means to allow them to see a positive return on their investment in the near future—and in April 2003 she closed on a 2nd round investment.

Critical Success Factors

Cindana's ability to turn a potential disaster into a success story is a clear demonstration of her ability to address all of the dimensions of the Circle of Success:

1. Following her passion and belief in herself and in her mission.
2. Understanding customer needs and finding a market niche in which the company could develop a meaningful product from which to build the business and generate revenue.
3. Identifying and building relationships with partners with whom she could create win-win relationships and leverage resources.
4. Getting the team to expand and leverage their competency and expertise and work together toward a common goal.
5. Creating a positive return for the investors and securing the next round of needed financing.

In reflecting upon these key factors for success, Cindana maintains that it all begins with people's "commitment and empathy" for what they are doing. "You can't give up," she says. "You have to believe in what you are doing. If you don't believe in what you are doing, you should be doing something else."

"People who become entrepreneurs do it because they want to do it," she asserts. "Nobody else is telling them to do it. Fundamentally, people who are entrepreneurs live to work. They don't live for a salary. They live to make a contribution. We all do that. And we wouldn't do it unless we enjoyed it."

For Cindana, the enjoyment comes from seeing the results of your effort with respect to your customers. "I always tell everybody, the real satisfaction comes when somebody else uses your product to their benefit; for the achieving of something they did not know was possible because of the tools you provided them."

"I'll never forget at Nortel," Cindana recalls, "I kept telling everybody, 'When the first optical networks go live with our optical amplifiers we will all be jumping up and down with joy.' Because it is such an amazing feeling of satisfaction."

"I guess that is why I wanted to be a civil engineer," she adds. "There is a deep sense of satisfaction when people drive over the bridge for the first time." "Every product is like that," Cindana goes on to say, "That's why I tell people it is not important if you go public or your company is acquired. What is most important is that your idea comes to fruition and becomes a reality. Keeping people focused on that is the real key to any company's success."

In order to find successful product ideas and make a genuine contribution, Cindana believes it is important to explore with customers what is important to them. "Don't just ask questions," she advises. "Demonstrate that you want to listen." Taking notes in front of them, for example, shows respect. According to Cindana, understanding customers' needs requires that you are able to put yourself in their shoes. "Unless you put on a 2nd position," she claims, "you cannot accomplish anything." This skill is something we will be exploring in great detail throughout this work.

"The customer never knows what they need," she explains. "Your job is to find out what they are doing and need in order to do things better and accomplish more. What is the solution set that improves what they have today?"

Getting appropriate support is another key success factor that Cindana believes is necessary to bring ideas and products to fruition and become a reality. "People have been successful through blind tenacity," she points out, "but it is not a guaranteed success. It is more important to understand what you really are the best at and what you can do that others cannot do, but admitting when you need some help."

According to Cindana, to be successful, entrepreneurs need to "admit what they know and what they don't know." Sometimes the biggest challenge for an entrepreneur is acknowledging that they need some help. "They love their idea and in many respects they love themselves," she explains, "so sometimes [acknowledging they need help] is the most difficult. But that is the key."

"You have to believe in what you are doing," says Cindana. "If you don't believe in what you are doing, you should be doing something else."

"People who become entrepreneurs do it because they want to do it," she asserts. "They don't live for a salary. They live to make a contribution."

VISION
Customers/Market
Key to Cindana's pattern of success is her focus on providing value to customers. As she points out, "Your job is to find out what they are doing and need in order to do things better and accomplish more. What is the solution set that improves what they have today?"

To be successful, Cindana claims it is important to develop "traction" and get validation from others "who are respected."

According to Cindana, "Entrepreneurs need coaching to help talk through difficult situations and turn them into positives."

"Entrepreneurs can be too internally focused," says Cindana. This can disconnect them from the key elements of the Circle of Success. "That is why venture capitalists make them look out and find their competition," she emphasizes. "Because every entrepreneur is going to say, 'We don't have any competition.'"

Getting validation is an area where finding partners can be important. "You can have a great idea but unless you get some traction you can't take it anywhere," explains Cindana. " Traction is about validation. It is not just your opinion." She maintains that it is important to "seek validation from people who are respected." Make sure you have "somebody or a group of people who are respected who have validated that concept."

Similar to Mark Fizpatrick, Cindana underscores the importance of effective communication as a critical success factor. "Entrepreneurs know they have a great idea," she points out, "but are frequently not presenters." According to Cindana, having the confidence to stand in front of people is essential. "How you say it is important," she points out. "Present it with desire."

This brings up the need for entrepreneurs to get support in the form of coaching and mentoring. "No one can get to an executive position without mentoring," claims Cindana. "Entrepreneurs need coaching to help talk through difficult situations and turn them into positives." According to Cindana, successful entrepreneurs "don't jump to conclusions." "Every single conversation needs to end up in a win-win," she concludes.

The Role of Women as Entrepreneurs

An important additional element of Cindana's success story is the fact she is a woman. Reflecting on the role of women as executives and entrepreneurs in the technology industry, Cindana claims "Women are definitely capable of being entrepreneurs, but they need more encouragement than men . . . The key is reinforcing what it takes to win."

Cindana maintains that there are some natural differences between men and women. "Men set goals and do what is necessary to reach them," she says. "Men like to win." According to Cindana, "men will do anything to win" (and go even as far cheating, for instance). If they fail to win, they can "lose face."

According to Cindana, "That drive does not exist to the same degree in women. Women's strengths are frequently in nurturing and multi-tasking." Cindana sees these as equally important and powerful success factors as the will to win. "Focus on what you can do that others cannot do," she recommends. "A lot of women are succeeding in cottage industries."

Rather than seeing men as adversaries or competitors, Cindana believes that "men value a woman's participation" and respect that "the female element is healthy."

"Don't try to play the 'man's game'," Cindana advises women who want to become entrepreneurs, "And, at the same time, don't feel left out."

Cindana advises women who want to be entrepreneurs to "focus on what you can do that others cannot do."

"Don't try to play the 'man's game'," Cindana says, "And, at the same time, don't feel left out . . . Women's strengths are frequently in nurturing and multi-tasking."

Conclusion

Since 2003, Cindana has been running her own company *Cindana, Inc.* whose focus is on introducing new products and services into the Telecommunications Carrier Network.

Like many other entrepreneurs that have achieved a high degree of success, Cindana also has a passion for supporting other entrepreneurs. In January of 2004, Cindana joined the Keiretsu Forum angel investor group. "Angels truly invest because they invest in people," she says. "They want the entrepreneur to reach his or her dream." Proper investment allows the entrepreneur to "focus on what you can do that nobody else can do" and "buy in everything else."

Cindana's main advice to aspiring entrepreneurs and angel investors? "Develop broad experience but keep learning and growing. Don't stagnate." It is clear that this advice reflects the story of her success.

Cindana's advice to aspiring entrepreneurs is, "Develop broad experience but keep learning and growing. Don't stagnate."

Cindana Turkatte's Circle of Success

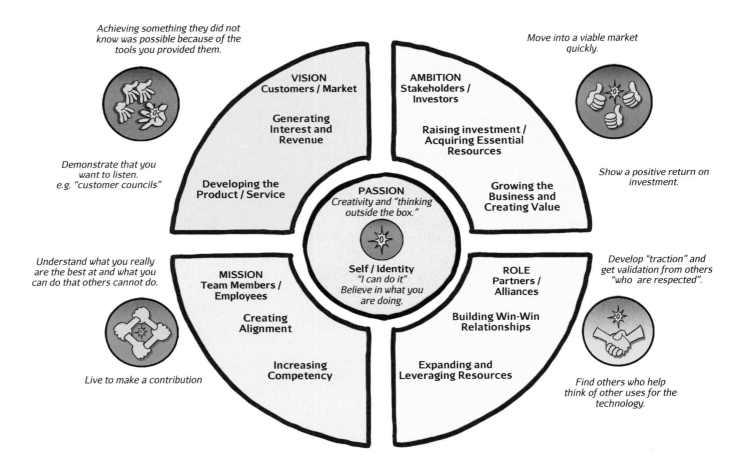

Achieving something they did not know was possible because of the tools you provided them.

Demonstrate that you want to listen. e.g. "customer councils"

Understand what you really are the best at and what you can do that others cannot do.

Live to make a contribution

Move into a viable market quickly.

Show a positive return on investment.

Develop "traction" and get validation from others "who are respected".

Find others who help think of other uses for the technology.

VISION
Customers / Market

Generating Interest and Revenue

Developing the Product / Service

AMBITION
Stakeholders / Investors

Raising investment / Acquiring Essential Resources

Growing the Business and Creating Value

PASSION
Creativity and "thinking outside the box."

Self / Identity
"I can do it"
Believe in what you are doing.

MISSION
Team Members / Employees

Creating Alignment

Increasing Competency

ROLE
Partners / Alliances

Building Win-Win Relationships

Expanding and Leveraging Resources

CINDANA TURKATTE'S CIRCLE OF SUCCESS

VISION
Customers / Market

* ACHIEVING SOMETHING THEY DID NOT KNOW WAS POSSIBLE BECAUSE OF THE TOOLS YOU PROVIDED THEM.

* DEMONSTRATE THAT YOU WANT TO LISTEN
* E.G. "CUSTOMER COUNCILS"

AMBITION
Stakeholders / Investors

* MOVE INTO A VIALBLE MARKET QUICKLY

* SHOW A POSITIVE RETURN ON INVESTMENT

MISSION
Team Members / Employees

* UNDERSTAND WHAT YOU REALLY ARE THE BEST AT AND WHAT YOU CAN DO THAT OTHERS CANNOT DO.

* LIVE TO MAKE A CONTRIBUTION.

ROLE
Partners / Alliances

* DEVELOP "TRACTION" AND GET VALIDATION FROM OTHERS "WHO ARE RESPECTED".

* FIND OTHERS WHO HELP THINK OF OTHER USES FOR THE TECHNOLOGY.

PASSION – Self / Identity

* CREATIVITY AND "THINKING OUTSIDE THE BOX"

* I CAN DO IT
* BELIEVE IN WHAT YOU ARE DOING

Reflections on the Success Factor Case Examples

Mark Fizpatrick and Cindana Turkatte are not examples of rare "rags-to-riches" stories, nor were they "born with a silver spoon in their mouths." Both individuals were average Americans who set out to make a difference in their lives and the lives of others and succeeded by following some basic principles for personal and professional progress.

Cindana and Mark should not be viewed as the exceptions to the rule, but rather as examples of what can be achieved by applying some of the basic rules we have begun to outline in this book. These principles include:

1. Take steps to improve yourself.
2. Create win-win relationships.
3. Discover and provide effective solutions for your customers.
4. Keep on the lookout for opportunities.
5. Be persistent and believe in yourself and your vision.

Cindana Turkatte and Mark Fizpatrick are not "exceptions to the rule," but rather are examples of what can be achieved by applying some of the basic principles of Success Factor Modeling.

Knowing Yourself and Finding Your Passion

The Success Factor Case Examples of Mark Fizpatrick and Cindana Turkatte highlight the fact that becoming a success all starts at the center of the Circle of Success— with one's *Self*. As the famous inscription above the entrance to the ancient Oracle at Delphi stated, the primary step to achieve wisdom, intuition and success is to "Know Yourself." This involves understanding what you are best at, admitting where you need some help and taking steps to improve yourself.

Another way of describing this quest is to "passionately follow your truth." Personal truth, of course, is a difficult goal to attain. Many of us go through our entire lives without every really feeling that we have discovered, let alone, pursued our own truth.

Bronnie Ware is an Australian nurse who spent several years working in palliative care, caring for patients in the last 12 weeks of their lives. In her book *The Top Five Regrets of the Dying*, she recorded her conversations with people about any regrets they had or what they would do differently in their lives. Most had not honored even half of their dreams. They went to their death realizing that this was a choice they had made, and they deeply regretted having never really lived their dreams, or even part of them. As Irish playwright George Bernard Shaw said, *"most people go their graves with their music still in them."*

The top five regrets were:

1. I wish I had the courage to live a life true to myself, not the one others expected of me.
2. I wish that I hadn't worked so hard.
3. I wish I had the courage to express my feelings.
4. I wish I had stayed in touch with my friends.
5. I wish I had let myself be happier.

At the beginning of this chapter we identified the emotional basis of "success" as the feelings of gratitude and generosity. It seems clear that these are the opposite of the feelings of regret. Our feelings of gratitude and generosity come from our capacity to "let our music out." This capacity involves connecting into our identity and passion and expressing it outwards to the various dimensions of the Circle of Success in the form of vision, ambition, mission and role.

By applying the principles of Success Factor Modeling, we can transform the "Top Five Regrets of the Dying" into Five Lessons for a Successful Life:

1. Live *your* life.
2. Work in balance and flow with passion.
3. Express who you really are and what you feel.
4. Develop sponsoring relationships that last a lifetime.
5. Give yourself permission to experience all forms of happiness.

Most people go their graves with their music still in them.

– George Bernard Shaw

According to Success Factor Modeling, satisfaction in life comes from connecting into our identity and passion and expressing it outwards to the various dimensions of the Circle of Success in the form of vision, ambition, mission and role.

5 LESSONS FOR A SUCCESSFUL LIFE

WORK IN BALANCE AND FLOW
WITH PASSION.

DEVELOP SPONSORING RELATIONSHIPS
THAT LAST A LIFETIME.

LIVE YOUR LIFE

EXPRESS WHO YOU REALLY
ARE AND WHAT YOU FEEL.

GIVE YOURSELF PERMISSION TO
EXPERIENCE ALL FORMS OF HAPPINESS

Accomplishing this all begins at the center of your Circle of Success. Through exploring and clarifying our identity and passion, we can release the energy and creativity that comes from connecting with our purpose and motivation.

Our sense of identity transcends our behaviors, capabilities and beliefs. It is the underlying foundation of all other levels of achievement. It is our perception of our identity that organizes our beliefs, capabilities and behaviors into a single system. Our sense of identity also relates to our perception of ourselves in relation to the larger systems of which we are a part, determining our sense of "role," "purpose" and "mission." Thus, perceptions of identity have to do with questions such as "Who am I?" "What are my limits?" "What is my purpose?" and "What is my passion?"

In the remainder of this chapter we will explore exercises to help you:

- Find and clarify your identity and passion.
- Become clear about the beliefs that support your identity and those which limit you.
- Understand what you are best at and where you need support.

Identity Level Elicitation Process

One way to help clarify your identity and passion is to explore the different levels through which the "deep structure" of identity reaches its surface manifestations and expresses itself. Starting at the most concrete expressions of one's identity, at the level of the environment and behavior, the following exercise systematically takes you through the successive levels (capabilities, beliefs, values, mission and vision) associated with both shaping and expressing identity.

Start by putting yourself into the COACH state that we defined in Chapter 1 so that you are maximally ready tune into yourself deeply. Then reflect on the following questions.

The Identity Level Elicitation Process helps you to explore and clarify your identity at and passion by examining a number of different levels of expression.

1. "What is an *environment* in which you are able to fully be 'yourself'?"
   "*When* and *where* do you feel most like yourself?"

   The contexts in which I am able to be most "myself" are _____

   _____.

2. "What specific *behaviors* and activities expresses the most about who you are?

   "*What*, specifically, do you do that makes you feel most yourself?"

   I feel most "myself" when I am _____.

3. "What *capabilities* do you associate most with yourself?"

   "What skills and competencies do you think most represent who you are?"

   The thoughts and capabilities I associate with "me" are_____

   _____.

4. "What *beliefs* and *values* most reflect and drive who you are? Why do you do what you do?"

"What values are you most passionate about?"

I value _____.

"What beliefs support and motivate your thoughts and activity?"

I believe _____.

5. "How do you perceive yourself?"

"*Who* are you, given the beliefs, values, capabilities and behaviors that you have defined?" "What do you consider to be your 'essence'?" (Think in terms of a metaphor or symbol.)

I am _____.

"What is your mission?"
My mission is to _____.

6. "What is your purpose within the *larger system* in which you are operating?"

"What is your *vision* with respect to the larger system in which you are pursuing that mission?"

This mission is in the service of the larger vision to _____

_____.

Reflect upon your answers to the different levels of questions.

What did you learn about yourself?

What seemed to be the common factors (the "red thread") running through all of the different levels?

Which level(s) of answers came most easily to you?

Which level(s) would be useful for you to explore further or strengthen?

What did this exercise help you to clarify about the center of your Circle of Success—i.e., your Self/Identity and your Passion?

As a point of comparison, our recent studies indicate that successful next generation entrepreneurs typically see their *Self/ Identity* as some combination of:

Explorer

- Trailblazers seeking new territories and new alternatives

Catalyzer

- Triggers for change
- Deliverers of new ideas (a "postman" of possibilities)

Connector

- Generators of energy and links between people
- Bridges between the existing and the possible
- Doors or passageways to new potentials

Enabler

- Facilitators of transformation

Builder

- Foundational stones for constructing something new and concrete
- Landmarks for the expression of particular principles and values
- "Syngineers" – Creators of something innovative that balances usefulness and beauty

Carrier

- Vehicles that take people somewhere new
- Drivers who negotiate challenging curves (risks)

Co-Creator

- Encouragers of collective realizations
- Promoters of interaction and collaboration

In relation to Passion, our research shows that successful next entrepreneurs share a strong passion for:

Empowerment

- Achieving freedom and autonomy – i.e., Control of one's own destiny
- Effectively overcoming challenges and difficulties
- Enhancing people's ability to navigate the world with honesty and clarity versus fear and manipulation
- Pursuing self-development and attaining self-actualization
- Expanding both individual and collective excellence

Change

- Changing the rules – changing the "game"
- Improving the world – on personal dimension, community dimension and global dimension
- Inspiring others to try something different and grow
- Increasing or augmenting pleasurable experiences

Creativity

- Doing something new
- Creating something concrete that makes a difference
- Innovating a process (e.g., solving a problem)
- Making something that is both useful and beautiful (i.e., aesthetically pleasing)
- Participating in and encouraging generative interactions

Use the major representational systems (verbal, visual and somatic) to create "reminders" that will help you connect with your identity and passion.

Expressing and Anchoring Your Passion

Key to the center of the SFM Circle of Success is continually *connecting to purpose and motivation*. As you begin to become clearer about your identity and passion, it can is very useful to deepen your connection with them and "anchor" them by experiencing and expressing them in different ways. Applying the principles of NeuroLinguistic Programming, we encourage people to employ each of the three major sensory representational systems: verbal, visual and somatic.

One of the primary abilities of successful entrepreneurs is their capacity to connect with and clearly communicate their passion. This is one of the necessary "intangibles" that attracts investors, team members, customers and partners. As Cindana Turkatte pointed out, entrepreneurs have to learn to present their ides "with desire." Identity and passion can be expressed in multiple ways: through *words*, through *images* and through *gestures*. Each of these forms of expression can stimulate and deepen an emotional connection with your passion for yourself and others.

As a practice, reflecting on what you have learned about your identity and your passion in the previous exercise, explore experiencing and expressing your passion through each of these modalities. As with the previous exercise, begin by putting yourself into the COACH state.

1. *Verbal* – Complete the following statement:

My deepest desire and passion is _____

As with the statements of your vision, ambition, mission and role in the first chapter, be succinct. Use as few words as possible, keeping your answer to no more than ten key words. Be sure, however, that those words are deeply "resonant." That is, that when you say them, you emotionally feel their meaning.

For example, Steig Westerberg's passion was "creating global solutions to common problems." Ed Hogan's passion was "travel to exotic places." Barney Pell's passion was "learning and artificial intelligence." Samuel Palmisano's passion was to "leave it in better shape than you found it." Mark Fizpatrick's passion was to "refine things and come up with a newer and better way." Cindana Turkatte's Passion was "helping people achieve something they did not know was possible."

2. *Visual* – Now create an image that expresses your passion. The image can be either literal or symbolic.

Barney Pell for example, described his practice of clearly visualizing his outcomes. Ed Hogan's passion to "travel to exotic places" could be represented by an image of an island with palm trees. It is sometimes easier to picture one's passion in symbolic way. For instance, the passion "refine things and come up with a newer and better way" could be visualized as a diamond in the rough becoming cleaned and cut to reveal many beautiful facets.

What is most important is that the image resonates or touches you emotionally and brings up a felt reminder of your passion, like Disney's "big and glittering" image of the future.

3. *Somatic model* – Make a gesture and/or movement that expresses your passion. Obviously, this gesture is to represent not so much the content of your passion but rather the feeling. Barney Pell, for example, recounts how, when he would finish visualizing his future goals, anchored it with his "arms up in the air in triumph." It could also be a gesture of gratitude or expansiveness. The purpose of such a somatic expression is clearly to create a connection with a felt sense of your passion.

We will be applying these representations of the center of your Circle of Success throughout the rest of this work. The COACH state and your connection to your purpose and motivation are the generative source of your vision, ambition, mission, role and ultimately your venture. You will need methods of entering the COACH state and connecting or reconnecting to your passion countless times during your journey as an entrepreneur, especially with things are challenging, uncertain, boring, confusing, etc. Barney Pell's description of his "Zen Warrior" approach to get his company through a time of crisis and Mark Fizpatrick's mention of the importance of "prayer" in order to "keep grounded and to keep it all in perspective" are a good testament to this.

Your connection to your passion and purpose are also the foundation of your ability to inspire others to listen to you and ultimately join you or support you. In our SFM coaching sessions and workshops, we have people practice expressing these three representations of their passion to one another as an exercise. People often describe how hearing someone else congruently express their passion gives them "chills" in their arms or spine. I encourage you to try this yourself with friends, family and team members.

Successful entrepreneurs are able to consistently connect with and clearly communicate their passion.

Your connection to your passion and purpose is the foundation of your ability to inspire others to listen to you, join you and/or to support you

Exploring the Center of Your Circle of Success Through the Identity Matrix

The Identity Matrix (Dilts, R., 1998, 2000) is another tool that we use to help people and organizations learn about themselves as a starting point and ongoing method for exploring the center of their Circle of Success.

The *Identity Matrix* is a framework for defining key beliefs that we hold about ourselves, our team or our venture. While our beliefs are at a different level of experience than our identities, beliefs can support or restrict various aspects of our identity. In a way, these beliefs reflect our self-observations that can also serve to freeze our deeper "superposition" or that of our team or organization and, alternatively, reveal new facets of that superposition to us.

The Identity Matrix describes the map that we make of our identity that is primarily formed from beliefs about our potential and our limitations. It includes those features of ourselves, team or organization that we perceive as desirable, as well as those that are undesirable. The Identity Matrix is a means of identifying a cross-section of core beliefs about ourselves and/or our venture which influence the actions we take and do not take.

The Identity Matrix involves identifying your beliefs about 1) what you are and will continue to be, 2) what you could become, and 3) what you are not or cannot be. These beliefs are explored in relation to what you (a) want to be and (b) do not want to be. The result provides you with some powerful cues about identity level goals, values and resources, as well points to areas in which you may have limiting beliefs. The result is a powerful framework from which to better understand yourself, your strengths and your potential as well as your limitations and areas for development.

	Am Not	Could Become	Am
Want to Be			
Do Not Want to Be			

The Identity Matrix Creates a Road Map of Key Beliefs About Yourself
That Forms a Foundation for Understanding Your Strengths and Areas for Development

The basic elements of this matrix are:

Core: What you "want to be" and believe "you are" constitutes your *core*. When we are in contact with our core, we feel *proud* and *content* – the sense of "humble authority."

Potential: What you "want to be" and believe "you could become" (or become more of) defines your *potential*. When we are connected with our potential, we feel *hopeful* and *excited*.

Limitation: What you "want to be" but believe that "you are not," are prevented from being or cannot be anymore establishes your *limitation*. When we experience our limitations we feel *frustrated* and *trapped*. Other times we will feel *grief* for what we used to be, but cannot be any longer.

Boundary: What you "don't want to be" and believe that "you are not," "will not be" or are no longer creates your *boundary*. When we put up a boundary or let go of who we believe that we no longer are, we feel *resolute* or a sense of *release*.

Weakness/Defect: What you "don't want to be" but are afraid that "you could become" indicates our *weakness* or *defect*. When we perceive our weaknesses or defects, we feel *fearful* and *anxious*.

Shadow: What you "don't want to" be but believe that "you are" points to your *shadow*. When we are aware of our shadow, we typically feel *ashamed* and *guilty*.

These same elements can clearly also apply to the identity of a team or organization as well as an individual.

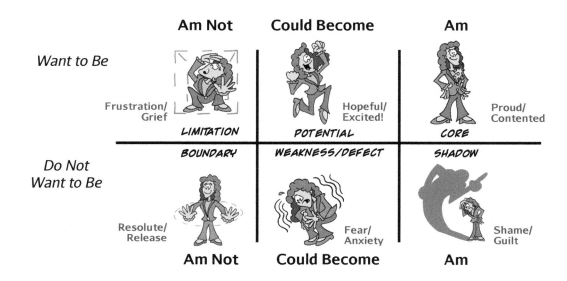

Generative Complementarities

For ourselves as individuals, all of these elements together make up the center of our Circle of Success. In fact, one way to look at the Identity Matrix is as three sets of complementary aspects of our identities:

1. Our *core* (what I want to be and I am) and *shadow* (what I don't want to be but I am) form one pair.

2. Our *potential* (what I want to be and could become or become more of) and our weakness or *defect* (what I don't want to be but could become) form another pair.

3. Our *limitation* (what I want to be but am not able to be) and *boundary* (what I don't want to be and am not) form yet another pair.

The Key Elements of the Identity Matrix Form Pairs of Complements

Instead of creating conflict or struggle, these offsetting dimensions of ourselves can become "generative complementarities" that provide a rich source for creativity and motivation. When we can acknowledge and create the space for these seeming polarities, and hold them with awareness in the proper way, they open the possibility for something new and energizing to emerge. Again, what is true for ourselves as individuals is also relevant for teams and organizations.

An iconic example of both the power and challenges of such "generative complementarities" is that of the late comedian and actor Robin Williams. World famous for his high energy, stream of conscious humor, Williams had an equal degree of darkness – struggling throughout his career with addictions and depression. It is quite likely that Williams' energy and humor would not have been nearly so intense if his depression and anxiety had not been equally present in his life.

The key, of course, is the ability to hold them both (especially the shadow side) without becoming overwhelmed. One of the positive intentions behind addictions is most likely the attempt to reduce the affects of the shadow side of such complementarities. Of course, their negative consequences just end up making things worse. This is why practices like the COACH state and connecting your passion are so important. It is in fact significant to note that, during the most productive stage of his career, Williams used exercise and cycling to help deal with his depression claiming "cycling saved my life."

Many of the examples of successful people in this book and the "famous failures" mentioned earlier in this chapter also imply the underlying dynamics of such generative complementarities. We have noted several times how Captain Sullenberger's commitment to save lives came from the devastation he experienced from his father's suicide. The brilliance of people like Elon Musk and J. K. Rowling clearly emerged as balances to the darkness of their depression, transforming it into inspiration. It was Musk's bout with depression that led him to the conclusion that "the only thing that makes sense is to strive for greater collective enlightenment." Rowling's depression even inspired the characters known as Dementors, soul-sucking creatures introduced in her third Harry Potter book.

As we will see in the next chapter, these types of generative complementarities were also the foundation for the success (and struggles) of people like Steve Jobs. An important conclusion of our Success Factor Modeling studies is that one of the key attributes and skills of highly successful people is the capacity to recognize and be with their limitations, weaknesses and shadows without becoming them. We will continue to explore and provide suggestions and practices (like the COACH state) for how to do this throughout these volumes.

The test of a first-rate intelligence is the ability to hold two opposed ideas in the mind at the same time, and still retain the ability to function. One should, for example, be able to see that things are hopeless and yet be determined to make them otherwise.
— F. Scott Fitzgerald

When seemingly conflicting aspects of our identity can be acknowledged and balanced, they become "generative complementarities" that provide a rich source for creativity and motivation.

Often, we are tempted to try to ignore our limitations and weaknesses or deny our shadows, but that does not make them go away. In fact, it is more likely to intensify them. The key is to find practices, projects and ventures that take us on a journey to:

a) Deepen and strengthen our *core* in a way that integrates or transforms our *shadow*.

b) Achieve our *potential* by effectively compensating for or neutralizing our *defects* and *weaknesses*.

c) Transcend or offset our *limitations* while clarifying or strengthening our *boundaries* and letting go of what no longer serves us.

We can see some of these dynamics in the success examples of Barney Pell, Samuel Palmisano, Mark Fitzpatrick and Cindana Turkette.

Barney Pell reconnected to his core and adopted a "Zen warrior" attitude to get himself and his company through a time of intense pressure and crisis. This allowed him to recognize and neutralize the shadows of "hype," "pressure," "arrogance" and "doubt" and refocus the mission of the team in order to achieve their potential.

By deepening and strengthening his own core as "the temporary steward of a wonderful enterprise" and his commitment to "leave it in better shape than you find it," Samuel Palmisano deepened and strengthened the core of IBM as an organization. Submersing himself in the company's roots and legacy, he was personally inspired by the mission to play a role in "solving social challenges." This led him to a new vision of offering complete solutions tailored to customers' needs and launch the "Smarter Planet initiative." It meant, however, that he also had to address and transform the shadow of the company's existing command-and-control culture and organizational structure, in which product silos and geographic entities operated independently and in a way that was more competitive than collaborative.

Mark Fizpatrick sought to develop and achieve his *potential* by taking steps to improve himself and continually looking for opportunities. Mark worked to bolster areas in which he did not have natural strengths and offset certain weaknesses he was aware of in himself, such as those relating to language, logic skills, clear communication, and being able to detach emotionally from situations.

Cindana Turkette's journey was one of continually transcending *limitations* whether they related to traditional roles for women or the challenge of relaunching a company that was in a market that had died. Her mission was helping people achieve things they did not know was possible and was supported by her ability to "think outside the box."

For next generation entrepreneurs, their ventures are a journey that helps them to integrate and harmonize the various dimensions of their identities.

This of course, meant building strong *boundaries* and being clear and honest about who she was and who she was not, admitting what she knew and what she didn't know and *letting go* of what was either not ready or no longer useful.

To explore your own Identity Matrix, consider your answers to the following questions. While your answers to the questions may be literal, you may also want to use symbols or archetypes to represent your answers when addressing identity level issues.

Again, begin by putting yourself into the COACH state. Then follow the instructions below.

1. Reflect upon your sense of who you are. Bring your awareness to your feelings as well as your thoughts. What are the things that you feel proud of and content with about yourself? What is it that you want to be and believe that you are (your *core*)? [This should be very similar to the symbol you identified at step 5 in the Identity Level Elicitation Process.] Find a somatic model and a symbol for your core.

   e.g., *"A volcano of light."*

2. Continuing to reflect upon your deep sense of yourself, tune into what makes you feel hopeful and excited about your life. What do believe that you could become or become more of that you would really like to be (your *potential*)? What is your somatic model and symbol for your potential?

   e.g., *"A shining star or sun."*

3. Now, shift your focus to the areas in your life where you feel trapped or frustrated. Reflect upon what you want to be or be more of but believe you cannot be or are prevented from being. What stops you (your limit or limitation)? Find a somatic model and symbol for what is in your way.

   e.g., "A locked gate."

4. Bring your attention to the places in your life where you feel resolute about making a change in your old identity, or where there are aspects of your identity that you do not want to be anymore or and are ready to let go of. Focus on your feeling of determination to change or of your willingness to release what is no longer you. Find a somatic model and symbol for your commitment to take a stand or to let go (your *boundary*).

   e.g., *"A sword and a shield."*

Exploring your Identity Matrix is a way to clarify some of the resources and challenges at the center of your Circle of Success.

5. Shift your awareness to the areas of your life where you feel fear or anxiety about the potential for you to become something you don't want to be but are afraid that you could become (your *defect/weakness*)? What is the somatic model and symbol for this weakness or defect?

> e.g., "A thick fog."

6. Take some time to focus on the places in your life where you feel ashamed or guilty about yourself. What is it you don't want to be or like to be but believe that you are (your *shadow*)? Find a somatic model and symbol for your shadow.

> e.g., "A dark tunnel."

Reflect on your answers. What polarities or "complements" emerge in the relationship between your core and your shadow? Your potential and your weakness or defect? Your limitations and your boundaries?

Transforming Polarities Into Generative Complementarities

Seeming polarities can be transformed into "generative complementarities" when they are able to be experienced as complementing processes with many combinations and variations of expression.

1. Choose one of the pairs of complements that has emerged from making your Identity Matrix; e.g., "I want to be full of energy." "I don't want to be tired and fatigued."

2. Create a somatic model (physical gesture and movement) of the desired quality (e.g., energy).

3. Shift locations and create a somatic model for the problem quality (e.g., fatigue).

5. Put yourself into the COACH state and practice moving from one of the polarities to the other, slowly, gracefully and mindfully, withough any contraction or CRASH. Notice how they complement rather than conflict with one another. Also notice how there are many combinations and variations of expression between the two polarities

6. Find and image or metaphor that allows to you to recognize and resourcefully balance or blend the qualities of both sides of the complementarities.

The Identity Matrix helps you to be clearer about your strengths and your areas for development.

In the coming sections of this chapter and the other chapters of this book we will continue to revisit and work with these key elements of the Identity Matrix and show how they are at the foundation of entrepreneurial success. To begin with, however, it is important to use them simply to enhance your own self-awareness. As Cindana Turkatte pointed out, in order to reach one's vision and fulfill one's mission, it is important to "understand what you really are the best at and what you can do that others cannot do, but admit when you need some help." This comes from the ability to "admit what you know and what you don't know."

Identity Assessment Template

The following is an example of an Identity Assessment Template that we use when coaching entrepreneurs in order to help them apply the results of the Identity Matrix to clarify their strengths and areas for development.

Strengths will most likely relate to the Core, Potential and Boundary aspects of the Identity Matrix. Areas for development will be linked with your Limitations, Weaknesses and the Shadow.

Strengths	Areas for Development
What do you have a lot of ?	What do you not have enough of?
What comes easily to you?	What do you find to be a struggle?
What resources do you have to offer?	What resources do you need?
What are your strongest personal qualities?	Which personal qualities would you most like to develop more fully?
What are your core competencies?	Which competencies do you need to develop more fully?

Following the lessons learned so far from Barney Pell, Samuel Palmissano, Mark Fizpatrick and Cindana Turkatte, reflect on your answers to the questions above.

- *What resources and qualities do you have that would be most beneficial to others?*
- *What do you have most to contribute to your vision and the visions of others?*
- *What are some of the areas in which you need to develop yourself?*
- *What types of partners would be most important for you to seek in order to succeed in your project or venture?*
- *What types of team members would be most necessary for you to recruit in order to succeed in your mission and vision?*

Chapter Summary

Success has to do with reaching desired goals on a variety of levels and producing win-win results in our interactions with others who can support us to reach our desired goals. It also has to do with our participation in and contribution to something larger than ourselves. That is, it is about "living our dreams" *and* "helping to create a better world." Balancing and aligning these two pursuits is the essence of success for next generation entrepreneurs.

"Becoming a success" begins by developing and enriching the center of the Circle of Success—your Self. True success at this level produces an inner sense of gratitude and generosity.

Key to the implementation of Success Factor Modeling is the "spirit of prosperity" which comes from enriching widening and enriching impoverished maps of the world to create an awareness of an abundance of resources on different levels. This creates a deep recognition that—rather than be at odds with developing a sense of purpose, meaning and the devotion of oneself to contribute to the lives of others—pursuing win-win success and healthy prosperity propels us toward reaching our visions and purposes.

The path to becoming a success begins by being true to yourself and your dreams. This involves the willingness to take risks and face the possibility of failure and the ability to transform perceived failure into feedback. The capacity to do this results from the development of a compelling vision and the strong belief in the vision and yourself. These success factors are necessary to be able to persist in spite of opposition and to learn from what initially appear to be failures.

As successful entrepreneur Don Pickens pointed out, if you do not initially succeed it is important to understand what part of it you did get right, and what you can learn from what you got wrong. As Pickens also advised, it is important to seek sponsorship, move ahead with those who will support you and avoid being held back by those who do not.

It could be said that to become a success you need a certain degree of luck. The principles and tools of Success Factor Modeling help you to improve your chances of getting "lucky" by preparing and developing yourself in order to be ready take advantage of opportunities when they do arise and by staying on the lookout for opportunities that may not yet be visible to others.

These principles are echoed by the Success Factor Case Example of Mark Fizpatrick, whose path to remarkable financial success began as a result of developing himself, looking for opportunities and applying his vision to create win-win results with potential customers.

Cindana Turkatte's Success Factor Case Example illustrates that, whether you are a man or a woman, entrepreneurial success comes from discovering what you can do that no one else can do and then acknowledging and seeking support in areas where you need it. Cindana's example also illustrates the importance of the driving force of the desire to make a contribution and the ability to understand the needs and motivations of those who make up your Circle of Success.

Knowing yourself is thus one of the first steps to becoming a success. Like the notion of *superposition* in quantum physics, our core identity can be many things at the same time; some which have been expressed and others that are still latent within us as potentials. The Identity Level Elicitation Process is a way to explore yourself and your interests on a number of levels.

Knowing yourself and finding your passion is thus one of the first steps to becoming a success. Through exploring and clarifying your identity and passion, you can release the energy and creativity that comes from connecting with your purpose and motivation. The Identity Level Elicitation Process is a way to explore yourself and your interests on a number of levels.

Along with the COACH state, Expressing and Anchoring Your Passion verbally, visually and somatically is essential to stay connected to your purpose and motivation. This is especially important when things are challenging, uncertain, boring, confusing, etc. It is also the foundation of your ability to inspire others to listen to you and ultimately join you or support you.

The Identity Matrix is a tool that can be used to help you identify beliefs that empower you as well as those that potentially hold you back. Rather than being a source of struggle, these seeming polarities can become generative complementarities that support you to learn about yourself and express your sense of identity, motivation and mission in the form of compelling projects and visions that can stimulate personal growth and transformation.

The Identity Assessment Template helps you to clarify and summarize your strengths and areas of improvement. Both are crucial factors to be aware of in order to take the next steps in becoming successful and creating the future.

As you will see, creating the future involves transforming your sense of identity and passion into a vision, mission, ambition and role aligned to the quadrants of the Circle of Success.

References and Further Reading

Why I am Leaving Goldman-Sachs, Smith, G., New York Times, March, 14, 2012.

Tools for Dreamers, Dilts, R. B., Epstein, T. and Dilts, R. W., Meta Publications, Capitola, CA, 1991.

Outliers: The Story of Success, Gladwell, M., Back Bay Books, Little, Brown and Company, New York, NY, 2008.

The Cambridge Handbook of Expertise and Expert Performance, Charness, N.; Feltovich, P.; Hoffman, R.; Ericsson, A., eds., Cambridge University Press, Cambridge, 2006.

The Luck Factor, Wiseman, R., Random House, London, UK, 2003.

The Top Five Regrets of the Dying: A Life Transformed by the Dearly Departing, Ware, B., Hay House, Carlsbad, CA, 2012.

04
Creating the Future

"The future belongs to those who see possibilities before they become obvious."
John Sculley

*"If you want to build a ship, don't herd people together to collect wood
and don't assign them tasks and work, but rather teach them to long
for the endless immensity of the sea."*
Antoine de Saint-Exupery

*"The companies that survive longest are the one's that work out what they uniquely
can give to the world—not just growth or money but their excellence, their respect for
others, or their ability to make people happy. Some call those things a soul."*
Charles Handy

"Where there is no vision the people perish."
Proverbs 29:18

The Journey of Identity

To the person who does not know where he wants to go there is no favorable wind.

– Seneca

Being an entrepreneur is a journey of self-discovery and service to yourself, others and the world.

In his book *Hero With a Thousand Faces*, Joseph Campbell talks about the three life paths that we can take: the village, the wasteland and the journey. *The village* represents the life that has been mapped out for us by our society and culture: We are born, go to school, graduate, get a job, get married, have children, work until we retire, get a gold watch and finally we die. This path has a lot of security and safety, and doesn't disrupt the norm or "rock the boat" very much. We do as we are expected. It is essentially the path of the ego. For many people, this is a satisfactory way to live their lives.

For others it is not so simple. For some reason, either they do not fit in (because they are the wrong color, gender, shape, sexual preference, etc.) or they feel called to something more. The village to them is, in Thoreau's words, "a life of quiet desperation." Rather than thrive in the village, they feel caged, suffocated or repressed. For these people, according to Campbell, there are two other possible paths.

The *wasteland* represents the path of the rebel, outlaw or outcast. It is a life on the fringe of society, one's family, one's career, etc.; beyond the edge of what is considered appropriate and normal. It is an attempt to flourish by rejecting and escaping the village (into sex, drugs, rock n'roll, etc.). While it is an attempt to find a context in which to thrive, it usually produces the opposite. It may ultimately end in something like addiction to alcohol or drugs, perhaps some kind of "criminal" activity, or maybe just a type of life of isolation or dereliction.

The other path is that of the *journey*. On the journey, we follow our hearts, vision and calling to find our own way and discover something new. This is the path of all great leaders, entrepreneurs and pioneers. Through the challenges and discoveries along the path we acquire courage, insight, wisdom, resiliency and greater awareness of ourselves and the world. When we return to the village we are able to make our own unique contribution to others and become recognized and acknowledged for who we really are. The journey is not always an external one. Sometimes we travel internally even as we stay within the physical context of the village. As a result of our growth, we bring new ideas and new life to the village, making it possible for more to thrive there. We may even find it possible to bring healing and transformation to the wasteland.

Being an entrepreneur is about taking this third path; the journey to find how to thrive by developing the skills to discover and travel your own path and live your own life as the best version of yourself in service to yourself, others and the world.

In this chapter, we will revisit the key success factors of vision, mission, ambition and role and apply them to the four quadrants of the Circle of Success in order to more specifically define your project or venture.

Entrepreneurial Vision

While all of the levels of success factors are important for beginning your journey to creating a successful venture, vision is one of the most paramount. In Chapter 1 we defined *vision* as "A mental image of what the future will or could be like." Such images frequently emerge when we direct our passion towards the future from a state of open curiosity. This produces a picture of how our lives or our world could be enriched or improved in some way. Such visions of the future provide guidance and direction for our lives and our work, furnishing the motivation and impetus for change on many levels.

Entrepreneurial vision is the product of directing the passion from the center of one's Circle of Success outward towards the needs and desires of customers and potential customers. It is from the center of the Circle of Success that the aspirations, insights, experience and passion of the entrepreneur create the initial foundation for building a new venture from conception to manifestation. If you ask investors why they have chosen to invest in a particular company, it is often on the basis of "intangibles" such as the entrepreneur's vision, passion or confidence. Investors know that technologies will change, markets will change, team members will change; the constant will be the entrepreneur's vision. This is because the entrepreneur's vision:

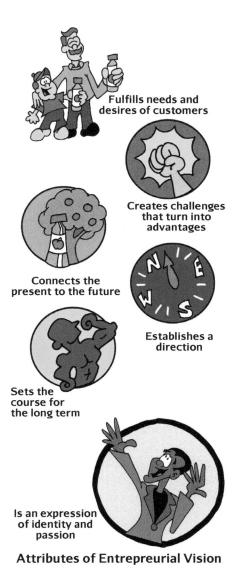

Fulfills needs and desires of customers

Creates challenges that turn into advantages

Connects the present to the future

Establishes a direction

Sets the course for the long term

- Establishes a direction and inspires motivation and creativity.
- Sets the course to be followed on the long term— in particular, what type of world you are attempting to create for customers.
- Creates challenges that turn into competitive advantages.
- Connects the present to the future.

Steve Artim, for example, is a Silicon Valley entrepreneur with many years of high tech marketing and business development experience in communication and multimedia. He helped found and launch the Real Time Visualization division of Mitsubishi Electric. He has also held senior marketing and business development positions at Phillips and Sierra Semiconductor. In 1999 he became co-founder and CEO of DoOnGo, a company offering a powerful suite of wireless infrastructure software products providing "intelligence and personalization" to wireless carriers and advanced mobile devices. Steve describes the importance of vision in the following way:

Is an expression of identity and passion

Attributes of Entrepreurial Vision

Steve Artim
CEO of DoOnGo

An entrepreneur's vision creates a "stake in the ground in the future" that forms a focal point for all of the activities of the venture and the team.

Entrepreneurial success also relies on a type of "peripheral vision" that operates like a radar to track ongoing changes and influences that may affect the entrepreneur's strategy and actions.

I believe vision is absolutely critical to a young start-up. You have to take a stake and drive it into the ground in the future, and do everything in your power as a leader of a company to drive your engineers, your sales and marketing people, and your financial people to go make that happen. Without that there is no differentiation between you and other large companies that can go out and do the same thing—and frankly they probably can—but you are wholly focused as a team and as an entity on going out and making it happen.

Steve Artim's description of a "stake in the ground in the future" implies that there is a clear quality of focus in entrepreneurial vision. His comments indicate that the entrepreneur's vision of the future becomes the focal point for all of the activity of the entrepreneur and his or her team as well as the "attractor" for those making up the entrepreneur's Circle of Success. As Steve explains:

For a start-up it takes a lot of partnerships to move yourself forward. It takes a lot of ability to get in there and solve a couple of problems very, very well for your lead customer. And picking your customer is critical for driving your company forward into the mainstream.

In addition to forward focus, there is also a lateral dimension of entrepreneurial vision; a type of "peripheral vision" that operates like a radar sensor to pick up ongoing influences in the current environment. As Steve explains it:

You have to be completely customer focused. You have to be outward facing at all times. You have to completely understand everything that is happening. There are large players in the market that are moving things, but there are also a lot of small players that are below the radar screen, that are just coming up on the radar screen. You have to understand what they're doing, how they are funded, and what their strategic backgrounds are to really understand and to make the right fit for your company.

Both of these dimensions of vision—forward focal vision and wider peripheral vision—are necessary for entrepreneurs to effectively manage uncertainty and change and stay on a successful course of action. Both types are essential in order to be able to navigate to accommodate a global marketplace, foresee changes and make adjustments, and to anticipate competition. This is not always an easy balance to maintain. One reason that some start-up companies fail is because, by looking too closely at their competitors, they lose sight of their real customers' needs.

In summary, our work with start-up companies and investors has shown us that strong technology alone will not make a company successful for the long-term. The development of concrete products, services and tools needs to be guided by a clear and inspirational vision that provides direction and ensures authentic value to customers.

Our research has shown that successful "next generation" entrepreneurs have a vision that is:

1. Human centered

- Promotes growth of people and society
- Includes personal development as well as practical competencies
- Perceives money as a means (not an end) to be used for human development
- Fulfills real needs of people
- Supports human centered values – i.e., health, harmony, education, etc.

2. Systemic

- Supports community development through the development of the individual
- Presupposes that individuals are a whole and part of a bigger whole ("holons") – i.e., improving oneself (or benefiting team/company) leads to improving a community of customers which leads to improving the world
- Nurtures skills and values that are useful for the community
- Serves more than an immediate need
- Takes into account social and environmental consequences
- Produces a positive social benefit beyond the scope of the business

3. Authentic

- The human centered and systemic characteristics are:
  - at the foundation for the venture
  - integrated in the business model and the strategy
  - shared and supported at all levels of the company
- Concrete resources are dedicated to the bigger vision even if they do not directly increase profits
- The venture is perceived as a contributing part of something bigger

The visions of next generation entrepreneurs are human centered.

Next generation entrepreneurs also have visions that are systemic, taking into account social and environmental consequences.

The visions of next generation entrepreneurs authentically integrate human centered and systemic characteristics into the business model of the venture.

Next generation entrepreneurs are strongly customer oriented.

Identifying Potential Customers and Their Needs

As Steve Artim pointed out, a successful entrepreneur has to be "completely customer focused." He also maintained that "picking your customer is critical" for the success of your venture and that it was necessary to "solve a couple of problems very, very well for your lead customer."

Tidal Wave Technologies founder Mark Fizpatrick claimed, "Our vision was centered on what our customer needs were" and that he and his team "applied our vision to that need, and we used a lot of customer feedback to constantly adjust the vision."

Cindana Turkatte pointed out that in order to find successful product ideas and make a genuine contribution, it was necessary to explore with customers what was important to them. This requires developing empathy by putting yourself in the shoes of potential customers.

Samuel Palmisano shifted the emphasis of IBM from selling customers computers and software to offering complete solutions tailored to customers' needs, helping them use technology to solve their business challenges.

Barney Pell ensured the success of his company by focusing on a "truly more user-centered test" for his product.

As these examples illustrate, identifying potential customers and their needs is a critical success factor for entrepreneurs. In fact, our research with successful next generation entrepreneurs has shown that they are:

Customer Oriented

- Maintain a strong ongoing feedback loop with customers

- Establish structures and infrastructures that create exchange and mutual feedback with customers

- Base their products and services on customer-oriented values: e.g., safety, comfort, intuitive, reliable, etc.

- Co-create products and services with customers instead of "selling"

- Ensure that the economic growth of the venture comes from increasing the quality of products or services versus marketing and hype

- Include customer needs and desires in their business decisions and management policies

Emotionally Intelligent

- Maintain a strong empathy ("second position") with customers
- Develop their products and services based on "living" customer experience versus surveys
- Take customer capabilities (knowledge, skill level, etc.) into account when developing their products and services
- Communicate customer benefits of their offerings simply and in the customer's own language
- Verify that their products and brand are felt as emotionally relevant by customers
- Take actions to assure that their products and brand trigger positive emotions in customers

Focused on Evolving Needs

- Constantly look ahead and anticipate future needs of existing customers and the needs and desires of new customers
- Distinguish between short-term fads versus long-term customer needs
- Consider a wide diversity of customers when developing their products and services
- Connect customers who are trendsetters and early adopters with developers and pioneers in the company
- Respect the ecosystem of their customers in their offerings – i.e., take into account chains of effect and the long-term consequences on the customer's larger context

Clearly, identifying your own customers and potential customers and their needs and desires is an essential step in the success of your venture. Often potential customers are those who share your passion. Pleasant Hawaiian Holiday's founder Ed Hogan's passion for travel to exotic locations, for instance, allowed him to attract and provide value for others who had the same passion for travel. Further, Ed's own experiences as a traveller gave him a strong empathy understanding of the needs and desires of his customers. Similarly, a person with a passion for video games is likely to find customers in other video game players.

Next generation entrepreneurs are emotionally Intelligent and maintain a genuine empathy with thier customers.

Next generation entrepreneurs are focused on the evolvoing needs of their customers, anticipating potential future wishes and desires.

Identifying customers and potential customers who will benefit from your passion and vision, and getting to know their needs and desires, is an essential step in the success of a new venture.

Sometimes we *are* our own lead customer. Airbnb co-founders Brian Chesky and Joe Gebbia, for example, came up with the idea for their venture in response to their own difficulties in finding affordable temporary housing. In such cases, we as entrepreneurs have the direct experience of customer needs and desires.

Other times, our customers are the object of our passion. Your passion may be naturally directed toward children, students, musicians, women leaders, new families, entrepreneurs, etc. In other instances, it might be slightly more indirect. A person with a passion for horses, pets or vintage automobiles may find customers among their owners.

Many times, our passion and vision leads us to find a solution or fill a need for a certain type of customer. In that case, we need to seek to identify who will most easily and clearly benefit from our product or service. In some cases, it is a current need that is felt by potential customers. In others, as Cindana pointed, we are able to help potential customers "do something they didn't know was possible." Barney Pell's "conversational computing" is a good illustration of this.

Frequently, as in Mark Fizpatrick's case, we are already in touch with a certain type of customer with a clear need and are able to use our passion and vision to find a solution that fulfills that need.

Customers do not necessarily have to fall into a traditional demographic group. When Bandler and Grinder were founding NLP, they identified the primary customers for their work as "professional communicators." This group includes anyone for whom communicating effectively is an essential part of the success of their work.

Take a moment to reflect upon and identify the customers and potential customers for your venture.

- Who are the *potential customers/clients* who share your passion or who could benefit from your passion and personal *vision*?

- What *types of people* would be most interested in either receiving those benefits or passing those benefits on to others?

- What types of people are most likely to be your *"early adopters?"*

- Do you have *existing customers* to whom your passion and personal vision could bring new solutions or benefits?

- What types of customers will have the biggest influence on making your potential products or services *visible to others?*

- Who is your *"dream customer?"*

The next step is to apply your passion and vision to begin to create or refine products or services that will bring a real benefit to your customers and potential customers. As we go through the next exercises, keep in mind the visions and ventures of next generation entrepreneurs are human centered, systemic and authentic.

Generative Vision Exercise

In Chapter 1, you began to explore your personal vision by considering the questions: "What do you want to create in the world through you that is beyond you?" "What do you want to see more of and less of in the world?" "What is the world to which you want to belong?" In Chapter 2, we pointed out that a vision for a venture or project emerges when we direct our passion from the center of our Circle of Success toward a particular group of customers or a particular market. This focuses our bigger vision and begins to generate the specific products and services that the venture will produce and that will become the "stake in the ground" in the future that Steve Artim described earlier.

The following exercise will assist you to begin to generatively apply your passion to create a vision for a project or venture.

The specific vision for a venture or project takes shape when an entrepreneur directs his or her passion from the center of his or her Circle of Success toward a particular group of customers or a particular market.

1. Put yourself in a relaxed and open state (i.e., the COACH state) in which you can feel fully yourself and connected with the sense of identity and passion at the center of your Circle of Success. Reconnect with your passion, your core and your potential that you discovered and clarified in the previous chapter. Recall and the words, image and gesture that you created as the anchor and expression of your passion.

2. With your eyes closed, create a space for "Vision" in your mind's eye. Imagine a vast inner "landscape." Notice where the horizon of your inner landscape is. Also notice the "point of convergence" or "vanishing point" related to your focus with respect to the inner landscape.

3. Restate the vision you explored in Chapter 1 in fewer than 10 key words. *e.g.*
   "People helping other people."
   "Women awakening to their leadership potential."
   "People growing and contributing through business ventures."
   "People living their dreams and creating a better world."
   "Children supported to be the best of themselves."

4. Vision begins to take shape when we direct it towards a customer or potential customer. Bring your focus to a potential beneficiary or "customer" for your vision that you identified in the previous reflection: i.e., families, executives, entrepreneurs, patients, students, or some other demographic group.

5. Visualize the customer and the various situations they encounter and continue to restate your vision. Open your imagination and transform the words into an image. What does the expression of your vision look like when applied to that customer and his/her/their situations? Consider the questions:

What do you want to create for your customers through your venture or project?

What services, benefits and contributions will your venture or project make to customers, society, the environment, etc.?

What do you want to make possible for them?

Let yourself dream. Don't try to figure it out. Tune into the "field" of that customer and let your creative unconscious show you some possibilities. Remember, the words you are using to express your vision are connected to wisdom and desires deep within you that are naturally generative.

Be careful not to become too rational or mental. Stay connected to the feelings of inspiration and motivation that come from your core and your potential and keep your imagination open. A vision is something that continues to evolve over time.

Directing your vision towards a potential customer begins to generate images of specific products and services that the venture will produce and that will become its "stake in the ground" in the future.

Creativity Catalysts

Creativity catalysts are activities that produce special internal states that allow us to access the "creative unconscious."

Many well-known creative geniuses developed their own forms of creativity catalysts.

Creativity catalysts help to develop special states for access to what we have referred to as the "creative unconscious."

Most highly creative people directly acknowledge the importance of unconscious processes in their work. For instance, a number of the entrepreneurs my brother John and I interviewed in our Success Factor Modeling studies reported something to the effect of, "I stuff my mind full of the information that I can find until I am completely exhausted and I can't fit anything more in there. Then I go to sleep. When I wake up, I have the answer!" Others claimed they got their best ideas when they were in the shower in the morning.

In my study of *Strategies of Genius* I discovered out that almost every well-known creative genius in history, from Leonardo da Vinci to Einstein to Mozart to Michael Jackson and Steve Jobs, maintain, in some way or another, that their most creative works and ideas come "through" and not "from" them as individuals. Of his musical ideas, for example, Mozart wrote, "Whence and how they come, I know not; nor can I force them." He did, however, mention that these ideas came most easily when he was in certain types of internal states, in which the creative process unfolded "in a pleasing lively dream." These states emerged most easily while he was engaged in simple activities such as "traveling in a carriage or walking after a good meal." It is these types of activities that we call "creativity catalysts."

It is interesting to note that other successful composers have also mentioned a dreamlike, largely unconscious, quality to their creative process. For example, in an interview with Rolling Stone magazine in 1983, popular music composer and performer Michael Jackson reported, "I wake up from dreams and go, 'Wow, put this down on paper.' You hear the words, everything is there in front of your face. . . . That's why I hate to take credit for songs I've written. I feel that somewhere, someplace, it's been done and I'm just a courier bringing it into the world."

In his notebooks, Leonardo da Vinci described how he would stare at "walls spotted with various stains or with a mixture of different kinds of stones" in order to "stimulate and arouse" his mind "to various inventions." Leonardo claimed he was able to see in the walls "various different landscapes adorned with mountains, rivers, rocks, trees, plains, wide valleys, and various groups of hills" as well as "figures in quick movement, and strange expressions of faces, and outlandish costumes, and an infinite number of things."

Thanks for shopping with us.
Kindest Regards, Customer Care

RETURNING GOODS

Please re-pack, in the original packaging if possible, and send back to us at the address below. **Caution!** Don't cover up the barcode (on original packaging) as it helps us to process your return.

We will email you when we have processed your return.

✂ ....

PLEASE complete and include this section with your goods.

Your Name _____

Your Order Number _____

Reason for Return _____

Would you prefer: Refund ☐ or Replacement ☐

(Please note, if we are unable to replace the item it will be refunded.)

Return to:
✂ ....

RETURNS
801 Penhorn Avenue, Unit 5
Secaucus
NJ
07094

While working on his classic works *Origin of Species and Descent of Man* Charles Darwin constructed a sand-covered path at his estate known as "the sandwalk." He strolled it daily, deep in thought, referring to it as "my thinking path." Often he would stack a few stones at the path's entrance, and knock one away with his walking stick upon completing each circuit and then head home when all the stones were gone. He talked about various issues a "three-flint problem" or a "five-flint problem" (just as Sherlock Holmes had "three-pipe problems").

Albert Einstein claimed his ideas and theories arose spontaneously from certain types of "thought experiments" that were primarily images and feelings and "did not grow out of any manipulations of axioms" or rational, cognitive forms of thought. His "creativity catalysts" included playing the violin and sailing.

These descriptions imply methods of connecting to creative intelligence beyond the confines of the rational, conscious cognitive mind. As we will see later in this chapter, successful entrepreneurs like Steve Jobs mention similar dynamics regarding their creative process. Jobs, for example, talked about following "your heart and intuition" and described how he listened to music as a way to stimulate his creative process.

The founder of a large shipping company who I interviewed claimed that when faced with complex and challenging problems, he would stop thinking about it and go ride his bicycle. At the end of the ride, he would frequently have an answer. For other problems, he would go out and play golf in order to get into the frame of mind required to deal with the issues. He was so specific about which type of "creativity catalyst" to use that he would say, "You can't golf on that problem. That's one that you have to ride your bicycle on."

What are some of your creativity catalysts? What are some of the things you do to stimulate your own creative unconscious? They can be as simple as riding a bicycle, taking a walk, listening to music or gardening. As an example, I run every morning. It helps me connect to my "core" and activate my nervous system.

As you are considering the exercises in this and the following chapters, use your creativity catalysts, or try some new ones, in order to involve your creative unconscious in the process. It is an essential resource for you. Time and again, we have heard successful entrepreneurs say, "If I had thought about it rationally, I never would have done it."

It is important for entrepreneurs to discover and develop their own creativity catalysts in order to activate and involve their creative unconscious as an ongoing resource.

Knowing how to dream is an important part of being an entrepreneur. Dreams, both sleeping and waking dreams or "daydreams," arise from the field of the creative unconscious. The cognitive, conscious mind is more of a witness to what has been created. What we have been calling "vision" begins to form when the conscious cognitive mind joins and helps direct the creative unconscious. When vision becomes applied to create a project, the process becomes primarily driven by the cognitive mind, with typically less ongoing contribution from the creative unconscious.

The next exercise will help you to begin to move from dreaming to visioning and give more shape to your vision for your customer and market.

An entrepreneur's vision emerges from the interaction between his or her cognitive mind and creative unconscious.

"More of/Less of" Chart

Vision can come from either inspiration or desperation. *Inspiration* is defined as "the process of being mentally stimulated to do or feel something; especially to do something creative. It literally means the act of breathing in; coming from the Latin *in* ("into") and *spirare* ("breathe"). *Desperation* is defined as "an act or attempt made in despair or when everything else has failed; having little hope of success." It comes from "a hopeless sense that a situation is so bad as to be impossible to deal with." It originates from the Latin *de* ("deprived of") and *sperare* ("hope"). We can say that inspiration comes from the drive to create while desperation comes from the drive to escape. One is towards a positive future, the other is away from a negative past or present.

Both of these drives can be legitimate sources for a vision for the future. To be too driven by desperation, however, can lead to a type of ungrounded "false hope." In fact, the most powerful visions are those that create the possibility of moving away from a difficult or unwanted situation and toward a desired or enhanced future state.

A useful tool for helping explore these two dimensions of your vision is the "more of / less of" chart. This chart invites you to describe the future that you want to create for your customer in more detail, listing what you expect to see *more of* and *less of* in their future environment. You will want to begin to describe the future conditions for your customers in behavioral terms.

Begin by writing the words expressing your vision at the top of the chart. Then, write down your potential customer. Reflect upon the future environment of your customer, taking into consideration both potential opportunities and constraints.

With this snapshot of the future in mind, list what you expect to see more of and what you expect to see less of in the future environment. In some cases, the two aspects may be correlated ("more time for creative exploration" and "less time spent on busy work"). In other cases, you can simply complete one side of the chart first and the other side of the chart later.

The "More of / Less of" Chart is tool that helps you to describe the future that you want to create for your customer in more detail, listing what you expect to see more of and less of in their future environment in behavioral terms.

VISION_____

CUSTOMER_____

BEHAVIORS

MORE OF   *LESS OF*

_____   _____

_____   _____

_____   _____

_____   _____

_____   _____

Formulating A Vision Statement

When formulating a vision statement, it is important to keep in mind that expressing a vision is more about pointing to a particular direction than describing a specific destination or objective. A good example of expressing a compelling vision is Martin Luther King's famous 1963 "I have a dream" speech. In it, he says:

> I have a dream that one day this nation will rise up and live out the true meaning of its creed, "We hold these truths to be self-evident; that all men are created equal."

> I have a dream that one day on the red hills of Georgia the sons of former slaves and sons of former slave-owners will be able to sit down together at the table of brotherhood.

> I have a dream that one day even the state of Mississippi, a desert state sweltering with heat of injustice and oppression, will be transformed into an oasis of freedom and justice.

> I have a dream that my four little children will one day live in a nation where they will not be judged by the color of their skin but by the content of their character.

These statements provide a helpful formula for expressing vision. King uses language not to describe the details of a particular objective but rather to paint a kind of mosaic of different images and experiences of different types and levels that define the shape and dimensions of a possible future:

Martin Luther King's "I Have a Dream" speech provides a helpful formula for expressing a vision.

1. King begins by defining the *core beliefs and values* associated with his vision, i.e., that "all men are created equal."

2. He then uses a more *metaphorical* way of communicating the vision, talking about "the sons of former slaves and the sons of former slave-owners" sitting together at the "table of brotherhood."

3. The next statement defines the vision in the form of the *transformation* of "injustice and oppression" into "freedom and justice" — a type of expression of the previous "more of/less of" exercise.

4. Finally, King provides a more specific example of one of the positive outcomes of the vision for one of the key "customers" or beneficiaries of that vision—children. He makes it all the more personal by referring to his own children.

I HAVE A DREAM!

"A DESERT STATE SWELTERING WITH HEAT OF INJUSTICE AND OPPRESSION, WILL BE TRANSFORMED INTO AN OASIS OF FREEDOM AND JUSTICE."

"THE SONS OF FORMER SLAVES AND SONS OF FORMER SLAVE-OWNERS WILL BE ABLE TO SIT DOWN TOGETHER AT THE TABLE OF BROTHERHOOD."

"WE HOLD THESE TRUTHS TO BE SELF-EVIDENT; THAT ALL MEN ARE CREATED EQUAL."

"MY CHILDREN WILL ONE DAY LIVE IN A NATION WHERE THEY WILL NOT BE JUDGED BY THE COLOR OF THEIR SKIN BUT BY THE CONTENT OF THEIR CHARACTER."

ANTONIO MEZA

Try out this formula with your own vision by filling in the following statements:

• *My vision is that one day people will live* _____.
   [which values? which benefits?].

• *My vision is that one day* _____.
   [what is a metaphorical way of describing your vision?]

• *My vision is that one day* _____
   [what problems and challenges]

   will be transformed into_____.
   [what desired state].

• *My vision is that one day* _____
   [what is a specific example of what this future will look like or a specific
   outcome that it will bring about for one of your key customers?]

Connecting Your Vision with Your "Charisma"

As Martin Luther King's speech illustrates, a vision is more than just an image or an objective. It is a reference point in the future that inspires motivation and releases energy, both in yourself and others. Communicating vision, then, is thus more than describing a goal. As successful entrepreneur Cindana Turkette claimed, "How you say it is important," and that it necessary to, "Present it with desire." This brings up the importance of communicating with "charisma" in order to create the future.

Charisma is defined as a "personal magnetism or charm" and a "unique personal quality attributed to leaders who arouse fervent popular devotion and enthusiasm." The term comes from the Greek *kharisma*, meaning "gift" or "favor," which in turn is derived from *kharis*, meaning "grace." Charisma is closely related to *presence*, which is defined as "a quality of poise and effectiveness that enables a performer to achieve a close relationship with his or her audience." The abilities to be poised, effective and achieve a close connection to those with whom we are interacting are important resources for entrepreneurs.

Your ability to communicate your vision with authentic charisma is another significant factor for entrepreneurial success.

The dictionary defines *authenticity* as: "an emotionally genuine, appropriate, significant, purposive, and responsible mode of human life." Thus, authentic charisma comes from the capacity to be present, centered in yourself and in relationship and harmony with individuals and the environment around you. The quality of charisma is frequently the "difference that makes the difference" in our ability to exert influence, collaborate generatively and contribute to the growth and transformation of others.

One of the goals of Success Factor Modeling is for people to be able to live their lives with passion and a sense of meaning that brings an exceptional level of energy and vitality into their everyday experience. As we have already established, one of the most common characteristics of successful people is their passion for what they do.

While charisma is typically considered a special gift, our experience has been that it is also a function of skills that can be learned. Applying the process of Success Factor Modeling, we have identified some of the key ways in which successful people intentionally strengthen their charisma and use their passion to bring more satisfaction and determination into their daily activities and into the lives of others. Some of these strategies include:

Authentic charisma comes from connecting with your core and your passion – a process that can be learned and practiced.

- Connecting to the center and "source" of your identity (your *core* and *potential*)
- Feeling centered in yourself and open to new possibilities around you
- Connecting what you care about to what you do and linking future goals to concrete examples of past successes
- Getting a clear picture of your goals and their connection to the "big picture" of your life
- Managing your energy and bringing positive energy into all that you do
- Creating a sense of alignment and connection to your vision, mission and core values
- Fostering a feeling of contribution to something important that will in some way "change the world"

As we continue this book, we will explore how to apply these strategies to release more authentic charisma and passion in your personal and professional life.

Communicating Your Vision with Authentic Charisma

Releasing your charisma, connecting to your passion, living your dream and creating a better world all begin with communicating your vision. According to Success Factor Modeling, a vision is something that mobilizes and enlivens all three of our minds: cognitive, somatic and field. Communicating your vision with authentic charisma involves expressing yourself to others with your "channel open."

The following exercise is a way to ensure that your vision is more than just an idea or wish, and that it lives deeply in your nervous system. Its purpose is to help you to stay connected with yourself and authentically touch others when you communicate. Try it for each of the statements you came up with in the Formulating A Vision Statement exercise.

There are three phases of communicating a vision:

The three phases of communitcating your vision with authentic charisma involve (1) knowing it; (2) feeling it; and (3) freeing it into the field.

1. Know It

Be clear and succinct with your language. Begin with the words, "My vision is . . ." and express your vision in five to nine (7+-2) words.

Repeat your statement of your vision several times until you feel that you can say it with simplicity, ease and clarity.

2. Feel It

From the COACH state, bring your awareness to your body and somatically center yourself in your experience of your *core* and your *potential*. Feel the sense of pride, confidence, hope and excitement with them. Express your vision again, speaking *from* your core and the center of your Circle of Success. Feel the words and their meaning as you say them, making sure your voice stays connected and resonant with your core and potential.

Repeat this several times until you feel that you can express your vision with congruence, passion and confidence.

3. Free It into the Field

The next step is best to do in front of a group. When we coach entrepreneurs, we have them begin expressing their vision in this way to us first and then to progressively larger audiences. It is also possible however, to practice this out loud but with an audience in your imagination.

Keeping your awareness on your body and your center, open your field of attention to include your audience. As you speak, sense your energy and the energy of your vision extending beyond yourself and touching the hearts and minds of your listeners. Make a gesture and movement that somatically expresses your vision as you say the words. Speak from your center to the field surrounding you. Feel the resonance both within and around you.

Repeat this several times until you feel that you can stay present and connected with yourself, your vision and your audience the whole time you are speaking.

Clarifying the Mission of Your Venture

As we established in Chapter 1, *Vision* relates to our *direction* and desired future state we want to see in the world. *Mission* relates to our *contribution* to moving in that direction and reaching that desired future state. In other words, mission relates to the purpose an individual or group serves in relationship to their vision for the larger systems of which they are a part — i.e., what their purpose is, in relation to *who and what else*. Vision is about something bigger than ourselves and beyond ourselves. Mission is about ourselves and the actions we take to participate in reaching the vision.

Clarifying your mission and the mission of your venture is another important success factor for entrepreneurs.

Martin Luther King's dream or vision of an "oasis of freedom" and a world his children were judged by the "content of their character" instead of the "color of their skin" was about something much larger than himself personally. His mission, on the other hand, was to lead non-violent demonstrations and other public events that brought awareness to places where change was needed in order reach the vision.

Mission is about the actions we take to participate in reaching the bigger vision.

Similarly, Barney Pell's vision of "conversational computing" was much bigger than himself or his company. It was an image of a world where people could interact with computers and other technologies using everyday natural human language, rather than technical commands or "keywordese." Barney's vision was not about him personally. It was about "the power of the idea to make a better world." In fact, he maintained, if some other person or company brought about this desired state before him or better than him, it would be "all the better." He would be happy because "the world is a better place and that is what is most important to me." The vision was clearly not about himself or his ego.

You've got to think about big things while you're doing small things, so that all the small things go in the right direction.

– Alvin Toffler

The mission of a particular venture relates to its identity and the unique contribution it makes to achieving a vision that benefits its customers.

A mision expresses itself in the form of a variety of specific tasks.

Barney's mission and ultimately the mission of his team and venture, on the other hand, had to do with his personal contribution to bringing the bigger vision of conversational computing into reality. This mission was quite personal and related to his identity. In fact, Barney felt it was the "completion of his journey." He even asserted that "You have to be me in order to do this thing. You have to have my history, which brings together all the right elements. Otherwise it just won't happen." This mission expressed itself concretely as developing algorithms in order to create "the best possible natural language search," and more particularly, to create "a superior user experience compared to Google."

As Barney's comments indicate, a person's or group's sense of mission relates to their identity and is thus an expression of the *core* and *potential* as defined by the Identity Matrix. Mission is also clearly an expression of one's passion, which is why mission is usually defined as a "strongly felt aim or calling." Barney's passion for learning and artificial intelligence fueled his vision of conversational computing, but also his sense of mission to create a fully functioning natural language search engine.

In the same way vision is about direction and spawns many specific objectives, mission is about contribution and becomes expressed as many specific tasks. Clarifying your mission is an essential step for moving into action. It is especially important for defining and prioritizing the critical path of steps that will realize the vision. As futurist Alvin Toffler pointed out, "You've got to think about big things while you're doing small things, so that all the small things go in the right direction."

Your mission for your project or venture has to do with the way in which your core, potential and passion at the center of your Circle of Success manifests itself in relationship your contribution to your vision for your customers. It relates to the questions:

- *What capabilities and qualities are you passionate about that you can bring into the service of others?*

- *How can your core and potential (from the Identity Matrix) be used to benefit potential customers?*

- *What is your contribution and service (as an individual and a team) with respect to the vision for your customers?*

- *What are the special resources, capabilities and actions that you will develop, apply and mobilize (as an individual and a team) to reach the vision for your customers?*

To clarify your mission, it is important to distinguish it from your ambition and your role. It is essential to keep in mind that even though the *mission* of a person or group is about their unique identity and capabilities, it has to do with the purpose they serve or contribution they make to some larger system *beyond themselves*. To say, "My mission is to be successful," is both too vague and too self-serving to be a "mission" statement. A mission statement defines the contribution the individual or group makes, and the purpose they have, within the larger system they serve or in which they participate. Even for an organization or association to say, "Our mission is to serve our members," is not yet a well-formed mission statement. It is not stated with reference yet to a larger system beyond the organization or its members. Such a statement may be an important values statement, but is not yet a true mission.

To become concrete, a mission needs to be defined with respect to the specific customer or demographic group and the vision that the venture or team serving. A statement such as, "Our mission is to provide the best services we can and be profitable," is too generic and clarifies no real service or contribution by the venture or team. So, similar to your vision, one of the main things to keep in mind with respect to defining the mission of your venture is: "Who is my specific customer?" *Athletes? Families? Organizations? Governments? Children? Executives? Women?*

Use the following two questions as a way to clarify more about the relationship between your vision and the mission of your venture or team.

1. "What is your vision with respect to the larger system or community (customers) in which you are operating?" (This should just be a matter of repeating the statement you practiced in the *Formulating A Vision Statement* exercise.)

My/Our vision is _____

2. "What is your service or contribution with respect to that system and vision?"*

My/Our mission is to_____

_____

---

* It can also be helpful to clarify your mission to explore making statements of what the mission is *not*. This helps to set boundaries and clarify purpose with respect to other roles within a system; i.e., "It is not my/our mission to _____."

A mission statement defines the contribution the individual or group makes, and the purpose they have, within the larger system they serve or in which they participate.

To become concrete, a mission needs to be defined with respect to the specific customer and the vision that the venture or team serving.

As an example, the winter sports company I mentioned in Chapter 1 was eventually able to reconnect with and express their vision for their customers as "people living and playing on the 'Mountain' in comfort and in harmony with their environment." This allowed them to clarify their mission as to, "Create next-generation gear, as a natural extension of the body, which makes every moment the most enjoyable."

As another example, the clean energy company I mentioned, whose vision was "a world in which people used 'green', sustainable energy," defined their mission as to "help businesses and governments put policy into action in order to transform waste into energy."

In support of his vision of complete solutions tailored to customers' needs, Samuel Palmisano established the "smarter planet initiative" whose mission was applying computer intelligence to create more efficient systems for governments and social organizations (such as utility grids, traffic management, food distribution, water conservation and health care).

Ed Hogan supported his vision of affordable travel to exotic places for the average person with his mission to create travel packages that included both the flight and hotel fees at a reduced package price.

Identifying Potential Team Members

Key to expressing your passion as a vision is the identification of potential customers. Similarly, expressing your passion as a mission takes shape with respect to your venture as you begin to identify potential team members. Your team is a major part of your "sangha" – those who are sharing the same methods and working with you towards the same goals (i.e., of fulfilling your purpose and achieving your highest potential).

The most dedicated team members will obviously be those who share your passion and vision. The most helpful team members will be those who have essential and complementary skills and capabilities required to fulfill the mission of the venture. When team members share your passion and vision *and* have the necessary skills and capabilities, it is clearly a winning combination.

IBM's Samuel Palmisano recognized this when he shifted the company's top-down structure to one based instead on a shared mission to provide the motivation and direction for people's actions. The three values of (1) Dedication to every client's success, (2) Innovation that matters, for our company and for the world and (3) Trust and personal responsibility in all relationships provide a powerful description of the company's mission and contribution. The shared perception of the company's mission served to guide decision-making throughout the organization and support the creation of a powerful collaborative interaction between team members.

The mission of a venture takes further shape as you begin to identify potential team members.

Team Members/ Employees

Creating Alignment

Increasing Competency

Mission

In assembling his team for Powerset, Barney Pell described how he was constantly posing the questions, "What do we need?" and "Who is the best?" These are good questions to ask yourself as you put together your own team. As Barney also wisely advised, to create excellence, whoever is chosen to join the team should "be as good at what they do as you are at what you do." As Cindana Turkatte pointed out, entrepreneurial success requires "respect and appreciation that the team can do it."

Keep these guidelines in mind as you reflect upon and identify the team members and potential team members for your venture.

- What are the core activities that need to be done in order for you and your venture to succeed in fulfilling your mission and contributing to the vision?

- Who are (or could be) your team members and co-workers on this project?

- Who else will you need to join you in order to fulfill your mission and support the vision?

- What competences will be best to have "in house" and which can be outsourced?

- Who would be your "dream team?"

The best team members are those who share your passion and vision and have the necessary skills and capabilities to effectively contribute to the mission of the venture.

Communicating Your Mission

To both attract and align team members, it is essential to communicate the mission as well as the vision of your venture. Your mission and mission statement also help to differentiate yourself from competitors and clarify who you are (i.e., your brand). As we have said before many ventures may have a similar vision. It is your unique contribution to reaching that vision in the form of your mission that distinguishes you and your venture.

To be effective, a mission needs to be communicated in such a way that it can be put into practice in a variety of different situations and under changing circumstances. To communicate the mission of the venture or the team effectively, an entrepreneur needs to:

- Identify the "Customer" (What System Are You Serving?)
- Establish the Essential Service (What is Being Provided or Promoted?)
- Reflect Core Values (Why Are You Doing What You Are Doing?)
- Express Core Competence (What Technology or Methodology Makes You Unique?)

If you review the examples of mission statements provided earlier in this section, you will see how they fulfill these various guidelines. Some other examples of mission statements from entrepreneurs in our study for their ventures include:

Help people in organizations through group educational experiences to develop capabilities, heart and vision and to overcome obstacles.

Produce massive improvement of people's lives all over the world through e-learning and on-line education in leadership and management skills

Design collective projects for people in developing countries through which they discover that they can find their own solutions.
Create art projects involving people in poor suburbs that gives them and the public a new perspective on their capacities and identity.

Discover and share practical behavioral methods that support health and well-being for people of all ages.

To help make the mission more concrete, it is useful to identify examples of projects, events or situations that characterize the successful expression of the mission; i.e., *"A past example of the successful implementation of my/our mission is . . ."*

Companies that sustain long-term success – like Disney, Apple, IBM, etc. – keep such past successes alive as part of their culture and company "lore" as examples of their mission in order to inspire new generations of employees.

Of course, an ongoing project that is a clear expression of your mission can be a powerful way to ground the mission in a concrete example.; i.e., *"A current project that expresses my/our mission is . . ."**

---

* For contrast, it can also be useful to identify projects, events or situations that characterize examples in which the mission would not be or was not appropriately applied; i.e., *"An example of a project that does not fit my/our mission is . . ."*

In situations in which there is not enough history to have good examples that typify the mission, people can draw upon instances that have similarities from other systems or circumstances. This can be done by either making a comparison or usivng a metaphor; i.e., *"A metaphor for my/our mission is . . ."*

Metaphors in particular have the advantage of being concrete and easy to visualize on one level, yet are also able to capture complex and abstract relationships. They are often the most effective way of representing deeper level issues relating to values and identity. Thinking of the identity and mission of a company in terms of being like a "machine," a "bee-hive" or a "football team," for instance, will each bring a different understanding of the focus of organization and its mission. As an example, we could say, "The mission of Success Factor Modeling is to create the 'mental software' that next generation entrepreneurs need in order to succeed. While this is not literally true, it clarifies certain things about the mission.

Companies will also sometimes use comparisons with other companies as a metaphor for their mission, referring to themselves as being "the 'Apple' of the sports equipment industry," for example. Such a metaphor would give the implication that they had values and a mission similar to Apple; i.e., providing an innovative, diverse product line that is user friendly and aesthetically pleasing.

Visual symbols have a similar effect of being concrete and easy to visualize on one level, yet are also able to capture deeper values and relationships; i.e., *"A visual symbol for my/our mission is . . ."*

The image of a flock of geese or a team of horses, for instance, says a lot about the way a team works and their purpose. A picture of a group of people holding hands and standing around the planet or a light bulb, for instance, conveys things about how and for what a team is working that could be more complicated to try to express in words.

The following worksheet provides an opportunity for you to describe and present your mission for yourself, your team or your venture using several different modes of expression.

You can express your mission with a metaphor. For example "our company is like a well organized bee-hive".

Mission Statement Worksheet

1. A direct statement of your mission:

   My/Our mission is to _____ *for* _____
   (provide which service)   *(which larger system/customer)*

   in order to _____.
                    (achieve what purpose)

2. A past example or reference experience related to this mission.

3. A current project that reflects or expresses the mission.

4. A metaphor for the mission.

5. A visual image or symbol for the mission.

Ambition, Vision and Motivation

As we have been exploring, the most inspiring visions are those which are associated with a sense of purpose or contribution to a vision of something beyond and bigger than ourselves. They stimulate our sense of *mission* and "calling." In order to release energy and initiate action, it is also important that they connect to our ambition and our role. One of the classic examples of this was expressed by President John F. Kennedy at the beginning of the 1960s in the form of the vision of the human exploration of space. To bring energy and action to the vision, Kennedy established the ambition to "put a man on the moon and return him safely to earth by the end of the decade." Kennedy's comments about the selection of this ambition help to reveal the link between vision, motivation, ambition and the center of the Circle of Success.

> But why, some say, the moon? Why choose this as our goal? And they may well ask, "Why climb the highest mountain?" "Why, thirty-five years ago, fly the Atlantic?" . . . We choose to go to the moon in this decade and do the other things, not because they are easy, but because they are hard. Because that goal will serve to organize and measure the best of our energies and skills. Because that challenge is one that we are willing to accept, one we are unwilling to postpone and one we intend to win.

As Kennedy's reflections indicate, ambitions serve to "organize and measure the best of our energies and skills." This implies that, when connected with a bigger vision, an ambition is a type of "attractor" whose purpose is to stimulate the drive for growth and mastery. This, and Kennedy's statement that the challenge created by the goal is "one that we are willing to accept, one we are unwilling to postpone and one we intend to win," also illustrates the intimate connection between goals and ambition.

A "vision" captures an overall sense of direction rather than a particular objective; it is a "stake in the ground in the future" that becomes the focal point for many other activities. Kennedy's vision of the human exploration of space was source of many specific manifestations; lunar landings, space stations, space shuttles, etc. When we connect one of these manifestations to our ambitions it becomes a compelling goal, project or venture.

The Kennedy example also brings out another key aspect of vision. As we have pointed out, a vision transcends the individual who forms and communicates it. Kennedy, for instance, sadly never saw any of the expressions of his vision come to fruition. It is clear, however, that the vision survived beyond him as an entity in and of itself that gave direction, purpose and meaning to the actions of many people. Thus, while ambitions are what you want to achieve for yourself and your mission is completely unique to you as an individual or organization and cannot exist without you, a vision—while it may come from oneself—goes beyond oneself as an individual and stimulates a sense of mission and ambition in many others.

Vision is not enough. It must be combined with venture. It is not enough to stare up the steps, we must step up the stairs.

– Vaclav Havel

John F. Kennedy's goal to "Put a man on the moon and return him safely to earth by the end of the decade" is a classic example of combining vision with ambition.

Setting Your Ambitions

Ambition is a major force in creating the future. Our ambitions arise from our innate desire to do or to achieve something and from what psychologist Gilbert Brim calls our "drive for growth and mastery." Kennedy's statement that the goal of putting a man on the moon was a way to "organize and measure the best of our energies and skills" is a perfect expression of this drive. In general, we are not content with what we already know we can do; we want to find growth-opportunities that "raise the bar" and allow us to explore and expand our competence and mastery. No matter what we have achieved, there is inevitably the question, "What's next?" As Brim points out, young or old, we want to be challenged. We want to shape, form, and build our own lives.

Studies of very young infants (Bower, 1985) in the first weeks and months of life, for instance, provide an interesting insight into the nature of ambition. In a typical experiment, a child is sat in front of an "attractive" toy such as a mobile. The toy moves depending on the child's activity. To stop the mobile the baby has to lower its foot, breaking a light beam and preventing the mobile from turning. To start it again, the child has to lift its foot out of the light beam. Most babies become interested in the stopping and starting of the mobile, analyze the situation quite quickly, and then notice the movement is caused by something they've done with their foot. They play around with both feet, and rapidly realize what to do to make the event – the starting and stopping of the mobile – occur.

In the past, psychologists assumed that the child was most interested in the external object: i.e., the "reinforcement" or reward was thought to be the mobile. But researchers observed that once a baby has figured out what to do, it became bored quite rapidly with the toy, except occasionally to check that it still has the power to influence it. They concluded that it was *figuring out how to control what was going on* that was important to the child. The reinforcement was realizing how to interact with and influence the outside world – i.e., the drive for growth and mastery – rather than desire for the physical object related to the interaction. In other words, the baby is not interested in accumulating mobiles. It is more interested in what interacting with the toy teaches it about its capability to influence its world. We have all no doubt observed the child who becomes more interested in the box his or her gift came in than in the gift itself.

As this research with infants illustrates, learning to master one's environment is inherently self-reinforcing and is one of the foundations for our ambitions throughout life. It is important for next generation entrepreneurs to keep in mind that the objects of our entrepreneurial ambitions (i.e., money, prestige, accomplishment, etc.) are also not necessarily the primary motivations of our ambitions. Rather they serve as a feedback or reflection of our own growth and mastery.

The greatest danger for most of us is not that our aim is too high and we miss it, but that it is too low and we reach it.

– Michelangelo

Achievement is largely the product of steadily raising one's levels of aspiration and expectation.

– Jack Nicklaus

At the opposite end of our life spectrum from infancy, Judith Rodin and other psychologists who study aging find that growth and mastery are also central to older people's sense of well-being. Rodin (1986) cites a relationship between health and a sense of control in elderly people. Her studies showed that there were detrimental effects on the health of older people when their control of their activities was restricted; in contrast, interventions that enhanced options for control by nursing home patients promoted increased health and wellbeing.

Studies relating to job satisfaction give similar evidence that challenge and autonomy make work more satisfying. Even in a work situation that is potentially confining, repetitive, and boring, people frequently create a way to grow. If people are not challenged enough they may set a shorter timetable, raise expectations of how much they can achieve, or expand or add to their goals. They will try to accomplish something earlier or faster, and to get more or better results.

The economist H. F. Clark has reported, for example, that no matter what level of income Americans reach, they want, on the average, about 25 percent more. When they achieve that, they want another 25 percent. People in all social classes, regardless of their income, set goals for about 25 percent more than they have. Other research in economics shows that when people get tax cuts, they put more into savings at first but then gradually increase their spending. People react the same way to wage increases: instead of putting money away in savings, they are inclined to spend it.

Achievement and success thus tend to enlarge rather than satiate our desire and drive for accomplishment, growth and mastery. As visionary inventor Buckminster Fuller said, "Evolution is a result of the innate desire on the part of all living creatures to live beyond their means."

Ambition, then, is a generative force in our lives, pushing us to continually strive for something new or more in order to feel fulfilled. This means creating a gap between our present state and some desired state. According to psychologist Nicholas Hobbs, when we set ambitious goals in our lives, we intuitively seek a level of *just manageable difficulty.* If the level of challenge or difficulty is too little, we can become bored, lazy or edgy. Once we master a particular job or task, it no longer takes most of our effort to do it well and we set our sights higher and push on to more demanding activities.

If the level of challenge or difficulty is too much, on the other hand, we can become overwhelmed, stressed and defeated.

Achievement and success tend to increase our ambitions and our desire for accomplishment, growth and mastery.

Our ambitions create a gap between our present state and our desired state. It is important to callibrate that distance so it is within the range of "just manageable difficulty" so our goal is not perceived as "too easy" nor "overwhelming".

Research with respect to artificial tasks shows that people are most strongly motivated to try to achieve success when they know the probability of success or failure to be about fifty-fifty. The satisfaction of achievement is actually enhanced by the risk of failure. Activities that involve no risk do not provide the same degree of satisfaction. Too much risk, however, creates a deterrent to take action.

Another consideration is the relationship between the effort we put into a project or activity and our actual capacity to do it. This relationship is known as our *performance/capacity ratio*. In situations where we already have a good deal of experience and mastery, things go easily and it requires little effort. In other situations, we are pushed to our limits and forced to draw upon all our reserves in order to either learn a new capability or make up for a deficit in our ability.

Our ambitions in one part of our life can also influence those in other areas. If we are expending a lot of effort in one area of life that stretches us over a long period – i.e., a situation demanding a high performance/capacity ratio – we will probably need to reduce our ambitions in some other area of life during the same time frame. If we are at or beyond our limit in several areas, we can be overcome by stress.

One of the challenges facing entrepreneurs, as they set their personal ambitions and their ambitions for their ventures, is to determine the level of difficulty that is "just manageable." It is the amount of gap between our present state and desired state that determines the level of difficulty. The optimal gap is one that serves to "organize and measure the best of our energies and skills" as Kennedy pointed out.

As an example, Kennedy's ambition of going to the moon within a decade probably would not have sparked the same level of enthusiasm and effort had it been expressed twenty years earlier in 1942. The world and country would not have been ready. The performance/capacity ratio would have been too great. The Second World War was taking a lot of resources in terms of money, energy and focus. Technology was not yet evolved enough for such a project to be within reach of achieving.

This is where a certain level of intuition and artistry comes into setting ambition for oneself and one's venture. Both vision and ambition involve being able to tap into a larger "field" and perceive weak signals that give indications about what is coming and what is within reach of the present state. It is another area where the creative unconscious plays a significant role.

Ambition, Passion, Belief and the Identity Matrix

In setting our ambitions for ourselves and our project or venture, *our beliefs about ourselves and our capacities* – especially those defined by the Identity Matrix – also exert a great deal of influence. Our beliefs about who we are, could be, cannot be, want to be, etc., determine much about the model of the world that we create and act from.

Beliefs and belief systems have been a major area of my life work. I have always maintained that the main purpose of belief is not to validate what we already know about the past or present, but rather to create the future. We set our future targets and estimate the level of effort we take to achieve them as a consequence of our beliefs about (1) what is possible, (2) what we and those we work with are capable of, and (3) what we feel we deserve.

Our ambitions will also be influenced by (a) how intelligent, how strong, how healthy, how creative, how attractive, etc., we believe we are and (b) what degree of these qualities we believe we need to have or achieve in order to achieve fulfillment, acknowledgment or acceptance.

Of course, ambition, like vision and mission are also expression of our passion. The most powerful ambitions emerge when we connect our beliefs with our passion.

Cindana Turkatte, for example had the belief "I can do anything" and a passion to create tools that helped people "achieve something they did not know was possible." These clearly spurred her ambition to take on ever greater challenges, overcome limitations and stretch her level of growth and mastery.

Mark Fizpatrick had the passion to continually improve himself and "to refine things a little bit better." He also talked about his belief that "if you feel that something has a chance to be successful, you've got to jump on it." The two together formed the foundation of his ambition to push his potential, take a major risk and create his own software company.

Barney Pell's belief that he "had a major role to play in the world," combined with has passion for learning and artificial intelligence, lead to his ambition to create a "game changing" search engine.

As I pointed out in Chapter 1, however, our ambitions can also be fueled by the need to compensate for our perceived weaknesses, defects and shadows. We can build ambitions as an attempt to hide or make up for perceived deficits and limitations. As mentioned earlier, these attempts at compensation are frequently a consequence of having created an "idealized self" – i.e., who we believe we should be or have to be in order to be acknowledged, loved or accepted. An idealized self always casts a "shadow" in the form of behaviors and characteristics that are excluded.

Our ambitions for our ventures are strongly influenced by our beliefs about what is possible, the capabilities of ourselves and our team members and what we deserve.

Inflated ambitions can become a problem when we overcompensate for perceived lacks and deficits. Such perceptions are frequently created by limiting beliefs.

According to Carl Gustav Jung, it is important to embrace both the "light" and the "shadow" sides of our personality.

Sometimes we try too hard and overcompensate for perceived lacks and deficits. This frequently occurs because the form of compensation we are attempting is not adequately addressing the underlying cause and, as a result, we are left constantly striving but never fulfilled. In other cases, we create limiting beliefs that hold us back in an attempt to avoid pressure or disappointment.

The psychologist Carl Jung claimed that one of the functions of our unconscious was to compensate for the biases and prejudices of our conscious ego (our idealized self). For example, if one is fasting or on a diet in order to lose weight, one might dream of having a feast or eating a whole box of chocolates. Similarly, shadows such as "doubt" and "helplessness" may emerge as unconscious responses if we are determined that we must always feel "confident" and "in control." The lifelong fight with depression of comedian Robin Williams that I mentioned in the previous chapter is another example of this.

Psychologist Deborah Phillips talks about the *illusion of incompetence* in which people underestimate their actual abilities. Her studies of 3rd, 5th and 9th grade students showed that approximately 20 percent had beliefs about themselves that were significant underestimates of their actual competence in various subjects and tasks.

Of course, limiting beliefs imposed by our society, culture or family systems can suppress our ambitions. As the quote from Marianne Williamson at the beginning of Chapter 3 points out: "We ask ourselves, 'Who am I to be brilliant, gorgeous, talented, fabulous?'" The implication is that we don't feel that we have the inner or external permission to be ourselves and express our uniqueness or greatness.

At the same time, we are inundated by messages—both overt and covert—on television, magazines and other media urging us to continually want and expect something more; particularly in the form of material goods and performance levels linked to money, power and prestige. Of course, increased performance expectations can simultaneously bring a greater sense of inadequacy. This can lead to the need for even more compensation in the form of more material wealth, possessions or socially recognized accomplishments. This can create a vicious cycle of materialism that we observe in some individuals, industries and societies.

An inflated sense of confidence may emerge in the attempt to balance the belief that we are inadequate or incapable. One study indicated, for example, that 95 percent of American men estimate that they are in the top 50 percent in social skills. Other surveys report that people feel on average about nine years younger than they really are, and that they believe they look about five years younger than they actually are.

Ambition as a form of denial or reality escaping fantasy in order to protect our egos prevents us from being realistic. Instead, it creates a "mirage" that sets us up for inner struggle or failure. On the other hand, ambition as an expression of optimism and empowering beliefs can set up healthy aspirations that align with our drive for growth and mastery. They support us in finding the proper degree of "just manageable difficulty."

From the COACH state, reflect on your own vision, mission and venture and your ambition and "drive for growth and mastery." Write down your answers to the questions below. As with your vision and mission, keep your answers succinct, limiting yourself to less than 10 words.

What is your ambition for your venture or project?

1. *What type of status and level of achievement do you want your venture or project to reach (e.g., first, best, fastest, biggest, etc.)?*

   I/We want to be or become _____

2. *How do you want your venture or project to be viewed by potential investors, stakeholders, advisors and competitors?*

   I/We want to be seen or known as _____

3. *How big do you want your venture to be?*

   I/We want to grow to be _____

4. *What past personal accomplishments you would like to surpass and in what way?*

   I/We want to achieve greater _____

5. *What is the specific time frame in which you are committed to reach your ambition?*

   I/We plan to accomplish my/our ambitions within _____

   _____

Ambition as an expression of optimism and empowering beliefs sets up healthy aspirations that align with our drive for growth and mastery and support us to find the proper degree of "just manageable difficulty."

Healthy and realistic ambitions are aligned with our vision and mission and support us to achieve satisfaction and success in a way that contributes to the success and happiness of others.

Perhaps the key to ensuring that we have a healthy and realistic ambition is to be sure that it is *aligned with our vision and mission.* Ambition and success are not just the result of selfish individualism. The price of one person's success and happiness is not someone else's failure and unhappiness. Next generation entrepreneurs have a vision of a world in which individuals achieve happiness and success by cooperating with others to increase the happiness and success of all, rather than by winning at others' expense and lessening their opportunities for success and happiness. Their vision is creating a world to which people want to belong.

As you reflect upon what you have defined as your ambitions above, be sure to consider in what ways your ambition aligns with and supports your vision and mission.

Role Models, Competitors and Advisors

Because our self-beliefs are subject to the distortions of compensation and enthusiasm, we often also set or clarify our ambitions by comparing ourselves to those we consider role models and equals. It is significant and telling, for example, that Kennedy claimed that the goal of putting a man on the moon was "one we intend to win." The clear implication is that part of the ambition was to get there before the Russians did. This is where competition plays a significant role in our ambitions.

Standards are always in comparison to something. Many of our ambitions come from observing, interacting with and comparing ourselves to others, both role models and competitors. We tend to observe the actions and accomplishments of those we think are most like us. From these observations we set and concretize our levels of aspiration. In this sense, role models operate as a type of metaphor as we discussed in the previous section on making a mission statement. When an entrepreneur says, "I want to be the 'Disney' of my industry," it creates a more concrete picture of their values and aspirations for their venture.

Our role models and competitors provide a type of "benchmark" for our ambitions. This is why potential investors and stakeholders want entrepreneurs to identify potential competitors. As Cindana Turkatte pointed out, identifying competitors keeps entrepreneurs from being too "internally focused" and unrealistic, and helps to provide validation and create "traction" or credibility. In some ways, to say that you have "no competition" is like saying you have no real ambition or an unrealistic ambition.

Some people are made uneasy by talking about "winning" or about "ambition" as if they were taboo words meaning something selfish, egotistic, arrogant or aggressive. But this presupposes a "zero sum" attitude. In healthy competition, the goal is to match or outperform another in order to demonstrate competence, "raise the bar" or, in fact, "make the pie bigger." This is different from simply attempting to make the other person "lose" in order to feel triumphant. When an individual with an entrepreneurial attitude sees a person with a big house on a hill, they think to themselves, "Someday, I am going to have a house on a hill like that person," as opposed to "Someday, I am going to drag that person down off the hill."

Competitors can also sometimes become partners if they can find complementary capabilities and create win-win arrangements. A good example of this (as we shall revisit later in this chapter) is the partnership that Apple made with Microsoft in 1997 to adapt Microsoft Office for the Macintosh; a move that brought the struggling Apple back from the brink of bankruptcy.

Role models and competitors provide a type of "benchmark" that allow us to more clearly define and and gauge our ambitions.

"I want to be the Disney of my industry!"

Competitors can become partners if we can identify complementary capabilities and create win-win arrangements.

Advisors are individuals who have expertise or experience in some area that is essential to the success of your venture and can validate and mentor you with regard to your ambitions.

Sometimes our most important competitor or role model is ourselves. We try to do something faster than before or to get more or better results than we have previously. We set our ambitions with respect to our past "personal best" in order to stretch ourselves.

As Cindana Turkatte pointed out, "traction" or credibility with respect to investors and stakeholders "is about validation. It is not just your opinion." She claimed that it is important to make sure you have "somebody or a group of people who are respected who have validated that concept." This has to do with identifying mentors and sponsors who can make up a board of advisors. Gathering a good advisory board is key to the success of any new venture. An *advisory board* is a group of individuals who usually have expertise or experience in some area that is essential to the success of the venture. It is invaluable to have the advice of people from different backgrounds who can validate and mentor you with regard to your ambitions. It is also a good test of the attractiveness of your ambition.

A start up's board of advisors is frequently one of the first group of "stakeholders" for a new venture. This is usually because, rather than payment, entrepreneurs offer a small "stake" in their company in return for the advisors' contributions. In a traditional company, this stake takes the form of a small amount of stock, which can become quite valuable if the venture becomes a big success. Since advisors are generally not paid directly for their services, the ambition for success of the entrepreneur becomes quite important. If advisors help the company to succeed, then they benefit from its success.

The benefit to advisors (and other stakeholders), of course, is not always stock. It could be visibility for themselves or an enhancement of their reputation as a result of being involved with a new venture. The benefit could also be in the form of some type of exchange.

Identifying Potential Stakeholders

In addition to an advisory board, you will want to identify other potential stakeholders (who will also be as interested in your ambition as they are in your vision and mission). As we have already established, potential stakeholders are individuals or groups that could affect decisions or who provide key resources or skills that can significantly affect your success in achieving your ambition for your project or venture. They are also those who will benefit primarily as a result of your creating a successful venture through your ambition, as well as your vision and mission.

From the COACH state, reflect on the questions below to begin to identify some of your potential stakeholders:

- What are the essential resources that you will need in order for you to accomplish your ambition?

- Who are (or could be) interested in, or who do you need, to *provide funding, advice or other key resources* in order for you to succeed?

- Who has a "stake" (i.e., *could be effected positively or negatively*) by your achieving your ambition?

- Who has an investment in your success?

- How will reaching your ambition create value for your stakeholders? What types of benefits will your success provide for your stakeholders?

- Who do or will you compare yourself with as a role model for your ambition?

- Who are your competitors – i.e., others who have similar ambitions to you?

Summarize your reflections below.

1. Who are your sponsors and mentors (potential advisory board members) who have validated or can validate that your ambition for your venture is achievable?

_____

_____

Stakeholders are individuals or groups that support you and/or provide key resources or skills that significantly impact your success in achieving your ambition. They are also those who will benefit most if you reach your ambition.

2. *Who are your potential investors or stakeholders that could affect decisions or provide key resources or skills which can significantly affect your success in achieving your ambition for your project or venture?*

_____

_____

3. *Who are your Role Models?*

_____

_____

4. *Who are your Competitors?*

_____

_____

Ambition

Stakeholders / Investors

Raising Investment / Acquiring Essential Resources

Growing the Business and Creating Value

Assessing Motivation Worksheet

Our ambitions and motivations are one of our primary sources of energy and direction for creating the future. They are also what attract investors and other stakeholders to support us. A key success factor in attaining your project or venture is understanding your motivations for your endeavor and looking for others who share them and/or can support you.

The purpose of the following worksheet is to help you clarify your motivations for taking on your project or venture and explore how much they align with one another. It will also help you to reflect upon how much they overlap or conflict with those of other key individuals or groups that could significantly influence your success.

Write down the vision, mission and ambition that you have clarified in this chapter. Begin by rating the statements in the far left-hand column of the table on a scale of 0 - 5, where 5 is "extremely important" and 0 is "not important at all." Put your answers in the column marked "Self." It is important to be honest with yourself about your answers and really look at all your motivations for your project or venture.

Notice which motivations tend to be more "ego" oriented and which are more "soul" oriented. Are they balanced? If there is an imbalance, are there areas of overcompensation or inappropriate compensation that you need to look at or bring more into awareness?

Put yourself in the shoes of your role models, (potential) competitors, sponsors and mentors, and especially potential investors and stakeholders. As best as you can, imagine how you would rate the same motivations on a scale of 0 – 5 from their perspective and about their own actions and ventures? What is important to them and how much? List you answers in the appropriate column. If you don't know, you can just put a question mark ("?").

Look for resonances between your motivations and those of others:

1. Which motivations do you share with your role models? Which are different?

2. How about your (potential) competitors? Where are you alike and where do you differ in terms of your motivations?

3. Consider your sponsors and mentors (potential advisory board members). Where are there overlaps? Where are there potential mismatches?

4. Most importantly reflect on potential investors and other "stakeholders" that have key resources or skills which can significantly effect the results in your project or venture. What are their motivations? What motivations do you share with them? Where do you "resonate" with potential stakeholders? Which of your motivations will they be most interested in?

Vision: _____

Mission: _____

Ambition: _____

MOTIVATION	Self	Role Models	Competitors	Sponsors/ Mentors	Stakeholders/ Investors
Make a name for myself					
Prove myself to myself/ my family/ doubters					
Get acknowledgement from my family/ peers					
Please a significant other					
Contribute something to my community/profession/the world					
Change the world for the better					
Serve my community/ country/ planet					
Make enough money to support myself/ my family					
Make a lot of money					
Make money quickly					
Increase my financial security for the long-term					
Grow personally					
Enhance my mastery					
Overcome my fears and limitations					
Share my vision with others					
Learn something new					
Develop new capabilities and skills					
Create something that has never existed before					
Apply my knowledge and skills					

MOTIVATION	Self	Role Models	Competitors	Sponsors/ Mentors	Stakeholders/ Investors
Work together with others to create something / achieve goals					
Achieve something noteworthy					
Support others to learn and grow					
Be known as a successful person/ venture					
Become what I was meant to be in the world					
Live up to my potential					
Solve an important problem					
Do what I was put on this world to do					
Follow the footsteps of another					
Increase my sense of power/ control					
Bring greater balance into my life					
Do what I can to eliminate suffering (disease, violence, poverty)					
Connect with others					
Discover more about myself/ people/ the world					
Enjoy myself					
Have fun with others					
Accomplish something others consider impossible					
Other:					

As you reflect on this exercise, which of the motivations do you think will be the most important to emphasize when you speak with or present to potential investors or stakeholders? What about prospective advisory board members?

Your motivations are also going to be of interest to possible partners. Partners, however, will also need to know how the various roles your projects or ventures play will fit together in a complementary way.

Establishing the Role of Your Project or Venture

Having a clear understanding of the role of your venture, and how it supports the bigger vision and mission, helps you to identify establish win-win partnerships and alliances that leverage and augment resources.

A clear sense of role allows entrepreneurs to establish win-win partnerships that expand and leverage key resources. As with an individual, the *role* of a venture reflects its core competencies and actions. It is related to both *the position a venture occupies with respect to other ventures*, and the expected *capabilities and behaviors* attached to that position. People, teams and ventures are most successful in roles that are compatible with their missions, ambitions and competencies, and that support the achievement of their vision. Samuel Palmisano, for example, redefined the role of IBM to be more aligned with its core vision and mission and that made the best use of its core competences.

The primary questions related to establishing the role of your project or venture are:

What type of venture or team are you, or do you need to be in order to reach your ambition regarding the status and level of performance you want to achieve?

What core competences do you have that best allow you to achieve your vision, mission and ambition? What role best represents and applies those core competences?

Start by clarifying who you are, or want to be, as a venture with respect to achieving your vision. From the COACH state, consider the questions:

What kind of entity are you or are you becoming?

In relation to my/our vision, I am/we are _____

What type of things do you do in that role or position?

I/we provide _____

How do you do it? By what means do you provide those things?

I/we _____

Be as clear as possible about the things you do and the special competences you have. If you are too vague, it is difficult for potential partners to assess the benefits of an alliance. It is also difficult for prospective customers, stakeholder and team members to get a clear sense of what your venture is all about, where you are going and what you stand for. Remember that it is not possible to be "all things to all people."

In considering your answers, it is not necessary to limit yourself to the traditional roles of the "village" (i.e., butcher, baker, candlestick maker). The role of the project or venture may be innovator; custom solution provider; school; merchant; platform; association; network; producer; distributor; transformer; connector; liberator; etc. Walt Disney called his organization a "fantasy factory."

It can also be fruitful to think about what other company or entity could you compare yourself to in terms of role.

You might also want to try using a metaphor or symbol to answer this question if you experience difficulty answering it literally. In Chapter 1 we used the metaphor of super heroes and superpowers. What type of super hero would your venture be and what is the superpower that your venture has or would like to develop?

If that approach does not resonate with you, what other metaphor could you use (e.g., pioneer, lighthouse, orchard, oasis, etc.)?

The winter sports equipment company that I have mentioned several times, decided to define themselves as "The Mountain" sports company. In this case, mountains were, on the one hand, a literal environment for many winter sports. The metaphor of "the mountain," on the other hand, also symbolized purity, majesty and challenge, as well peacefulness and diversity of ecosystems, etc.

To consider and evaluate possible alliances, prospective partners need to have a clear idea of your core competences, where you are going and what you stand for.

It can be useful to think about your role in metaphorical as well as literal terms.

Identifying Potential Partners

Clarifying the role of the project or venture helps to attract and create partnerships and alliances with other entrepreneurs and ventures. Partners could be other people or ventures who have different roles that support or complement yours. Finding such partners involves creating win-win relationships for the purpose of leveraging and expanding resources. A good example of this that we presented earlier is Ed Hogan, founder of Pleasant Hawaiian Holidays, whose small travel company could not compete with larger airlines. By partnering with hotels to create a "vacation package," however, he was able reduce the overall cost to prospective customers and bring a significant benefit to those who had a dream of visiting "paradise."

As another example, Barney Pell was also able to use his venture's *role* as a provider of natural language capabilities to establish key partnerships and alliances to leverage resources such as public relations, scalable data infrastructure and cloud computing.

Thus, another important question to consider is "What fit does your project or venture have with respect to others?" Given the role and core competencies of your project or venture, what complementary roles and competences would be important or necessary for you to succeed in achieving your vision, mission and ambition? What other roles could your activities and competences provide a benefit to?

Again, it can be helpful to explore this metaphorically as well. If your metaphor for your role is an "oasis," for example, you could benefit from partnerships with "tent makers," "entertainers," "hydro-engineers," etc. You could provide benefits as a partner to "caravan leaders," "camel drivers," "military groups," etc.

Returning to the COACH state, take some time and reflect on the following questions:

- Who are (or could be) your *partners*? With whom could you make potential win-win *alliances*?

- What resources and competences that you have could be expanded or leveraged by partnering with someone else?

- Who could help to increase the value or benefits of your projects, products or services by linking them with their own?

- Who has resources and competences that would complement your own in a way that would greatly expand both of your potentials?

Partners are people or ventures who have roles, missions and ambitions that support or complement those of your venture is such a way that you are each able to leverage and expand key resources.

Make a list of the potential partners or alliances that you have identified.

Potential Partners/Alliances:

_____   _____

_____   _____

_____   _____

_____   _____

_____   _____

_____   _____

_____   _____

Exploring Win-Win Relationships

A next step is to identify potential win-win ways in which you and your potential partners could leverage resources. While there are many ways to do this, three of the main possibilities include:

1. Sharing Essential Resources and Costs (in order to reduce expenses, for instance)

2. Combining Capabilities (as Ed Hogan did with flight and hotel packages)

3. Exchanging Services or Products (such as trading one partner's service for the other partner's product, for example)

Sharing essential resources and costs works best with partners who have parallel projects or ventures in a start-up stage. What are known as start-up "incubators" are an example of this type of leverage. *Incubators* are made up of a group of entrepreneurs who join together and collectively share:

- Pro-active support, access to critical tools, information and contacts which may otherwise be inaccessible or unaffordable

- Resources such as lobby/reception, meeting rooms, copy and fax equipment, audio visual equipment, clerical services, and kitchen

- Private offices, cubicles, lab or manufacturing spaces

- Access to business and technical advice and introductions to a range of qualified service providers, potential mentors and financial resources

- An organized program of training, one-on-one counseling, or mentoring

Combining capabilities is a very effective strategy for creating alliances with partners who have projects or ventures that complement your role and capabilities. Such an alliance can leverage both partner's capabilities in a way that makes them more attractive to customers and potential stakeholders. A management consulting firm may partner with a financial firm to provide a greater range of service to customers, for instance. A photocopying company can partner with a delivery service to make a more efficient experience for customers. Barney Pell's partnership with Amazon, combining natural language search with online retail, is another example of combining capabilities. Similarly hardware and software companies frequently make effective win-win partnerships by combining their products together into a "bundled" package or solution.

There are three fundamental ways to create win-win alliances:

(1) sharing essential resources and costs

(2) combining capabilities

(3) exchanging services or products

Exchanging services or products, while not as powerful a leverage as combining capabilities, is always an option with potential partners, even if your projects or ventures do not have the potential for much if any synergy. A training institute could offer free training to a technology company in exchange for the use of that company's equipment; a law firm could exchange services with an accounting firm; a car dealer could exchange free automobile rental with an event planner in return for his or her services, etc.

Exploring these options can open the door to many possible win-win relationships that may not be obvious at first. As an example, at a recent Success Factor Modeling program I was conducting, a group of entrepreneurs were exploring potential partnerships. They had quite different projects and ventures and would probably not have normally thought about considering partnerships with one another.

Exploring win-win relationships can lead to surprising synergies that may not be obvious at first.

- One person's venture was about offering stress reduction for entrepreneurs.

- Another had an idea for a venture that would incorporate Chinese traditions (such as tea ceremonies) as an innovative way of teaching certain key communication and relationship skills to managers.

- A third person was in the process of building an Internet marketing company.

- Yet another was starting a coaching practice aimed at helping clients to "declutter" their lives by reflecting on which of their activities, possessions, expenses, relationships, etc., were truly essential and which ones were adding pressure or draining time and energy given the client's current life goals and circumstances.

- A fifth participant was setting up a business that sold electric cars.

At first glance, these widely different projects and ventures do not appear to have much obvious partnering potential.

Stress reduction for entrepreneurs
Using Chinese traditions as a way of teaching interpersonal skills
Internet marketing
Life decluttering coaching practice
Selling electric cars

Encouraged to explore possible ways they could share resources, combine products, services or capabilities, or exchange resources they began to find numerous potential win-win relationships. Since they were all in a start up phase and needed to be efficient and attentive to costs, they realized they could share certain types of office equipment and business services.

It was pointed out that combining *stress reduction* and *life decluttering support* made a potentially advantageous package for some customers. Either or both of those services could also be combined with *using Chinese traditions as a way of teaching interpersonal skills* to create a richer offering to certain potential customers and clients. The three entrepreneurs discussed putting on a several day retreat for entrepreneurs and managers in which participants would benefit from all three approaches.

It also became clear that all of the ventures could benefit from Internet marketing and could potentially offer their own service (or product in the case of the electric car business) in exchange for Internet marketing support.

Of course, any of the ventures could exchange their services with the founder of the electric car business (who could need stress reduction, more interpersonal skills, Internet marketing or decluttering support) in return for the use of an electric car or a discount on the purchase or lease of a vehicle.

The Internet marketing firm could easily come across certain of its own customers in need of the other services or an electric car. The founder of the Internet marketing firm could pass those referrals along to the other entrepreneurs in exchange for possible contacts and leads for people interested in Internet marketing services that the other entrepreneurs come across.

These are only some of the many possibilities that began to emerge as a result of the exploration of potential win-win relationships. Some valuable long-term partnerships were established as a result of this exploration that would have never happened had the five entrepreneurs not taken the time to intentionally explore partnering options.

Developing a win-win mindset and establishing the habit of constantly looking for mutually beneficial relationships is one of the most powerful things you can do increase your "luck factor" and guarantee the success of your venture. It emerges out of a fundamental attitude in which all parties are constantly asking:

"This my future, can you contribute?"

"What is your vision so I can contribute?"

Developing a win-win mindset and establishing the habit of constantly looking for mutually beneficial relationships is one of the most important ways to ensure the success of your venture.

Keeping in mind the various options and examples described above, explore potential partnerships for your own project or venture using the following form:

Potential partner: _____

Type of potential partnership (sharing, combining, exchanging):

_____

Benefit of partnership to you: _____

Benefit of partnership to them: _____

For each partner on the list that you created in the previous section, ask yourself the questions:

What resources or costs could we share? (e.g., office equipment, tools, meeting rooms, business services, etc.)

Is it possible to combine our products, services or capabilities in a way that would add value and make them more beneficial or attractive to customers or potential stakeholders?

Do we each have services, products, information or capabilities that the other partner could use or benefit from that could be exchanged?

As the earlier example of the five entrepreneurs illustrates, it can also be very powerful to actually sit down with potential partners and explore these questions together.

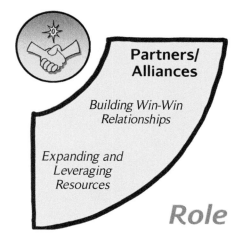

Partners/ Alliances

Building Win-Win Relationships

Expanding and Leveraging Resources

Role

Developing a win-win mindset involves constantly exploring the two questions:

"This my future, can you contribute?"

"What is your vision so I can contribute?"

HOW TO CREATE WIN-WIN ALLIANCES?

1) SHARING ESSENTIAL RESOURCES AND COSTS

A TRAVEL AGENT AND A SHOW BUSINESS COMPANY CAN SHARE OFFICE SPACE, INTERNET CONNECTION, PRINTING AND INTERNET COSTS, EVEN THE COFFEE MACHINE!

2) COMBINING CAPABILITIES

A PHOTOGRAPHER CAN TEAM UP WITH A MAKE UP ARTIST TO OFFER OUTSTANDING PROFESSIONAL PORTRAITS.

3) EXCHANGING SERVICES OR PRODUCTS

OUR FRIENDS PRODUCING APPLE JUICE CAN EXCHANGE SUPPLY OF THEIR PRODUCT IN EXCHANGE OF USING A SOLAR ENERGY VAN TO DELIVER THEIR PRODUCT AND PROMOTE THIS TYPE OF VEHICULES.

Vision and Ambition Worksheet for New Ventures and Projects

To integrate what we have covered so far in this chapter, summarize the explorations you have made regarding the vision, mission, ambition and role regarding your project or venture and relate them to the Circle of Success. Start by using the following worksheet to make an overview of what you have clarified so far.

Soul	EGO
Vision What do you want to create for your customers through your venture or project? What services, benefits and contributions will your venture or project make to customers, society, the environment, etc.? What do you want to make possible for them?	**Ambition** What type of status and level of achievement do you want your venture or project to reach (e.g., first, best, fastest, etc.)? How do you want your venture or project to be viewed by potential investors, stakeholders and competitors?
Mission What is your contribution and service (as a team) with respect to the vision for your customers? What are the special resources, capabilities and actions that you will develop, apply and mobilize (as a team) to reach the vision for your customers?	**Role** What type of team or venture do you need to be in order to reach the status and level of performance you want to achieve?

As you reflect upon the questions above consider them from the point of view of both a literal and a symbolic or metaphoric answer. (For example, "Our ambition is to be like a pyramid that stands for centuries.")

Review your answers. Which ones are clear for you? Are there questions you find difficult to answer at this point?

How well does your vision for your project or venture align with your ambition for the venture or project? How about the mission of your team and the role your venture or project plays in the bigger system?

Look back over your answers to these questions for you as a person that you expressed at the end of Chapter 1. How aligned are your personal vision and the vision of your venture or project? How aligned is your ambition with the ambition of your venture or project? How about the missions? Roles?

Clarifying your vision and potential customers, your mission and potential team members, your ambition and potential stakeholders, and your role and potential partners allows you to establish a rich and aligned Circle of Success.

Enriching Your Circle of Success

Now, review the Circle of Success that you started at the end of Chapter 2 and reflect upon who you have identified as your potential customers, team members, stakeholders and partners. Rewrite your answers to the previous worksheet in the template on the following page and reflect upon how the two sets of distinctions interrelate. The result should be a powerful and generative foundation for building your project or venture.

Enriching Your Circle of Success

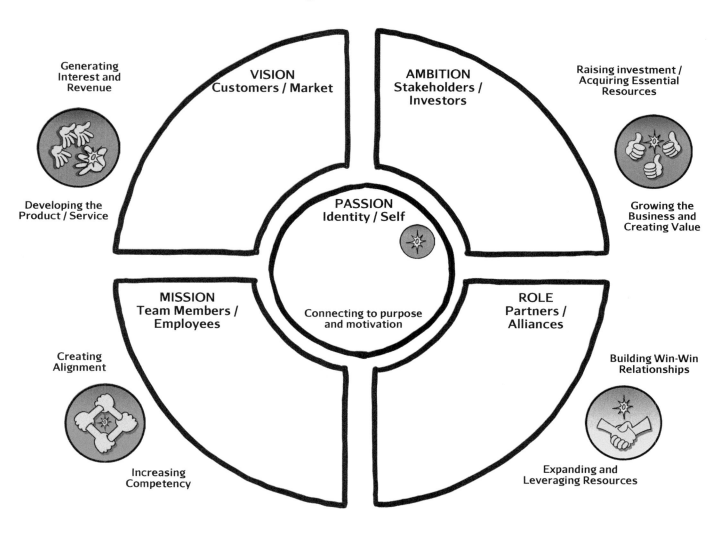

Generating Interest and Revenue

VISION
Customers / Market

AMBITION
Stakeholders / Investors

Raising investment / Acquiring Essential Resources

Developing the Product / Service

PASSION
Identity / Self

Growing the Business and Creating Value

MISSION
Team Members / Employees

Connecting to purpose and motivation

ROLE
Partners / Alliances

Creating Alignment

Building Win-Win Relationships

Increasing Competency

Expanding and Leveraging Resources

Examples of Defining a Generative Circle of Success

The following are a couple examples of answers to these questions that I and my partners have put together to form Circles of Success for several ventures that I have been involved in starting up. Each has reached a sustainable level of international recognition and success.

Example: Dilts Strategy Group

Dilts Strategy Group is a consulting, coaching and training company, with a global network of consultants in more than twenty-five countries. Founded by myself and my brother John Dilts, the purpose of the Dilts Strategy Group (DSG) is to bring together proven business criteria with strategic knowledge and behavioral skills, through the Success Factor Modeling™ process, in order to support the growth and development of individuals and their organizations on many levels. DSG's services include: modeling, training, consulting, coaching and hosting seminars and conferences in the application of the Success Factor Modeling™ process.

Vision:
A world in which people are fulfilling their aspirations and giving the best of themselves to produce a positive systemic impact through their ventures – More and more organizations, businesses and projects that promote the growth and mastery of the those involved and create a more healthy, harmonious and thriving planet and society.

Mission:
To discover and share the "differences that make a difference" in creating and growing successful ventures – Identifying and transmitting the key success factors necessary to build a sustainable and successful business, team or project.

Ambition:
To be a globally recognized pioneer and a leader in holistic business strategy – A respected source of methods, models and tools that strongly and positively influence the way teams, businesses and organizations around the world are managed and led.

Role:
An international group of consultants and coaches with experience in NLP and enterprise who collaborate to provide effective business strategies and the accompanying support – A network of entrepreneurial, forward thinking people who work together to assist teams, businesses, organizations and each other to significantly improve their performance in the areas of entrepreneurship, leadership, innovation, collective intelligence and communication.

http://www.journeytogenius.com/DSG/index.html

Example: Dilts Strategy Group SFM Circle of Success

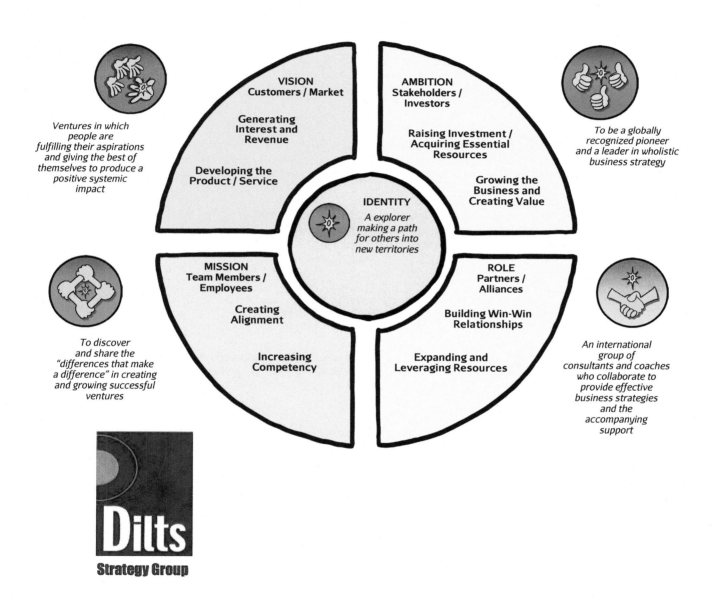

Ventures in which people are fulfilling their aspirations and giving the best of themselves to produce a positive systemic impact

VISION
Customers / Market

Generating Interest and Revenue

Developing the Product / Service

AMBITION
Stakeholders / Investors

Raising Investment / Acquiring Essential Resources

Growing the Business and Creating Value

To be a globally recognized pioneer and a leader in wholistic business strategy

IDENTITY
A explorer making a path for others into new territories

To discover and share the "differences that make a difference" in creating and growing successful ventures

MISSION
Team Members / Employees

Creating Alignment

Increasing Competency

ROLE
Partners / Alliances

Building Win-Win Relationships

Expanding and Leveraging Resources

An international group of consultants and coaches who collaborate to provide effective business strategies and the accompanying support

Dilts
Strategy Group

Example: NLP University

I established NLP University with Todd Epstein in 1991 as a new type of structure for providing the opportunity for a complete NLP education. Judith DeLozier joined us in 1992 and helped to shape the current NLPU curriculum. Together with NLPU coordinator Teresa Epstein and a group of highly competent and committed guest faculty, we strive to provide the highest quality presentation of fundamental NLP skills and the newest developments. NLP University is one of the best-known and respected international NLP training organizations hosting participants from more than 30 countries each session. NLP University offers a summer Residential curriculum for certification trainings in NLP. The home of NLP University is on the University of California Campus located in Santa Cruz, California—the birthplace of NLP.

Vision:
A world in which people have the models, skills and motivation to bring their unique and individual richness in service of the larger systems of which they are a part (family, community, profession, country, environment, etc.) – A world of empowered, innovative and wise individuals acting harmoniously and ecologically in support of their own growth and the sustainable growth of the planet.

Mission:
To develop and support high quality practitioners and trainers to spread the skills and tools of NLP – Create a context and infrastructure through which professionals of different professions, disciplines, fields and nationalities can learn, share and apply fundamental and advanced tools and applications of NLP relevant to their personal vision and professional vocation with a high level of integrity, skill and compassion

Ambition:
To be a primary reference point and global leader in spreading the best that NLP can bring into the world – Internationally recognized as a credible, creative and trustable source and role model with respect to the field of NLP.

Role:
A specialized school providing a comprehensive NLP education through training, community and technology – A unique educational institution supplying structures through which the necessary tools and strategies along with the required guidance and support can be brought to the people who are committed to manifesting the global potential of NLP; specifically in the form of conducting NLP Practitioner, Master Practitioner and Trainer certification programs.

http://www.nlpu.com

Hopefully, these examples will provide you with more clarity about these key dimensions for building a successful venture. Our Success Factor Case Example for this chapter is none other than Apple Inc. co-founder Steve Jobs. As you read through the account of his remarkable accomplishments, notice how they demonstrate many of the principles we have established so far in this book.

Example: NLP University SFM Circle of Success

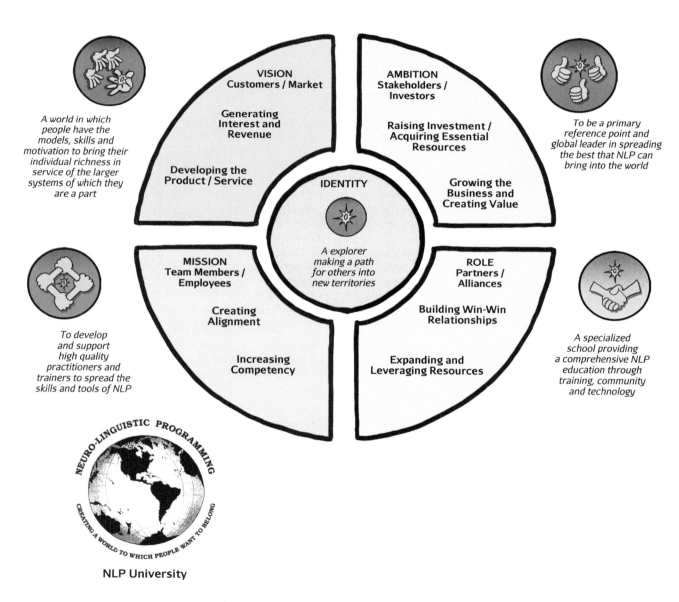

A world in which people have the models, skills and motivation to bring their individual richness in service of the larger systems of which they are a part

To be a primary reference point and global leader in spreading the best that NLP can bring into the world

VISION
Customers / Market

Generating Interest and Revenue

Developing the Product / Service

AMBITION
Stakeholders / Investors

Raising Investment / Acquiring Essential Resources

Growing the Business and Creating Value

IDENTITY

A explorer making a path for others into new territories

To develop and support high quality practitioners and trainers to spread the skills and tools of NLP

MISSION
Team Members / Employees

Creating Alignment

Increasing Competency

ROLE
Partners / Alliances

Building Win-Win Relationships

Expanding and Leveraging Resources

A specialized school providing a comprehensive NLP education through training, community and technology

NEURO-LINGUISTIC PROGRAMMING

CREATING A WORLD TO WHICH PEOPLE WANT TO BELONG

NLP University

Success Factor Case Example
Apple's Steve Jobs

Steve Jobs
Founder and former CEO of Apple

"Insanely great." Ambition in the service of Vision and Mission.

Perhaps no one in recent years has epitomized the ability to create the future more than Steve Jobs. Steve Jobs founded Apple Computer with Steve Wozniak in a garage in "Silicon Valley" in the San Francisco Bay Area, California in 1976. When the company went public in 1980, it generated more capital than any stock market launch since the Ford Motor Company in 1956, and created 300 new millionaires overnight. By the time of Jobs' death in October 2011, Apple had become the largest technology firm in the world with revenue for the year of $127.8 billion in sales. In March 2012 its stock market value had reached $500 billion. By any measure, Apple is one of the greatest success stories of the last century (at one point in the summer of 2011 Apple had more cash reserves than the United States government!), and it owes a great deal of that success to the leadership of the brilliant and enigmatic Steve Jobs.

Jobs, who was also founder of NeXT Computers and instrumental in turning Pixar into a computer animation giant, was in many ways the personification of the Silicon Valley entrepreneur. He stands out as one of the most successful people in modern history. More than 300 US patents are registered under his name; from computers to smartphones to electronic accessories and gadgets. He had a major hand in transforming seven industries: personal computers, animated movies, music, phones, tablet computing, digital publishing, and retail stores. There is no question that Stephen Paul Jobs left a significant mark on the modern world.

Having grown up in the San Francisco Bay area in San Mateo, very near to where Steve Jobs was raised in Cupertino, I have been aware of him, his story and his accomplishments for a long time. Steve Jobs was, in fact, a contemporary of mine. He was born in February 1955. I was born less than a month later in March of that same year.

It has always seemed a fascinating synchronicity to me that Apple's philosophy and products emerged in the same time frame and the same geographical area as NLP – the methodology that is at the foundation of Success Factor Modeling. As has been true in other periods in history, developments in our understanding of the human psyche mirror developments in technology (and vice versa). In many ways, NLP and Apple grew up side by side. Apple was bringing computing and technology out of the laboratory and institutionalized settings at the same time NLP was doing the same thing with psychology and personal development.

Steve Jobs had an exceptional ability to create the future. One of the most successful people in modern history, he was in many ways the personification of a new generation of Silicon Valley entrepreneurs.

NLP founders Bandler and Grinder contended that the most powerful "personal computer" was the one "between your ears," but that it comes without a user's manual. The purpose of NLP (and Success Factor Modeling) has been to help provide that manual.

Changing the World for the Better Through Technology

Steve Jobs' saw the personal computer as a way to extend and enhance the capabilities of the human brain and nervous system, similar to the way a bicycle enhances the efficiency of the human body. As he said in a 1990 interview:

> *I read a study that measured the efficiency of locomotion for various species on the planet. The condor used the least energy to move a kilometer. And, humans came in with a rather unimpressive showing, about a third of the way down the list. It was not too proud a showing for the crown of creation. So, that didn't look so good. But, then somebody at Scientific American had the insight to test the efficiency of locomotion for a man on a bicycle. And a human on a bicycle blew the condor away, completely off the top of the charts.*
> *And that's what a computer is to me. It's the most remarkable tool that we've ever come up with, and it's the equivalent of a bicycle for our minds.*

Jobs had a vision of "insanely great" technology products that would change the world for the better.

Prior to Steve Jobs and Apple, technology and computing had essentially been viewed as a tool of the "establishment," more likely to be considered as means for controlling and manipulating people and their minds than for empowering them and encouraging unique expression.

In contrast, Steve Jobs had what was then a radical vision: "Changing the world for the better through technology," with easy to use and "insanely great" products. This vision is dramatically embodied in the famous television commercial introducing the Macintosh. Directed by Ridley Scott, the ad aired during the third quarter of Super Bowl XVIII in January 1984. In the commercial, a woman, representing the coming of the Apple Macintosh, saves humanity from the technology driven prison created by "Big Brother" (an icon of control and conformity). The imagery is a clear reference to George Orwell's novel, *Nineteen Eighty-Four*, which described a bleak future society ruled by the ubiquitous, televised Big Brother. It is also a reference to IBM, known as "Big Blue," who was at the time Apple's major competitor in the personal computer market.

In the ad, the woman, dressed in colorful aerobic attire, runs through hoards of drab, gray men as she is chased by heavily armed and armored police.

Scene From Apple's "1984" Commercial

People being awakened from a life of monotony in Apple's "1984" Commercial

The heroine ultimately hurls a large hammer through the immense television screen carrying the image and the blaring, monotonous voice of the Machiavellian dictator. The screen explodes, bringing new color and energy into the lives of the people previously dominated by the despotic ruler.

This scene is a powerful metaphor for Job's passionate personality, provocative nature, innovative vision and his aspiration to be an "awakener." As he said in his legendary pitch to John Sculley, the successful Pepsi-Cola CEO Jobs brought in to run Apple in the 1980s: "Do you want to sell sugared water for the rest of your life? Or do you want to come with me and change the world?"

My Journey with Apple

NLP co-founders Bandler and Grinder (who were also passionate, provocative and innovative) were interested in the process and potential of programming as well, and were both quite attracted to the notion of a personal computer. To them, it was the perfect metaphor for the human brain. They were some of the first purchasers of Apple's products. In those early days, if you bought five or more Apple computers from the company, you were automatically a "dealer" and got a dealer discount. I got my first Apple II computer from them in the late 1970s (complete with a whole 8 kilobytes of memory). Since getting my first Apple II, I have always felt a close personal connection with the company, its products and Job's vision to positively influence the world.

Over the years, I have had a unique opportunity to be a close observer of Apple and Steve Jobs through times of both success and struggle. Through the past three decades, I have had a number of different connections with the company. In fact, Apple was my first corporate client in 1980, when I was brought in at the age of 25 to do a program on effective communication for managers.

A couple of years later, I designed and wrote a number of educational programs based on early applications of Success Factor Modeling to learning basic skills like spelling, math and typing. From 1982-1985 Apple sold my programs *Spelling Strategy, Math Strategy* and *Typing Strategy* for the Apple II computer as part of the Apple Special Delivery Software program. The program was terminated around the time Jobs was forced to leave the company.

From 1989 to 1990, I was deeply involved in a joint venture project between Apple and Lucasfilms to create interactive multimedia training products for managers. The project sought to combine high entertainment and production quality with innovative technology and practical and concrete skills, incorporating drama and storytelling with multimedia and explicit step-by-step learning formats. The final product, however, never materialized due to the unclear and changing vision of Apple at that time.

In the early 1990's I spearheaded a joint venture between Apple University and ISVOR Fiat, the internal business school for the Fiat Group. I was intensely involved in a major project on leadership and management development at Fiat as well as with Human Resource Development at Apple. Again, the project ended up fizzling out because of the lack of vision and direction at Apple without Jobs.

After Jobs' return in 1996, the next project I was involved in with Apple focused on identifying the success factors associated with the development of the iMac, which emerged from an unprecedented cross-fertilization between hardware engineers and software designers.

Most recently, I examined the success factors relating to the development of the iPod as an iconic example of "breakthrough innovation" in an article I published together with Benoit Sarazin.

These different interactions over the years have given me a unique perspective on Steve Jobs and his leadership style. Even when he was out of the company, for instance, Jobs' presence lived on in stories and anecdotes that the people who worked there told over and over.

As another interesting connection, my older brother Michael worked as a manager for Apple for more than 8 years, during the time that Steve Jobs was out of the company and when he came back. According him, there is no question that the company was only months or weeks from failing and that the return of Jobs saved it from going bankrupt.

Much has been written about Steve Jobs both before and since his death, and it is obvious that his success and the success of Apple was not based on him having a charming and likable personality. Jobs was frequently perceived as aggressive and demanding. *Fortune* magazine wrote that he was "considered one of Silicon Valley's leading egomaniacs." A former colleague of Jobs once said that he "would have made an excellent king of France."

So what were the key factors of his success?

Even when he was out of the company, Jobs' presence lived on at Apple in stories and anecdotes that the people who worked there told over and over.

A Transformational Leader

From the perspective of Success Factor Modeling, Steve Jobs is a perfect example of finding a role in which a powerful ambition is put in the service of mission and vision. At his best, Steve Jobs was an example of a *transformational leader*. He was passionate and enthusiastic about what he did, created visions and injected energy and motivation into the people he worked with. Driven, uncompromising and motivational, Jobs inspired his co-workers and organizations to ever greater heights of creativity, driven by his own remarkable vision of how things might be.

Steve Job's life, work and leadership style epitomize three of the key characteristics at the center of the SFM Circle of Success:

- Passion – The Desire to Achieve something great
- Vision – A Deep Sense of Direction
- Courage – Believing in the Vision, Yourself and the Team

It is clear that Jobs lived his passion. He claimed:

We don't get a chance to do that many things, and every one should be really excellent. Because this is our life. And we've all chosen to do this with our lives. So it better be damn good. It better be worth it.

In Jobs' case it couldn't even just be "damn good." It has to be *"insanely great."* As he advised people starting out in their careers:

You've got to find what you love... The only way to be truly satisfied is to do what you believe is great work. And the only way to do great work is to love what you do. If you haven't found it yet, keep looking. Don't settle. As with all matters of the heart, you'll know when you find it. And, like any great relationship, it just gets better and better as the years roll on. So keep looking until you find it.

Steve Jobs lived his passion to create innovative technology products that would make a positive difference in the world.

Discovering your "calling" and living from the passion it generates is one of the major success factors that we have found in successful entrepreneurs. Of course, the next step is that the passion has to be directed outward as a vision that is pursued with courage and determination; especially if it is something that takes you into new territory. Truly new ideas tend to meet resistance or disdain because they do not fit the current paradigms or business strategies.

Before setting up shop in their garage, for example, Jobs and Wozniak tried to get other companies interested in supporting them and their innovative "personal computer", but were met with resistance and skepticism. As Jobs described it:

> We went to Atari and said, "Hey, we've got this amazing thing, even built with some of your parts, and what do you think about funding us? Or we'll give it to you. We just want to do it. Pay our salary, we'll come work for you." And they said, "No." So then we went to Hewlett-Packard, and they said, "Hey, we don't need you. You haven't got through college yet."

In addition to passion and vision, succeeding takes a lot of trust and belief in yourself and what you are doing. In one of Steve Jobs most profound and revealing statements he claimed:

> Your time is limited, so don't waste it living someone else's life. Don't be trapped by dogma – which is living with the results of other people's thinking. Don't let the noise of other's opinions drown out your own inner voice. And most important, have the courage to follow your heart and intuition. They somehow already know what you truly want to become. Everything else is secondary . . .

Choosing to live his passion led Steve Jobs on an extrordinary life journey beyond the borders and confines of the "village."

This statement is clearly a message about self-empowerment and living congruently from the center of your Circle of Success. Jobs' advice to "have the courage to follow your heart and intuition" is an acknowledgment of the role of what we have called the "creative unconscious." He does not say to follow the rational mind nor the rules of the "village." It is clearly an encouragement to travel your own "journey" and discover your unique contribution to making the world a better place.

In a 1995 interview, Jobs explained it the following way:

> *When you grow up, you tend to get told that the world is the way it is and your life is just to live your life inside the world. Try not to bash into the walls too much. Try to have a nice family life. Have fun. Save a little money. But that's a very limited life.*
>
> *Life can be much broader once you discover one simple fact. And that is, everything around that you call life was made up by people who were no smarter than you. And you can change it. You can influence it. You can build your own things that other people can use.*
>
> *And the minute that you understand that you can poke life . . . and that if you push in, something will pop out the other side; that you can change it, you can mold it.*
>
> *That's maybe the most important thing. To shake off this erroneous notion that life is there and you're just going to live in it versus embrace it; change it; improve it; make your mark upon it.*
>
> *And however you learn that, once you learn it, you'll want to change it and want to make it better, because life is messed up in a lot of ways. Once you learn that, you'll never be the same again.*

Steve Jobs had a strong sense of being a "holon" – both a whole in and of himself and part of something bigger. He understood that there was an intimate interaction between himself and the larger system, and that he could "embrace it," "change it," "improve it," and make his mark upon it.

Jobs is implying that the journey of "living your own life" leads you to realize that you can "make a positive difference in the world." It is important to keep in mind that living your own life and following your heart and intuition does not mean to ignore everyone else and become a loner. On the contrary, it makes you an even more active participant, which connects you even more strongly and makes you more sensitive to the larger "field" in which you are living.

In fact, a major part of Jobs' success was his ability to position his businesses and their products at the forefront of the technology industry by foreseeing and setting trends with respect to that larger field and connecting them to his vision. As he explained it:

> There's an old Wayne Gretzky quote that I love: "I skate to where the puck is going to be, not where it has been." And we've always tried to do that at Apple. Since the very very beginning. And we always will.

In this regard, it is fascinating to note that Jobs' beloved iPad was the manifestation of a vision that he had from the earliest days of Apple. In 1983, Steve Jobs gave a speech in which he said:

> What we want to do is we want to put an incredibly great computer in a book that you can carry around with you and learn how to use in 20 minutes . . . And we really want to do it with a radio link in it so you don't have to hook up to anything and you're in communication with all of these larger databases and other computers.

Like Wayne Gretsky, Steve Jobs strove to "skate where the puck is going to be, not where it has been". He saw future possibilities before they became obvious.

The iPad was without a doubt Steve Jobs' crowning achievement. He introduced the tablet at a stage when no one else was even imagining doing it and succeeding. When it was launched in 2010 more than 3 million iPads were sold in first 80 days. Apple sold more than 28 million iPads in the following two years. In the initial nine months after the launch, more than 135,000 iPad apps were made by developers which generated more than $1 billion in revenue.

Yet, when asked how much money he spent on market research to develop the iPad, Jobs famously replied, "None. It's not the consumers' job to know what they want." He didn't need to do market research, he claimed, because he already knew it would succeed. Jobs' ability to have his "finger on the pulse" of the "weak signals" in his marketplace and link those signals to his vision was one of Jobs' most critical success factors. It is that combination that let him know "where the puck was going to be."

As an illustration, Jobs revealed that he began developing the iPad in 2004, but realized that it wasn't the right time to launch it as processor speed, screen resolutions and wireless networks of that time were not good enough to make it successful. Instead of hurrying up the launch, Jobs waited until all of the ingredients of the product were ready to give the level of performance necessary to be successful. He temporarily put the effort on hold, realizing that the ideas would work just as well in a mobile smartphone. He viewed the iPhone as a miniature version of the iPad that could be enlarged when the pieces were all in place.

By 2009, he had made almost all the preparations for launching the tablet; everything was in place from screens, processors and the all-important mobile networks. After the success of iPhone, Jobs was convinced that people would love the tablet he had been designing. And the rest is history

In addition to his own vision and ability to recognize the readiness of both technical capacity and people's interests, Jobs was able to convey and inspire his desire to stay ahead of the curve in others. This was another major factor in his success. In fact, people who worked with Jobs coined the term "reality distortion field" to describe Jobs' charisma and its effects on those working on projects with him. It has also been used to describe Jobs' sway over the public, particularly regarding new product announcements. The term refers to Jobs' ability to convince himself and others to believe almost anything, using "a mix of charm, charisma, bravado, hyperbole, marketing, appeasement, and persistence." Although sometimes the subject of criticism, Jobs' so-called reality distortion field had the effect of creating a sense that the impossible was possible. As he pointed out:

> It's like when I walk into a room and I want to talk about a product that hasn't been invented yet. I can see the product as if it's sitting there right in the center of the table. It's like what I've got to do is materialize it and bring it to life—harvest it.

Steve Jobs' capacity for vision and his ability to recognize the readiness of both technological development and people's interests allowed him to inspire and awaken others to believe that the impossible was possible.

This ability to bring visions to life, and get others as excited about them as he was, was one of Steve Jobs' most important leadership abilities. According to Jobs:

> Innovation has nothing to do with how many R&D dollars you have. When Apple came up with the Mac, IBM was spending at least 100 times more on R&D.* It's not about money. It's about the people you have, how you're led, and how much you get it.

The "it" that Jobs is referring to, of course, is not just the understanding of a goal or objective. It is the bigger vision of something exciting that will change the world. This is where ambition and vision connect with mission. Jobs even introduced the notion of "evangelism" into the company to describe the type of fervor he expected people to have for the products they were developing at Apple.

---

*As my father-in-law, who was a senior technology manager at IBM during this period, points out however, "Most IBM R&D was not aimed at the PC market. Cost also depends on the type of R&D you are doing. The fundamental technologies – Bell Labs and the transistor, Intel and the integrated circuit, Xerox and electrophotography, and IBM and the hard disk – required big bucks to get the innovation to market. Jobs statement would seem most applicable to design innovation [as opposed to fundamental innovation]."

Thus, while it is no secret that Steve Jobs could be notoriously difficult to work with, he was also equally inspiring. Jobs made *Fortune's* list of America's Toughest Bosses in regard to his leadership of NeXT. NeXT Cofounder Dan'l Lewin was quoted in Fortune as saying of that period, "The highs were unbelievable . . . But the lows were unimaginable." According to his biographer Walter Isaacson:

> *Everyone was eager to talk about Steve. They all had stories to tell, and they loved to tell them. Even those who told me about his rough manner put it in the context of how inspiring he could be . . . He could be petulant and rough, but this was driven by his passion and pursuit of perfection. He liked people to stand up to him, and he said that brutal honesty was required to be part of his team. And the teams he built became extremely loyal and inspired.*

If you ask people who worked with him, "How was it working with Steve Jobs?" they would probably answer that it was "very challenging," at least at times. If you ask, "Would you do it again?" a majority would say, "Absolutely." This was frequently because they felt like they grew or improved as a result of working with him. In the words of one Apple employee:

> *I was incredibly grateful for the apparently harsh treatment Steve had dished out the first time. He forced me to work harder, and in the end I did a much better job than I would have otherwise. I believe it is one of the most important aspects of Steve Jobs' impact on Apple: he had little or no patience for anything but excellence from himself or others.*

One of the most common statements I have heard from people who worked closely with Jobs is that "It is difficult to find someone who actually liked Steve Jobs, but everyone respected him." According to Jobs:

> *My job is to not be easy on people. My job is to make them better.*
> *My job is to pull things together from different parts of the company and clear the ways and get the resources for the key projects. And to take these great people we have and to push them and make them even better, coming up with more aggressive visions of how it could be.*

Even though Steve Jobs could be notoriously challenging to work with, people on his team typically felt that they grew or improved as a result of their interactions with him.

Steve Jobs felt that a key part of his role as a leader was to push people and "make them even better, coming up with more aggressive visions of how it could be."

Jobs also earned people's respect because it was clear that his primary focus was not on himself and his own benefit, but on the achievement of the vision and the success of the company. Jobs' salary as CEO of Apple, for example, was only $1 per year! In the age of outrageously high salaries for CEOs, Jobs' pay was clearly symbolic that he planned to only benefit if Apple succeeded. Jobs described the importance of this commitment to the larger vision and mission in the following way:

> When I hire somebody really senior, competence is the ante. They have to be really smart. But the real issue for me is, Are they going to fall in love with Apple? Because if they fall in love with Apple, everything else will take care of itself. They'll want to do what's best for Apple, not just what's best for them, what's best for Steve, or anybody else.

Jobs clearly understood that when people "fall in love" with the company – when their role and ambition is in the service of the vision and mission – then everything else falls into place. That is, the other levels of success factors (values, capabilities, behaviors, etc.) align to support the vision and mission. This was the essence of Jobs' leadership approach. And it is a powerful principle of leadership and entrepreneurship.

I frequently ask the top managers at the businesses I consult for if their company is something the people who work there can "fall in love with." This is a very revealing question and is frequently a major "difference that makes a difference" in the success of an organization. While it is true that people can be "in love" with their job, with money, their own personal advancement or even the leader, these can lead to conflicts with what is in the best interest of the larger system.

Jobs didn't want this sense of mission only from his senior people but from all the people who worked for Apple. He claimed, "I ask everybody that: 'Why are you here?'" It was not an uncommon experience at Apple to suddenly find yourself in the elevator next to Steve Jobs who would proceed to ask you your opinion on all types of things.

People could experience this as intimidating, especially given his impetuous nature and prickly personality. It was even more challenging given that he was the "boss." But Jobs did not have much respect for hierarchies, as the 1984 commercial clearly symbolizes. Rather, he felt the activity in the organization should be organized around a shared vision, mission and what was best for the company. Somebody who may have only been working at the company in a low level position for a couple of weeks might suddenly get an email from Jobs asking for their input about something. As Jobs put it, "Apple should be the kind of place where anybody can walk in and share his or her ideas with the CEO."

Steve Jobs' ambition supported his bigger vision and expressed itself in the form of a total commitment to his company's success.

Jobs' intensity and his disregard for traditional protocol could make people uncomfortable. Many people have pointed out that Jobs was a demanding perfectionist who liked to be in control. My former father-in-law was a carpet salesman in the Silicon Valley during the early days of Apple. He tells a revealing story about going to Apple to sell carpet. To his surprise, Steve Jobs came into the presentation. According to my father-in law, Jobs asked ten times more questions any other customer he had before or since that time. Jobs wanted to know the details of how the carpets were manufactured, what they were made of, why they were better than other options. Jobs inquired about the company, its suppliers and why he should choose them instead of someone else. While my father-in-law was impressed, he eventually found himself starting to wonder, "Don't you have a company to run?"

Clearly, Jobs was both intensely curious and exacting down to every detail. In his words, "We have an environment where excellence is really expected . . . My best contribution is not settling for anything but really good stuff, in all the details. That's my job – to make sure everything is great."

In his best-selling biography of Steve Jobs, Walter Isaacson includes a quote from Jobs that provides a revealing insight into his decision-making process. In the quote, Jobs is explaining how his family decided to choose a particular washing machine for their home. Though one would think it is a seemingly trivial purchase, Jobs' explanation of how the decision was made illustrates his well-known attention to detail.

> It turns out that the Americans make washers and dryers all wrong. The Europeans make them much better – but they take twice as long to do clothes! It turns out they wash them with about a quarter as much water and clothes end up with a less detergent on them. Most important, they don't trash your clothes. They use a lot less soap, a lot less water, but they come out much cleaner, much softer and they last a lot longer.
>
> We spent some time in our family talking about what's the trade-off we want to make. We ended up talking a lot about design, but also a lot about the values of our family. Did we care more about getting our wash done in an hour versus an hour and a half? Or did we care most about clothes feeling really soft and lasting longer? Did we care about using a quarter of the water? We spent about two weeks talking about this every night at the dinner table.

Steve Jobs expected everyone who worked at Apple to "fall in love" with the company and its products.

Like Barney Pell, Steve Jobs strove to create a culture of excellence. As he put it, "My best contribution is not settling for anything but really good stuff, in all the details. That's my job – to make sure everything is great."

When making decisions, Steve Jobs viewed details as expressions of key values and were not to be overlooked.

Steve Jobs also saw creativity as a necessary part of a culture of excellence. He established a working environment that encouraged cooperation, teamwork and open conversation between all levels of team members.

As we shall see, Jobs' focus on *design* and the *values* of the family are key themes in his pattern of success. But this attention to detail and emphasis on excellence is only part of the story. He also encouraged creativity, fostered collective intelligence and actively facilitated a leadership culture.

Jobs experimented with changes in organizational structure at Apple and when he started NeXT he abandoned conventional corporate structures altogether. Instead, the company was organized as a "community" with "members" rather than employees. There were only two different salaries at NeXT until the early 1990s; and which one people received depended upon when they joined the company as opposed to their position in the organization.

The success of Pixar is also considered to be a direct result of Jobs' attitudes and behaviors, including his inspiring of employees and his confidence in them. Jobs established an environment without strict management practices or a rigid hierarchy. He built a social workplace that encouraged cooperation, teamwork and open conversation between all levels of employees. The quality and aspirations of employees he hired ensured a high level of creativity and imagination of all individuals working at the company. Pixar personnel are known for having a deeper commitment to their work and creations than their desire for money.

These are all hallmarks of Steve Jobs' transformational leadership approach. As he said in the earlier quotation, "It's about the people you have, how you're led, and how much you get it." Jobs explained it the following way:

If [people] are working in an environment where excellence is expected, then they will do excellent work without anything but self-motivation. I'm talking about an environment in which excellence is noticed and respected and is in the culture. If you have that, you don't have to tell people to do excellent work. They understand it from their surroundings.

Jobs reference to "an environment in which excellence is noticed and respected and is in the culture" is a clear description of what we have referred to earlier as a "field." As Jobs mentions, the motivation and standards become a part of the environment and are "understood from the surroundings" rather than coming from the reinforcement of individual behaviors or stated rules. This type of field is crucial to the long-term success and sustainability of any venture, and it is critical that the core values and expression of this field be fully embodied by the leader of the venture. Just like the pilot in the earlier example of the Miracle on the Hudson, the responses and actions of the leader are the touchstone for others within the system.

Steve Jobs' unwavering commitment to the achievement of the larger vision and his constant focus on innovation and excellence were key success factors to his repeated success as a leader and to the success of his ventures. According to John Lasseter, chief creative officer at Pixar and Walt Disney Animation Studios, and Edwin Catmull, current president of Walt Disney Animation Studios and Pixar Animation Studios:

> Steve was an extraordinary visionary, our very dear friend, and our guiding light of the Pixar family. He saw the potential of what Pixar could be before the rest of us, and beyond what anyone ever imagined. Steve took a chance on us and believed in our crazy dream of making computer animated films; the one thing he always said was to "make it great." He is why Pixar turned out the way we did and his strength, integrity, and love of life has made us all better people. He will forever be part of Pixar's DNA.

According to Steve Jobs, an environment and culture of excellence created a type of field in which people would "do excellent work" without needing anything more than their own "self-motivation" to incentivize them.

To infinity and beyond! Steve Jobs was congruent with a vision that was going beyond designing computers, as he proved when he helped Pixar to take off as a 3D Animation studio.

An Orchestrator of Innovation

My current father-in-law, who was a senior technology manager for IBM in the 1980s, refers to Steve Jobs as an *orchestrator of evolution*. He saw Jobs major strength as having been "a selector, evolver and integrator of good ideas" rather than a developer of fundamental technologies. Jobs' embracing of this role of "orchestrator of innovation" in support of the vision, mission and ambition of his ventures was clearly a major key to his success. Consider the following comment by Jobs:

> So when a good idea comes . . . part of my job is to move it around, just see what different people think, get people talking about it, argue with people about it, get ideas moving among that group of 100 people, get different people together to explore different aspects of it quietly, and, you know – just explore things.

In some ways, this statement captures one of Jobs' most significant success factors: his ability to promote collective intelligence and generative collaboration within his team.

It is notable that Jobs said, "when a good idea comes." The clear implication is that the idea does not necessarily come *from* him, but rather *through* him. It is as if he were the channel for a field of possibilities. This is a quality I have found in every great entrepreneur and leader. No matter how egoistic and arrogant they are in other parts of their life, they are humble with respect to their vision, because it does not come from their ego. In the same way that when Martin Luther King said "I have a dream" he was not talking about a personal dream from himself, for himself, the vision of an entrepreneur like Steve Jobs is not from himself and for himself.

The most important thing, according to Jobs, is to "move the idea around," "see what different people think" and "get people talking about it." These activities promote the three crucial processes of collective intelligence: resonance, synergy and emergence (see *Success Factor Modeling Volume 2* for more on this).

The common commitment to a bigger vision creates a culture that can even hold a space for argument without getting caught in it or divided by it. That is what made it possible for Jobs to "argue with people" without it becoming a petty "ego trip" and regressing into conflict and struggle. As anthropologist Gregory Bateson said, "Wisdom comes from sitting together and truthfully confronting your differences, without the need to change them." When you can do that, something beyond any particular person's point of view emerges. This is clearly a key success factor in the capacity to "orchestrate evolution." As Jobs described it:

Steve Jobs was an "orchestrator of innovation," promoting collective intelligence and geneative collaboration among his team members.

Wisdom comes from sitting together and truthfully confronting your differences, without the need to change them.
– **Gregory Bateson**

My model for business is The Beatles: They were four guys that kept each other's negative tendencies in check; they balanced each other. And the total was greater than the sum of the parts. Great things in business are not done by one person, they are done by a team of people.

Interestingly, one of the benefits of Jobs' seeming lack of relational sensitivity may have been to avoid one of the potential negative consequences of strongly cohesive groups known as "group think." *Group think* is a mode of thinking that people in groups and teams engage in when "the members' striving for unanimity overrides their motivation to appraise realistically the alternative courses of action." The phenomenon of "group think," for example, has been considered responsible for a number of American policy "disasters" such as the failure to anticipate the Japanese attack on Pearl Harbor in 1941 and the Bay of Pigs Invasion fiasco in 1961. Jobs explained:

> *[Our culture] definitely rewards independent thought, and we often have constructive disagreements—at all levels. It doesn't take a new person long to see that people feel fine about openly disagreeing with me. That doesn't mean I can't disagree with them, but it does mean that the best ideas win. Our attitude is that we want the best. Don't get hung up on who owns the idea. Pick the best one, and let's go.*

Steve Jobs was not just interested in his own ideas; he wanted the "best" ideas. His approach to working with his team encouraged independent thinking and the acknowledgement of multiple perspectives. This served to bring out and filter for the highest quality and most innovative ideas.

Thus, in addition to brainstorming, Jobs' focus on vision and his strategy for harnessing collective intelligence and generative collaboration also helped him to keep his finger on the pulse of his customers evolving needs and motivations. The ability to collect and hold multiple, potentially conflicting perspectives helps to find the places of resonance as well as to appreciate differences. These places of resonance reveal common needs and motivations. As Jobs explained:

> *It's not about pop culture, and it's not about fooling people, and it's not about convincing people that they want something they don't.*
> *We figure out what we want. And I think we're pretty good at having the right discipline to think through whether a lot of other people are going to want it too.*

The "discipline" of mining and integrating multiple perspectives not only allowed Jobs and his team to more clearly identify conscious "felt" needs and desires, it also could point to more unconscious "latent" needs and desires that were in the "field" but not yet in people's awareness. Jobs claimed, "A lot of times, people don't know what they want until you show it to them."

Jobs' ability to foster collective intelligence and orchestrate evolution also brought him to embrace and practice "open innovation." The central idea behind *open innovation* is that in order to accelerate innovation and leverage resources, companies need to create win-win partnerships and alliances with other organizations and entities. Much of the fundamental technology for the graphical interface of the Macintosh computer, for instance, was developed at the Xerox Palo Alto Research Center (PARC). The computer mouse was pioneered by Douglas Engelbart and the Stanford Research Institute (SRI). I can vividly remember being given a demonstration at PARC in 1982 of the mouse being used on a computer with windows and pull-down menus while I was involved in a modeling project at Xerox. A short time later they fatefully gave a similar demo to Steve Jobs. Jobs' genius was to see the potential for these innovations in a personal computer and integrate them into an easy to use and aesthetically pleasing package.

Twelve years after the introduction of the Macintosh, in 1996, when Jobs re-emerged as CEO of Apple (after NeXT Computer was bought by Apple), the company was struggling and near bankruptcy. In 1985 Jobs had been removed from managerial duties at Apple as result of a power struggle with John Sculley, whom Jobs himself had recruited as Apple's CEO. As a consequence, Jobs resigned from the company that he had created. Eleven years later, Jobs returned to a company that was on the verge of failure. One of Jobs' first actions was to arrange a strategic partnership with the software giant Microsoft, with whom Apple, under Sculley, had been engaged in a drawn-out and costly legal battle over patent rights. In 1997, at the Boston Macworld Expo, Jobs took the stage to deliver one of his famous keynote speeches. He stunned his audience—for whom the world had become defined by the struggle between the "underdog" Apple and the increasingly "all-powerful" Microsoft Corporation—with the following announcement.

Steve Jobs also embraced the practice of "open innovation" which involves creating win-win partnerships with other entrepreneurs and ventures in order to accellerate innovation and leverage resources.

> *Apple lives in an eco-system and it needs help from other partners; it needs to help other partners. And relationships that are destructive don't help anybody in this industry as it is today. So during the last several weeks we have looked at some of the relationships, and one has stood out as a relationship that hasn't been going so well, but that has the potential, I think, to be great for both companies. And I'd like to announce one of our first partnerships today, a very very meaningful one. And that is one with Microsoft. . .*

> *We have to let go of this notion that for Apple to win, Microsoft has to lose . . . the era of setting this up as a competition between Apple and Microsoft is over as far as I'm concerned. This is about getting Apple healthy and . . . about Apple being able to make incredibly great contributions to the computer industry, to be healthy and prosper again.*

The deal set up a number of arrangements for the cross-licensing of patents. It guaranteed that Microsoft would continue to release Microsoft Office products for the Mac platform. Apple began to make Microsoft's Internet Explorer the default browser on all new Mac products. Microsoft also bought $150m of non-voting Apple shares at market prices with the agreement not to sell them for three years. This meant Microsoft was now also a stakeholder in addition to being a partner and had a vested interest in seeing Apple's share price increase, rather than collapse. When news of the deal reached the market, Apple's stock rose by 35%!

This example shows the power of partnerships and why they are such a key part of the Circle of Success. And, again, it was Jobs' commitment to the bigger vision and mission of Apple that was at the basis of the move. His claim that "This is about getting Apple healthy and . . . about Apple being able to make incredibly great contributions to the computer industry, to be healthy and prosper again," is a clear statement of the link between putting ambition into the service of the greater identity and mission of the company.

Steve Jobs encouraged "open innovation" and saved Apple from bankrupcy by creating partnership with Microsoft, who most people at the time considered to be Apple's mortal enemy.

Jobs' practice of the process of open innovation is also particularly well illustrated by the development of the iPod, a product that changed both Apple and the entire music business. Before its introduction, MP3 players were the realm of small companies with limited funds who were unable to provide content. After the iPod, the entire industry evolved and grew to the point where the largest computer companies in the world have major interests in the digital music industry.

When the iPod was designed, Apple lacked the internal resources necessary to make an attractive music device. Instead of trying to develop a whole new set of capabilities, Apple licensed the software platform from a 3rd party, PortalPlayer. Similarly, it acquired software from the outside to build iTunes and hired music software experts and hardware engineers from outside the company, integrating them with a team of Apple veterans. Apple contracted another company, Pixo, to help design and implement the user interface under the direct supervision of Steve Jobs.

The iPod is a clear example of how Steve Jobs applied open innovation and stimulated generative collaboration in order to create the future.

Jobs grew up in the period where rock and roll music was changing the world. He claimed that music was "good for the soul" and that he listened to music as a creativity catalyst to stimulate his own process of imagination and dreaming. He also saw the common love of music as a way to connect to a whole new generation of technology users.

Because of his passion with respect to the power of music, Steve Jobs took a very active role in the iPod project, scheduling frequent meetings with the designers. During these meetings he would tell them in detail what issues he had with the device, whether it was the interface, sound quality, or the size of the scroll wheel.

For Jobs, the iPod epitomized the vision and mission of Apple. He saw it as something that "really changed the world" by helping to "bring music back into people's lives in a really meaningful way." As he put it:

> *If there was ever a product that catalyzed what's Apple's reason for being, it's (the iPod). Because it combines Apple's incredible technology base with Apple's legendary ease of use with Apple's awesome design... it's like, this is what we do. So if anybody was ever wondering why is Apple on the earth, I would hold this up as a good example.*

Jobs' reference to "Apple's incredible technology base," "Apple's legendary ease of use" and "Apple's awesome design" is a clear and concise answer to the questions, "What is your unique contribution and service with respect to the vision for your customers? What are the special resources, capabilities and actions that you will develop and apply to reach your vision for your customers?" One of the great strengths of Apple as an organization is the clear sense of mission instilled by Steve Jobs as a leader.

The Importance of Aesthetic Intelligence

Job's well-known attention to detail, characterized by his role in the development of the iPod, points to another one of his major success factors that can best be labeled *aesthetic intelligence*. Apple products have long been known as much for their sleek and innovative design as they have for their functionality and ease of use. This is a direct expression of Jobs' values and respects the positive side of his meticulous rigor regarding the style and features of Apple products. As he explained it:

> In most people's vocabularies, design means veneer. It's interior decorating. It's the fabric of the curtains or the sofa. But to me, nothing could be further from the meaning of design. Design is the fundamental soul of a human-made creation that ends up expressing itself in successive outer layers of the product or service.

Similar to Leonardo da Vinci who strove for "harmony and proportion" in his inventions as well as his paintings and other works, Steve Jobs perceived that "design is the fundamental soul of a human-made creation."

Design is defined as "deciding upon the look and functioning of" some product. Functioning has to do with the pragmatic use of a product. Its "look" has to do with its aesthetic appeal. The most lasting and impactful contributions in any field are those where esthetics and artistry (elegance, harmony and beauty) are in integrated with pragmatics and utility (technical accomplishment and practical applications). This applies to everything from shoes and clothing to buildings to automobiles and even scientific theories.

A major factor in Steve Jobs' impact and success was his emphasis on aesthetic intelligence. He claimed, "Design is the fundamental soul of a human-made creation that ends up expressing itself in successive outer layers of the product or service."

The most lasting and impactful contributions in any field are those where esthetics and artistry are integrated with pragmatics and utility.

Aesthetic intelligence, then, is about bringing "harmony, balance and beauty" into what one is doing or creating. It can be defined as the "conscious use of skill and creative imagination to produce works of beauty." As anthropologist Gregory Bateson defined it, "the reasons of the heart" become "integrated with the reasons of the reason."

According to da Vinci, harmony and proportion were a result of the relationship between the parts of a system and their "intent" with respect to the whole system. Jobs understood and valued this perspective deeply. No part, no detail, was irrelevant. He explained:

> When you're a carpenter making a beautiful chest of drawers, you're not going to use a piece of plywood on the back, even though it faces the wall and nobody will ever see it. You'll know it's there, so you're going to use a beautiful piece of wood on the back. For you to sleep well at night, the aesthetic, the quality, has to be carried all the way through.

It was this level of aesthetic and quality "carried all the way through" that made something "insanely great."

Jobs applied the same values of passion, utility and aesthetics to his own life. These are what made it "worth it." As he put it:

> Being the richest man in the cemetery doesn't matter to me ... Going to bed at night saying we've done something wonderful... that's what matters to me.

Steve Jobs applied the same values of passion, utility and aesthetics that he fervently stressed in his ventures to his own life.

"WE'VE DONE SOMETHING WONDERFUL TODAY"

Summary of Steve Job's Success Factors

I said at the beginning of this case study that Steve Jobs was enigmatic:

- He could be aggressive and demanding, yet he was also intensely innovative and driven to do "something wonderful."
- Jobs was perceived as arrogant and egotistical, yet he was also recognized as being profoundly inspiring and motivating.
- He was controlling and obsessed with details, yet he was equally deeply aesthetic and promoted collective intelligence, open innovation and generative collaboration.

In the words of his biographer Walter Isaacson:

Steve was filled with contradictions. He was a counterculture rebel who became a billionaire. He eschewed material objects yet made objects of desire. He talked, at times, about how he wrestled with these contradictions. His counterculture background combined with his love of electronics and business was key to the products he created. They combined artistry and technology.

As Isaacson indicates, Jobs contradictions were actually one of the keys to his creativity. These seemingly opposing qualities of Steve Jobs' character are what we have called "generative complementarities." Both his strengths and his faults can be seen as necessary aspects of these complementary traits. In some ways, one does not come without the other; or at least the potential for the other. In the same way that to know joy is to know sadness (and vice versa), or to know love is to know suffering, Jobs' positive and negative traits necessarily went hand in hand. You don't get one without the other. Light always casts a shadow somewhere.

These complementary traits are essentially a similar characteristic that is being expressed on the one side through the Ego and on the other side through the Soul. Ambition, control, arrogance, obsession, anxiety, etc., are all Ego traits. Vision, contribution, inspiration, connection and appreciation of harmony and beauty are Soul traits. The key to success, as I have mentioned a number of times, is finding a role in which ambition is put in the service of mission and vision.

The example of Steve Jobs illustrates the power and importance of "generative complementarities." Both his strengths and his faults were essential aspects of his creative genius.

I like to point out that the greater your ambition is, the greater your vision needs to be in order to direct that ambition. Likewise, the greater your vision is, the greater your ambition needs to be in order to achieve that vision. When there is a lot of ambition and little or no vision, the consequence is selfish arrogance. When there is a lot of vision and no ambition, the result is unfulfilled dreams. When the two come together in a win-win partnership, the consequence is passion and enthusiasm about what one is doing, a clear direction, and a type of charisma that brings energy and motivation to the people one is working with. It also supports the ability to bounce back from adversity and transform failure into feedback. This certainly seems to have been the case with Steve Jobs. As he summarized:

When ambition is in the service of vision it is possible to both take risks and ask for help. As Steve Jobs claimed, "If you are afraid of failing you won't get very far."

I've never found anybody that didn't want to help me if I asked them for help . . . I called up Bill Hewlett (co-founder of electronics giant Hewlett-Packard) when I was twelve years old. He lived in Palo Alto. His number was still in the phone book. And he answered the phone himself. He said, "Yes?" And I said, "Hi, I'm Steve Jobs and I'm twelve years old. I am a student in Junior High School and I want to build a frequency counter, and I was wondering if you have any spare parts that I could have. And he laughed and he gave me the spare parts to build this frequency counter. And he gave me a job that summer at Hewlett-Packard working on the assembly line putting the nuts and bolts together on frequency counters. He got me a job in the place that built them. And I was in heaven.

I have never found anyone who said "no" or hung up the phone when I called. I just asked. And when people ask me, I try to be as responsive to pay that debt of gratitude back.

Most people never pick up the phone and call. Most people never ask. And that's what separates sometimes the people who do things from the people who just dream about them.

You've got to act, and you've got to be willing to fail. You've got to be willing to crash and burn, with people on the phone, with starting a company, with whatever.

If you are afraid of failing you won't get very far.

Steve Job's Circle of Success

At the center of the circle was Jobs' passion and desire to achieve "something wonderful," a deep sense of direction, and the courage that came from a strong belief in himself and his destiny. As he put it:

> You can't connect the dots looking forward; you can only connect them looking backwards. So you have to trust that the dots will somehow connect in your future. You have to trust in something – your gut, destiny, life, karma, whatever. This approach has never let me down, and it has made all the difference in my life.

This was linked to his aesthetic intelligence and commitment to *design* as a core value and guide in his life. These qualities, along with the ability to convince himself and others to believe almost anything, were what allowed him to create the so-called *"reality distortion field"* that could make the impossible seem possible. As he claimed in his "Think Different" ad, the people who are crazy enough to think they can change the world are the ones who usually do.

With respect to customers and the market, Jobs' passion expressed itself as a *vision of personal empowerment and enrichment through technology* and creation of *"insanely great" products* that combined *beauty and functionality.* Jobs' vision and passion gave him a strong sense of connection with his customers and the marketplace and the possibility to make a positive difference in people's lives. In a 1996 interview he explained:

> I felt it the first time when I visited a school. They had third and fourth graders in a classroom full of Apple IIs. I spent a few hours there and I saw these third and fourth graders growing up completely differently than I did because they had this machine.

> And what hit me about it was, here was this machine that a very few people designed; about four in the case of the Apple II. And then they gave it to some people that didn't know how to design it, but they knew how to make it, to manufacture it. They could make a whole bunch of them. And then they gave it to some people who didn't know how to design it or manufacture it, but they knew how to distribute it. They gave it to people that didn't know how to design, distribute or manufacture it, but they knew how to write software for it.

At the center of Steve Jobs' Circle of Success was his passion to make a positive difference in the world, a belief in himself and his destiny, and a deep aesthetic intelligence. This created a type of "reality distortion field" that allowed him to convince others that what appeared to be impossible was possible.

When expressed toward potential customers, Steve Jobs' passion produced a vision of personal empowerment and enrichment through technology and the creation of "insanely great" products that combined beauty and functionality

Gradually this sort of inverse pyramid grew, and when it finally got into the hands of a lot of people, it blossomed out of this tiny little seed. It seemed like an incredible amount of leverage. And it all started with just an idea. And here was this idea taken through all of these stages, resulting in a classroom full of kids growing up with some insights and some fundamentally different experiences which I thought might be very beneficial to their lives because of this germ of an idea a few years before.

And that is an incredible feeling; to know that you had something to do with it and to know that it can be done. To know that you can plant something in the world and it will grow and change the world ever so slightly.

With respect to his team members, Steve Jobs strove to inspire them to "fall in love with Apple'" and to "make them better." He established an environment and culture in which excellence was "noticed," "respected" and part of "the surroundings."

Jobs' had a knack for being able to plant the right "seeds." His preference for a lack of hierarchy and his ability to "move ideas around," "see what different people think" and "get people talking" about them ensured that he did not get caught in an "ivory tower" and allowed him to keep his *"finger on the pulse"* of people's needs, interests and desires. He also had the courage to continue to evolve the expression of his vision and not let it freeze into ideology or dogma.

With respect to his *employees and team members*, Jobs strove to inspire them and "make them better" and established a culture of excellence in which excellence was "noticed," "respected" and part of "the surroundings." His question *"Why are you here?"* is an example of his intense focus at the level of mission. His major concern was whether or not his team members would "fall in love" with the company and its vision. He promoted collective intelligence and generative collaboration through open communication between all levels of people in the organization and "evangelism."

Steve Jobs' ability to form and leverage win-win partnerships and alliances as an "orchestrator of innovation" allowed him to attract and integrate fundamental technologies from multiple sources

Jobs' ability to form and leverage *partnerships and alliances* was another key part of his success. His role of *"orchestrator of innovation"* made him an attractive partner to work with. As a "selector, evolver and integrator of good ideas," Jobs welcomed *open innovation* and brought in and linked fundamental technologies from multiple sources, as in the case of the Macintosh, iPod and iPad. His role of orchestrator of innovation also motivated him to partner with and encourage developers to create new apps and software. His groundbreaking partnership with Microsoft in 1996 saved his company when it was on the brink of disaster.

In terms of *investors and stakeholders*, Jobs' *ambition* to *stay ahead of the curve* and "go to where the puck is going to be" was attractive and ultimately paid off in a big way. Like many other "lucky" entrepreneurs, his ambition motivated him to stay active, take risks and ask for help. He also demonstrated a total *commitment to the success of the company.* His symbolic decision to receive a salary as CEO of one dollar per year is a dramatic statement in that respect.

Another way that Jobs created value for investors and stakeholders was through *discipline.* Like another entrepreneurial icon, Walt Disney, Steve Jobs could be a dreamer, a realist and a critic. As a dreamer, he was capable of anticipating trends and applying discipline to elicit and integrate multiple perspectives to develop and enrich new ideas. He was also a realist, showing extraordinary discipline with his teams in order to validate the readiness of the marketplace and ensure that all of the ingredients of the product were ready to give a high level of performance. For Jobs, there was also a clear connection between the big vision and attention to detail. This involved being a constructive critic and bringing the discipline of design to ensure that the "soul" and quality of his creations were "carried all the way through" each layer of the product. In Jobs' words, "To turn really interesting ideas and fledgling technologies into a company that can continue to innovate for years, it requires a lot of disciplines." As a critic, this also required the discipline to say "no." As Jobs explained:

> People think focus means saying yes to the thing you've got to focus on. But that's not what it means at all. It means saying no to the hundred other good ideas that there are. You have to pick carefully. I'm actually as proud of many of the things we haven't done as the things we have done.

Steve Jobs' ambition to stay ahead of the curve and "go to where the puck is going to be" motivated him to keep active, take risks and ask for help. It also brought a total commitment to the success of his company which was attractive to investors and other stakeholders.

Steve Jobs' Circle of Success

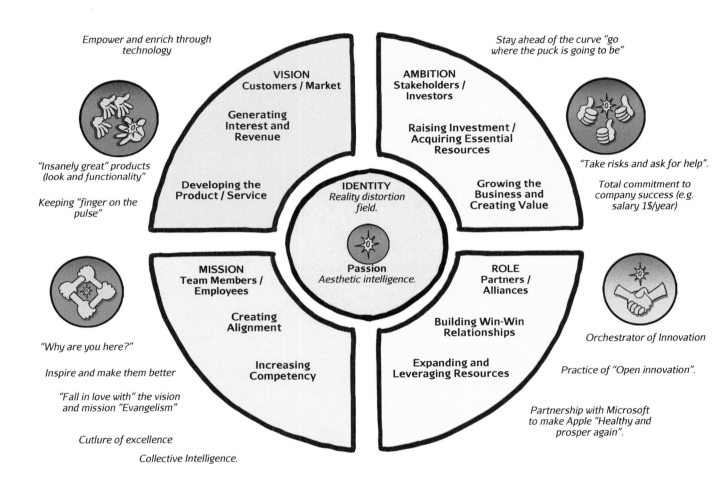

Empower and enrich through technology

"Insanely great" products (look and functionality"

Keeping "finger on the pulse"

VISION
Customers / Market

Generating Interest and Revenue

Developing the Product / Service

AMBITION
Stakeholders / Investors

Raising Investment / Acquiring Essential Resources

Growing the Business and Creating Value

Stay ahead of the curve "go where the puck is going to be"

"Take risks and ask for help".

Total commitment to company success (e.g. salary 1$/year)

IDENTITY
Reality distortion field.

Passion
Aesthetic intelligence.

MISSION
Team Members / Employees

Creating Alignment

Increasing Competency

ROLE
Partners / Alliances

Building Win-Win Relationships

Expanding and Leveraging Resources

"Why are you here?"

Inspire and make them better

"Fall in love with" the vision and mission "Evangelism"

Cutlure of excellence

Collective Intelligence.

Orchestrator of Innovation

Practice of "Open innovation".

Partnership with Microsoft to make Apple "Healthy and prosper again".

STEVE JOBS' CIRCLE OF SUCCESS

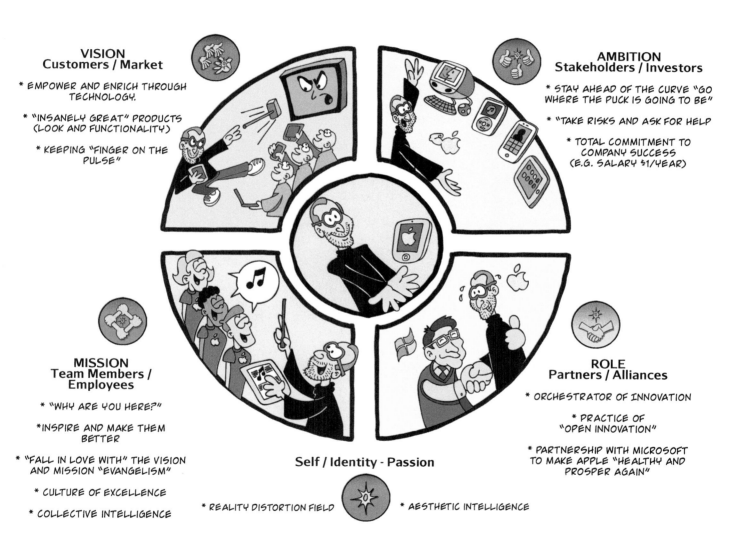

VISION
Customers / Market

* EMPOWER AND ENRICH THROUGH TECHNOLOGY.

* "INSANELY GREAT" PRODUCTS (LOOK AND FUNCTIONALITY)

* KEEPING "FINGER ON THE PULSE"

AMBITION
Stakeholders / Investors

* STAY AHEAD OF THE CURVE "GO WHERE THE PUCK IS GOING TO BE"

* "TAKE RISKS AND ASK FOR HELP

* TOTAL COMMITMENT TO COMPANY SUCCESS (E.G. SALARY $1/YEAR)

MISSION
Team Members / Employees

* "WHY ARE YOU HERE?"

* INSPIRE AND MAKE THEM BETTER

* "FALL IN LOVE WITH" THE VISION AND MISSION "EVANGELISM"

* CULTURE OF EXCELLENCE

* COLLECTIVE INTELLIGENCE

ROLE
Partners / Alliances

* ORCHESTRATOR OF INNOVATION

* PRACTICE OF "OPEN INNOVATION"

* PARTNERSHIP WITH MICROSOFT TO MAKE APPLE "HEALTHY AND PROSPER AGAIN"

Self / Identity - Passion

* REALITY DISTORTION FIELD

* AESTHETIC INTELLIGENCE

Concluding Comments on Steve Jobs

Steve Jobs' *role* of "orchestrator of innovation" allowed him to put his *ambition* to live his own life, stay ahead of the curve and keep moving to where "the puck is going to be" in the service of the *vision* of empowered individuals using "insanely great" technology and products. It also supported his *mission* to create those products through generative collaboration and aesthetic discipline.

In Jobs, who embraced Buddhism, we see the presence of the "three jewels" of zentrapreneurism we mentioned in Chapter 2: his *Dharma* (benefiting others through technology), *Buddha* (living his own life) and *Sangha* (doing something wonderful with others). What makes Steve Jobs an icon of success is not only his phenomenal business results, it is his desire to do "something wonderful" together with others and his commitment to living *his* life on his own terms, according to his values. As he said:

> For the past (38) years, I have looked in the mirror every morning and asked myself: "If today were the last day of my life, would I want to do what I am about to do today?" And whenever the answer has been "No" for too many days in a row, I know I need to change something.

Though clearly imperfect, Jobs lived his life striving to "go to bed at night saying we've done something wonderful" and waking each morning wanting "to do what I am about to do today." Whether or not we like Steve Jobs as a person or even appreciate what he created, it is interesting and inspiring to imagine living our lives bounded each day by these two criteria.

Steve Jobs' success could be viewed as the result of an epic journey of an entrepreneur on a quest to balance and integrate his ego and his soul. It is no wonder that his final words were, *"Oh Wow. Oh Wow. Oh Wow."*

Steve Jobs' role of "orchestrator of innovation" allowed him to put his ambition to live his own life, stay ahead of the curve and keep moving to where "the puck is going to be" in the service of his vision of empowered individuals using "insanely great" technology and products.

Chapter Summary

Vision is an important expression of the center of the Circle of Success outward toward customers. As the example of John Kennedy's vision to "put a man on the moon and safely return him to Earth" illustrates, a compelling vision stretches and tests the best of our abilities.

As entrepreneur Steve Artim pointed out, entrepreneurial vision is a type of "stake in the ground in the future" which serves as a reference point for coordinating the actions of the entrepreneur and his or her team. It is also important for entrepreneur's to have "peripheral" vision in order to perceive and track influences that are emerging on the "radar screen."

The Generative Vision exercise helps you to apply your vision to generate more specific contents and details of your project or venture by directing that vision towards a selected group of customers. The "More of/Less of" chart can then help you to focus the vision even more.

Communicating your vision with charisma is an essential skill for entrepreneurs. This involves the ability to "know it," "feel it" and "free it" into the field of awareness of your audience in a way that will touch and inspire them. Your authentic charisma comes from the felt connection to the sense of pride, confidence, hope and excitement that comes as a result of speaking from your core and your potential.

The most powerful visions are those which propel us to make a contribution to something beyond ourselves as individuals. This is related to a sense of purpose and *mission*.

The types of missions that drive us to success are more than just inspiring ideas, they are actionable. An actionable mission statement (a) reflects core values, (b) expresses our core competencies and (c) establishes the essential contribution we are making for whom and for what purpose.

Frequently, a mission is not easy to express or define in only literal terms. It is often useful to express a mission in multiple ways; citing a personal reference that relates to the mission, using a symbol and metaphor, creating a movement, or defining a project that embodies the mission in some way. The Mission Statement Worksheet can help you to describe and present your mission using several of these different modes of expression

In order to release energy and initiate action, it is also important that vision and mission are connected to our ambition and role. Our ambitions arise from our innate desire to do or to achieve something and from our "drive for growth and mastery." Entrepreneurs are not content with what they already know they can do; they want to find growth-opportunities that "raise the bar" and allow them to explore and expand their competence and mastery by finding the "just manageable difficulty."

Our beliefs about our capabilities influence our level of ambition. Empowering beliefs encourage us to take risks and push the edge of our performance/capacity ratio. Limiting beliefs can create "shadows," drive us to overcompensate for perceived lacks or weaknesses and create an "illusion of incompetence."

Identifying role models, advisors, competitors help us to find concrete references and comparisons from which to set, measure and validate our ambitions. The most important way to ensure that we have a healthy and realistic ambition is to be sure that it is *aligned with our vision and mission.* Next generation entrepreneurs have a vision of a world in which individuals achieve happiness and success by cooperating with others to increase the happiness and success of all by "creating a world to which people want to belong."

The Ambition Worksheet assists you to be more specific about your ambition and identify the relevant role models, sponsors and mentors and competitors to make it more concrete for yourself and potential investors and stakeholders. The Assessing Motivations Worksheet helps you clarify your motivations for taking on your project or venture and explore how much they align with one another. It also helps you to reflect upon how much they overlap or conflict with those of other key individuals or groups that could significantly influence your success.

Establishing a role that aligns and supports your vision, mission and ambition is another significant success factor for creating the future. Clarifying the role of the project or venture also helps to attract and create partnerships and alliances with other projects and ventures. When establishing the role of your project or venture, it is important to be as clear as possible about the things you do and the special competences you have. If you are too vague, it is difficult for potential partners to assess the benefits of an alliance.

The Vision and Ambition Worksheet for New Ventures and Projects assists you to summarize the vision, mission, ambition and role of your project or venture. You can then integrate them into your Circle of Success to get a solid synthesis from which to guide and create the future of your project or venture.

Perhaps no individual more personifies the new generation of entrepreneurs than Steve Jobs. Although, challenging and enigmatic as a person, Steve Jobs clearly embodied the majority of the success factors identified in the book up to this point. Steve Jobs' *role* of "orchestrator of innovation" allowed him to put his ambition to live his own life, stay ahead of the curve and keep moving to where "the puck is going to be" in the service of the *vision* of empowered individuals using "insanely great" technology and products, and support the *mission* to create those products through generative collaboration and aesthetic discipline.

References and Further Reading

The Hero With A Thousand Faces, Campbell, J., Fontana Press., London, UK, 1993.

The Origin of Species, Darwin, C., Mentor Books, New York, NY, 1958.

Photo of Martin Luther King
      http://www.drmartinlutherking.net

Ambition: How We Manage Success and Failure Throughout Our Lives, Brim, G., Basic Books, 1992.

Rodin, Judith; *Aging and Health: Effects of the Sense of Control*; Science Vol. 233, September 19, 1986, pp.1271-1276.

Imagined Worlds: Stories of Scientific Discovery; Andersen, P., and Cadbury, D., Ariel Books, London, 1985.

Steve Jobs, Walter Isaacson, Simon & Schuster, New York, 2011.

The Little Kingdom, Michael Moritz, William Morrow & Co., New York, 1984.

The Second Coming of Steve Jobs, Alan Deutschman, Crown Business, New York, 2001.

iCon: Steve Jobs, by Jeffrey S. Young & William L. Simon, Wiley, New York, 2006.

Success Factors of Innovative Disruptions, Robert Dilts & Benoît Sarazin, September 2008.

2005 Stanford Commencement Address by Steve Jobs

Steve at Work, Romain Moisescot; allaboutstevejobs.com, 2012.

Conclusion
Making your "Elevator Pitch"

"Determine that the thing can and shall be done and then we shall find the way."
Abraham Lincoln

ANTONIO MEZA

What is an Elevator Pitch?

An elevator pitch is a brief and concise description of your project or venture

You have now completed our first journey around the entire SFM Circle of Success – getting a sense of your identity and passion; your vision and customers; your mission and team; your ambition and stakeholders; and your role and partners. These are the fundamental pillars from which to build a successful venture. It is time to summarize this exploration and synthesize what you have learned regarding the various levels of success factors into what is known as an "elevator pitch" for your venture.

The notion of an elevator pitch evolved in the fast paced world of Silicon Valley. In such a dynamic context, an entrepreneur needs to be able to communicate the essence of his or her vision and venture to someone in the time it takes to ride up or down with that person several floors in an elevator. Sometimes that is the only chance you will get to interest a prospective investor, partner or team member in what you are planning. Thus, the term *elevator pitch* has come to mean a brief and concise description of your project, idea or venture.

An elevator pitch needs to be a succinct, carefully planned, and well-practiced description of you, your venture or your product/service that your intended listener can understand in the time it would take to ride several floors an elevator. Whether you are an entrepreneur with a start-up company trying to find investors, a recent graduate trying to find a job, a parent with ideas on how to improve the classroom, or a nonprofit looking for donations, a good elevator pitch can help you to generate interest in your project or venture.

An elevator pitch isn't about cramming as much information into as short a time as possible. As we explored in the exercise on communicating your vision with authentic charisma, a well crafted elevator pitch should evoke emotion as much as cognitive understanding. There are three fundamental characteristics of a successful elevator pitch:

1) *Precision*

  – You should be able to give your pitch in just a couple of minutes.

2) *Passion*

  – Customers, investors, team members and potential partners expect energy and dedication from entrepreneurs.

3) *A request*

  – At the end of your pitch, you must ask for something. Do you want their business card, to schedule a full presentation, to ask for a referral, etc.?

There are six questions your elevator pitch must answer:

1. *What is your project or venture?*

   State your vision and mission; i.e., what you intend to create in the world through your project or venture and how you will do it.

2. *Who is your customer/market?*

   Identify the demographic group to which your vision and mission are targeted. How large of a market do they represent?

3. *What is your revenue model?*

   Explain how you expect to make money or support the venture or project.

4. *Who is involved in the project or venture?*

   Talk briefly about yourself and your team's background and achievements. If you have a strong advisory board, tell the listener who they are and what they have accomplished.

5. *Who is your competition?*

   Identify and briefly describe any other projects or ventures that are doing something similar to you, who they are and what they have accomplished. Remember that competitors are validation that there is a need for your project or venture.

6. *What is your competitive advantage?*

   It is also important to effectively communicate how your company is different from your competitors and why you have an advantage over them. What is unique about you and why will you succeed?

A well crafted elevator pitch should evoke positive emotion as much as cognitive understanding.

Preparing Your Pitch

Get a piece of blank paper, or open your word processor, and write out a rough draft of your "elevator pitch."

Overview of the Project or Venture

Make a brief overview of the key elements of your project or venture (250 words or less). Answer the questions:

- *What is your overall vision for your project or venture?*
- *What is your ambition? What is your breakthrough? How are you "pushing the edge of the envelope?"*
- *What is your mission? What is unique about your project or venture and its possible results?*
- *What will your project or venture allow people to do more of, more quickly, better, less expensively?*
- *Why will you be a big success?*

If it is important, make sure you include your time line for completing your project or having your venture up and running successfully.

Needed Resources

State what type of resources or support you need for your project to be successful. Think in terms of clients/customers, investors, team members, information, contacts, web links, books, etc.

Partnering and Investment

Identify what type of partnering, investment or other form of collaboration you are open to and interested in.

Request

Make an explicit request. Begin your request with "What I am looking for is . . ."

Example of Pitch Prepration for the "Generative Venture Community"

The following is an example of a preparation for a pitch that I wrote up about the vision my brother John and I formed for what we termed a "generative venture community."

Overview of the Project or Venture

What is your overall vision for your project or venture?

> The vision is of a "generative venture community" (GVC) formed around the principles of Success Factor Modeling and the visions of its members. The community will expand and prosper through the passion and contributions of its members. It will be structured in such a way that there is a positive loop between the success of the individual and the growth of the community.

What is your ambition? What is your breakthrough? How are you "pushing the edge of the envelope?"

- Take Success Factor Modeling to the next level
- Establish a renewing network of at least 1000 next generation entrepreneurs each year.
- Build a website that provides an ever increasing number of success case examples
- Create international interest among existing organizations to support next generation entrepreneurship within their companies

What is your mission and what is unique about your project or venture and its possible results?

> Dilts Strategy Group will provide training and coaching in SFM to bring inspiration, focus and structure for next generation entrepreneurs to support one another in creating successful ventures. This will enable entrepreneurs to stay connected and maintain their ongoing collaborations in order to increase the value and chances of success of each other's ventures.

What will your project or venture allow people to do more of, more quickly, better, less expensively?

- Create a road map for a successful venture
- Develop optimal mindset
- Connect to their passion and express it as a vision
- Harness collective intelligence
- Discover their charisma and inspire others
- Enhance their leadership and resilience

Why will you be a big success?

Unlike a traditional incubator, GVC members will share the principles and models of Success Factor Modeling can continually exchange resources, including introductions, coaching, professional services, investor leads, etc., and to directly benefit from those efforts. They will also be able to share some level of ownership in one another's ventures.

Needed Resources

- Technical support for the website
- Help getting the message out to entrepreneurs
- Sponsors for Success Factor Modeling events and certification courses
- Skilled trainers, consultants and coaches that can provide ongoing support to GVC members
- Other ideas/input

Partnering and Investment

I am interested in getting a network of people together who are passionate about next generation entrepreneurship - i.e., living their dreams and making a better world - to help create the foundations for the GVC. In return, network members will get exposure, paid work with some of the entrepreneurs and sponsoring groups, and a stake in the GVC.

Request

What I am looking are partners who are willing to join me to help create products, build out the website, conduct Success Factor Modeling interviews and case studies and/or promote the vision to existing companies as well as new entrepreneurs.

Presenting with Passion

Once you have prepared the content of your elevator pitch, it is important to prepare yourself for the behavioral aspects of communicating it effectively and persuasively. Time and time again, we have seen the power and importance of the entrepreneur's ability to communicate his or her vision in a way that makes others as inspired and excited about it as the entrepreneur. Investors, for instance, rarely choose to invest in an idea, product or plan alone. They invest in the entrepreneur and his or her vision, mission, ambition, passion and commitment to make things happen. The same is true for other potential collaborators. Like Steve Jobs, you must create a type of "reality distortion field" in order to convince others that your dream for your project or venture is desirable and possible to achieve.

You will need to present your elevator pitch for your venture so that it captivates the attention of others. As we have explored, the power of your presentation is a result of behavioral skills and qualities such as:

Vision: *Inspiring and touching your listeners with your vision.*

Rapport: *Fully engaging with your audience and gaining their trust and respect.*

Empathy: *Demonstrating a comprehensive understanding of the needs and motivations of customers, stakeholders and/or other collaborators.*

Passion: *Conveying and transferring fervent enthusiasm for your project or venture.*

Clarity: *Communicating your ideas in a way that is sharp, clear and easy to understand.*

Confidence: *Projecting "humble authority" and being convincing about your ability to address risks and obstacles and to succeed in your project or venture.*

Alignment: *Expressing yourself and your message in a congruent, authentic and credible manner.*

Remember to use all three of the major representational modalities when presenting the key ideas of your elevator pitch: verbal, visual and somatic. Also, be sure to review the section in the previous chapter on Communicating Your Vision with Authentic Charisma. These same principles apply for your entire elevator pitch.

It is a good idea to practice with a friend or colleague who can give you feedback on both the clarity of your presentation and the passion with which you present it.

Key to delivering an effective elevator pitch is developing your ability to communicate your vision in a way that makes others as inspired and excited about it as you are.

Next Steps

While making your elevator pitch is the culmination of this first volume on Success Factor Modeling, it is in many ways just the beginning of your journey. In the next volume we will be exploring how to enrich, expand and bring more detail to your vision and venture through collective intelligence and generative collaboration. We will also provide models, tools and exercises to help you develop the capacities of resilience and leadership. We will be exploring topics such as Making the Pie Bigger, Doing the Impossible, Making Something Out of Nothing, Rebounding From Adversity and Developing Fitness for the Future.

I hope you choose to continue your journey into the exciting and rewarding world of next generation entrepreneurship.

Afterword

I hope you have enjoyed this exploration of Success Factor Modeling™ and the SFM Circle of Success™. If you are interested in learning about the principles and technology of Success Factor Modeling in more depth, other resources and tools exist to further develop and apply the distinctions, strategies and skills described within these pages.

Dilts Strategy Group

Dilts Strategy Group is an organization committed to providing the training, consulting and coaching in the applications of Success Factor modeling, including Next Generation Entrepreneurship, Collective Intelligence, Leadership and Innovation. Dilts Strategy Group also sponsors research projects promoting the development of new models and the identification of evolving success factors in the dynamic social and economic world in which we live. Dilts Strategy Group offers trainings and certification programs in Success Factor Modeling throughout the world.

For more information please contact:

Dilts Strategy Group
P.O. Box 67448
Scotts Valley CA 95067
USA
Phone: (831) 438-8314
E-Mail: info@diltstrategygorup.com
Homepage: http://www.diltstrategygroup.com

In addition to the training programs I offer through Dilts Strategy Group, I also travel extensively internationally, presenting seminars and workshops on a variety of topics related to personal and professional development.

For more information on scheduled programs, please consult my website: http://www.robertdilts.com or write for information to: rdilts@nlpu.com.

Journey to Genius

I have also written a number of other books and developed audio recordings based on the principles and distinctions of Success Factor Modeling and NLP. For example, I have produced several products based on my modeling of Strategies of Genius such as audio recordings describing the creative processes of geniuses such as Mozart, Walt Disney and Leonardo Da Vinci.

For more information on these and other products and resources, please contact:

Journey to Genius
P.O. Box 67448
Scotts Valley, CA 95067-7448
Phone (831) 438-8314
E-Mail: info@journeytogenius.com
Homepage: http://www.journeytogenius.com

NLP University

I am also a co-founder, director and trainer at *NLP University*, an organization committed to providing the highest quality trainings in basic and advanced NLP skills, and to promoting the development of new models and applications of NLP in the areas of health, business and organization, creativity and learning. Each summer, NLP University holds residential programs at the University of California at Santa Cruz, offering extended residential courses on the skills of NLP, including those related to business consulting and coaching.

For more information please contact Teresa Epstein at:

NLP University
P.O. Box 1112
Ben Lomond, California 95005
Phone: (831) 336-3457
Fax: (831) 336-5854
E-Mail: Teresanlp@aol.com
Homepage: http://www.nlpu.com

Success Factor Modeling illustrations and products

Antonio Meza and I have created this series of books with the intention of offering you something different, fun and visually rich. Through the pages of this book and the following volumes you will find many memorable illustrations and characters that will help you create a deeper connection with the content of the book.

We have created a special online store where you can find a variety of products like posters, t-shirts, mugs, etc that can help you to stay connected to the main concepts of Next Generation Entrepreneurship.

For more information on these and other products and resources, you can visit:

Success Factor Modeling website
Homepage: http://www.successfactormodeling.com

Success Factor Modeling product store
Homepage: http://society6.com/successfactormodeling

Antonio Meza illustrates books, articles, presentations and also performs as a graphic facilitator for conferences and seminars. He is also a business consultant, trainer and coach member of the Dilts Strategy Group.

If you are curious about Antonio's work as an illustrator, you can contact him at: t

Antoons
E-Mail: hola@antoons.net
Homepage: http://www.antoons.net

The Successful Genius Mastermind

The Successful Genius Mastermind is an exclusive, accelerated growth program for successful entrepreneurs and business owners. Successful Genius teaches the seven core strategies shared by the world's most successful people. This provides Participants with a clear roadmap and tremendous competitive advantage for greater success, accelerated growth, and positive impact. Current members include influential leaders from a variety of fields who have positively impacted the lives of hundreds of millions of people.

Successful Genius was created by author Robert Dilts, Mitchell Stevko (a Silicon Valley growth expert who has helped over 150 entrepreneurs achieve their dreams, raising over $5 billion in capital) and Dr. Olga Stevko (a Russian MD and Belief Medicine expert who specializes working with high level professionals). The Successful Genius mastermind program is available only by approved application and interview or member referral.

If you are ready to take your business and your abilities to an entirely new level of impact and influence, you can learn more and apply for membership at:

E-Mail: Mitchell@SuccessfulGenius.com

Homepage: http://www.SuccessfulGenius.com

Logical Levels Inventory

Logical levels inventory (*Ili*) is an innovative online leadership profiling tool based on the various levels of success factors that we have been exploring in this book. *Ili* identifies the key qualities that leaders need to possess in order take advantage of opportunities and remain successful in times of uncertainty and crisis. Developed as a direct result of the first Success Factor Modeling certification program, *Ili* takes you through a self-assessment process that helps you uncover the driving forces behind your actions and provides insight into what you can change to be a more successful leader in any area.

E-Mail: info@lld.uk.com

Homepage: http://www.logicallevels.co.uk

Appendix: Ongoing Success Factor Modeling Projects

As I mentioned in the Preface to this book, as of the beginning of 2015 there are several ongoing projects applying Success Factor Modeling to study important trends for new and existing businesses. One on "next generation entrepreneurship" is being sponsored by Institut REPERE in Paris. Another on "collective intelligence in organizations" is sponsored by Vision 2021 in Avignon. The following overviews summarize two of these projects and their purpose.

Next Generation Entrepreneurship

An entrepreneur is generally defined as "a person who organizes and manages an enterprise or venture and assumes significant accountability for the inherent risks and the outcome." The name is most frequently applied to a person who is willing to take on a new venture, project or enterprise, creating value by offering a product or service, and accepting full responsibility for the outcome. In essence, entrepreneurship is about taking personal, professional or financial responsibility and risk in order to pursue opportunity. In this sense, entrepreneurship is not only for individuals or small companies; it is an essential factor for success in today's rapidly evolving business world. Principles of entrepreneurship are necessary for all types of growth, innovation and change.

In recent years, a new generation of entrepreneurs has begun to emerge who are interested in more than just financial gain; they are also committed to living their dreams and making a better world through their projects or ventures. Many are people who have made a conscious decision to become more passionate, purposeful and creative. This translates into increased motivation, innovation and focus. Next generation entrepreneurs want to create both a successful and purposeful business, or career; combining ambition with contribution and mission, and the desire for personal growth and fulfillment. They also desire to attract and collaborate with others who share the same vision, mission and ambition. In other words, Next Generation Entrepreneurship involves creating a world to which people want to belong. This new generation of entrepreneurship is driving and changing the way business is done and paving the way to both our social and economic future.

The purpose of the study was to identify the latest trends adopted by this new generation of entrepreneurship in order to address challenges and take advantage of opportunities in the current economic environment. The learning gathered during the study is intended to enhance the productivity, profitability and satisfaction of a new generation of entrepreneurs and intrapreneurs.

The project involved interviews with 18 selected *"Next Generation Entrepreneurs."* Next Generation Entrepreneur was defined as:

Someone who creates a sustainable business or project to live one's own dream, while delivering a product or a service that makes a positive difference in the world and personally growing through it.

The four mandatory criteria of interviewee selection included:

- Living one's dream and passionate about something else than money
- Making a positive difference in the world
- Business is at least economically sustainable if not growing
- Delivering something new and innovative

Interviewees were selected to represent a wide scope of ventures including:

- Different Business Types

  Industry, Services, Technology, Environmental, NGO, etc.

- Different Business Sizes

  Small and middle sized companies, Intrapreneurs within large scale/ multinational companies, Social entrepreneurs, etc.

- Different Business Phases

  Start-up, Growth, Expansion, Maturity

- Different Entrepreneur's Reputation and Notoriety

  Reputation amongst peers could be local, regional, national, international

Major trends will be documented in articles published in selected business magazines and on the Dilts Strategy Group website.

This study was done in conjunction with Institut REPERE in Paris, France.

For more information, contact:

Institut REPERE

78 Avenue du Général Michel Bizot
75012 Paris, France
+33 1 43 46 89 41
commercial@institut-repere.com
http://www.institut-repere.com

Collective Intelligence

Working together with others in groups and teams is an increasingly important part of modern business success. High functioning groups and teams demonstrate the characteristic of collective intelligence; a phenomenon that greatly enhances both efficiency and creativity. Intelligence is defined as: The ability to interact successfully with one's world, especially in the face of challenge or change. Collective intelligence has to do with a shared or group intelligence that emerges from the collaboration and communication between individuals in groups and other interacting systems.

Practically speaking, collective intelligence relates to the ability of individuals in a team or group to share knowledge and think and act in an aligned and coordinated fashion to achieve critical outcomes. In organizations, this involves the process of people working cooperatively to reach common objectives by exchanging information and complementing one another's skills and experience. This accumulation and integration of individual know-how and competence also serves as a platform from which to develop new insights, ideas and capabilities. As a result, a major benefit of promoting collective intelligence is that group members grow more quickly and the creative problem solving capacity of the organization is improved through increased access to knowledge and expertise.

The purpose of this study is to identify current trends and ideas generated by teams and organizations to increase collective intelligence in order to address challenges and take advantage of opportunities in the current economic environment. Dilts Strategy Group members have contacted a number of teams and companies to participate in interviews and other activities ranging from one hour to several days. These teams and companies have been selected on the basis of their reputation as a strong leader in the area of collective intelligence among peers.

The following topics are being explored:

- What are the current challenges and opportunities the company or team is facing.
- How they view and value collective intelligence as a key means to succeed in today's business environment.
- How they modified their business strategy and management practices to encourage and increase collective intelligence.
- What specific steps they have implemented to support collective intelligence on a practical level.

As with the Next Generation Entrepreneurship study, major trends will be documented in articles published in selected business magazines and on the Dilts Strategy Group website.

This study was done in conjunction with Vision 2021 in Avignon, France.

For more information, contact:

Vision 2021
3 Avenue de la Synagogue
84000 Avignon, France
+33 4 90 16 04 16
Gilles Roy <gilles.roy2@orange.fr>
www.intelligence-collective.net

Glossary

Advisory Board: A group of individuals who provide advice and resources to start-up companies. These individuals usually have expertise or experience in some area that is essential to the success of the start-up.

Alignment: The placement of things in the "correct or appropriate relative positions." With respect to Success Factor Modeling, this has to do with the shared focus of team members on the larger vision and purpose of the venture in order to efficiently coordinate their actions. Alignment also involves ensuring that all levels of success factors support the larger vision of the project or venture. Specifically, that the vision is appropriately supported by the mission, ambition, role, values, beliefs, capabilities, behaviors and environment embodied by both the venture itself and the individuals involved.

Alliance: A union or association based on common interests and formed for mutual benefit. Forming effective alliances and partnerships is a key part of entrepreneurial success.

Ambition: The desire and determination to achieve success for oneself. It is defined as "a strong desire to do or to achieve something, typically requiring determination and hard work." Our ambitions in the form of aspirations arise from the drive for growth and mastery. Ambition is an essential force for entrepreneurs. It is one of the primary sources of energy for creating the future and is what attracts investors and other stakeholders.

Angel Fund: An angel fund is an early stage venture capital fund that typically puts small amounts of money in a number of different start-up companies. Angel funds are generally much smaller than traditional venture capital funds, but offer the potential of much greater reward, because they are able to purchase stock at a much cheaper price from companies that are in an early stage.

Angel Investor: A new breed of investors that has arisen in Silicon Valley and in other technology centers around the world. Angel investors often fill the "funding gap" for investment in new companies where such early stage funding is preferable over venture capital investment. Angels often invest their own money in start-ups, making a relatively small but significant capital investment in return for an equity position in the company. Angel investors are often also "value-added" investors, in that they use their relationships and expertise to support the company to succeed.

Behavioral factors: The specific action steps taken in order to reach success. They involve what, specifically, must be done or accomplished in order to succeed.

Behavioral Modeling: A process by which specific behavioral and cognitive patterns associated with successful performance are elicited and coded. Behavioral modeling involves observing and mapping the successful processes that underlie an exceptional human performance of some type. It is the process of taking a complex event or series of events and breaking it into small enough chunks so that it can be recapitulated in some way. The purpose of behavior modeling is to create a pragmatic map or 'model' of that behavior which can be used to reproduce or simulate some aspect of that performance by anyone who is motivated to do so.

Behavioral Skills: The cognitive and interpersonal processes which frequently make up the "soft" or intangible aspects of doing business. Behavioral skills include cognitive and interactive abilities such as communication, creative thinking, leadership and problem solving. Behavioral skills may be contrasted with business practices, which relate to the tasks which must be accomplished in order to sustain and grow a business. In order to be achieved effectively, business practices must be supported by behavioral skills. The most significant behavioral skills relating to the start-up of a new venture include vision, rapport, second position, passion, clarity, confidence and alignment.

Beliefs and Values: A level of inner programming that provides the reinforcement which supports or inhibits particular capabilities and actions. They relate to why a particular path is taken and the deeper motivations which drive people to act or persevere. Values, and related beliefs, determine how events and communications are interpreted and given meaning. Thus, they are the key to motivation and culture. The entrepreneur's belief in the venture, the team and himself or herself is a major success factor for a new business or venture.

Benchmarking: The process of dynamically establishing a standard by which something can be measured or judged. A particular product, for instance, might be said to "set the benchmark of quality." Thus, a benchmark is a reference point against which other related processes or phenomena may be compared and evaluated. In business, benchmarking is often related to performance measurement tools used in conjunction with improvement initiatives to measure comparative operating performance and identify Best Practices. In a dynamic environment, benchmarks cannot be held rigid, and must be continuously adjusted to account for changing situations and circumstances. Thus, benchmarking needs to be an ongoing practice. When combined with 'best practices' studies, benchmarking becomes a powerful form of modeling.

Best Practices: The process of sharing, discussing and comparing business practices or behavioral action steps, and searching for those that produce the best results. Best practice groups and networks compare the approaches that they have taken with respect to shared problems and goals in order to identify practices that will improve the overall operations of the members.

Board of Directors: The individuals chosen by shareholders to oversee the management of a company on behalf of the shareholders.

Branding: Establishing the unique characteristics or identity of a particular product, service or business. It usually expressed through an identifying symbol, words, or mark that distinguishes a product or company from its competitors

Burn Rate: For a typical rapidly expanding start-up company with negative cash flow, this is the rate of that negative cash flow, usually calculated per month. The amount of the burn rate determines the projected amount of funds necessary to build a product or service and enter a market, and determines the length of time a start-up can operate before needing an infusion of capital.

Business Practices: The fundamental activities (the "nuts and bolts") required to operate an effective business. Business practices include making business plans, forming marketing strategies, protecting intellectual property, recruiting employees, and so on. Business practices are tangible activities that are typically easy to measure and track. Business practices may be contrasted with behavioral skills, the dynamic cognitive and behavioral "human factors" that influence the way business practices are carried out. Successful companies need an integration of both effective business practices and behavioral skills.

Capabilities: The specific skills, mental maps, plans and strategies that lead to success. Capabilities determine how specific behaviors and actions are selected and monitored.

CEO--Chief Executive Officer: The executive who is responsible for a company's operations, usually the President or the Chairman of the Board.

CFO--Chief Financial Officer: The executive who is responsible for financial planning and fundraising for a company.

CMO--Chief Marketing Officer: The executive who is responsible for promoting brand awareness and other activities leading to the sale of a company's products or services.

COO--Chief Operations Officer: The executive who is responsible for the day-to-day management of a company's internal operations.

CTO--Chief Technology Officer: The executive responsible for developing a Company's technology strategy, development and implementation.

Circle of Success: A key model for entrepreneurs that defines the five fundamental elements founders of new ventures need to identify and give attention to in order to achieve success: 1) themselves and their personal passion in the form of their vision, mission and ambition, 2) their customers and products, 3) their investors and stakeholders, 4) their strategic partners and alliances and 5) their team members or employees. Successful entrepreneurs divide their focus of attention evenly between each of these five fundamental perspectives.

Coaching: Coaching is the process of helping another person to perform at the peak of his or her abilities. Personal coaching methods derive from a sports training model, promoting conscious awareness of resources and abilities, and the development of conscious competence. They involve drawing out another person's strengths through careful observation and feedback, and facilitating him or her to function as a part of a team. An effective coach observes a person's behavior and gives him or her tips and guidance about how to improve in specific contexts and situations. Coaching emphasizes generative change, concentrating on defining and achieving specific goals.

Core Competences: The key capabilities, skills and methodologies (such as leadership, communication, conflict resolution, etc.) necessary to establish a venture and successfully grow it into a sustainable business.

Customers: The first and most significant quadrant in the SFM Circle of SuccessTM. Customers are the recipients and primary beneficiaries of the entrepreneur's vision and the ones who typically buy or pay for the products or services of the venture. It is in relationship with their customers that entrepreneurs develop their products, services and ultimately their venture. To achieve sustainable success, entrepreneurs must generate enough interest and revenue to support their enterprise — establishing both sufficient "mind share" and market share.

Early Stage: As the name implies, the beginning stage of a new venture, generally before any significant venture capital has been raised (see Start-Up). Early stage investments are frequently risky, but offer the greatest opportunity for a return on investment because the valuation of the company is so low.

Ego: One of the key forces, along with the "soul," that form the identity of an individual or organization. It relates to one's sense of oneself as a separate independent entity. Ego motivations include survival, acknowledgement, self-benefit, safety and control. The "ego" of an organization is made up of its owners or shareholders, who are concerned with the survival and efficient functioning of the organization so that they can make a positive return on their investment. It is important and necessary for entrepreneurs and organizations to have a healthy ego. An inflated ego or an imbalance of motivation in the direction of the ego leads to selfishness, arrogance and conflict.

Elevator Pitch: A succinct and concise description of you, your venture or your product/service that your intended listener can understand in the time it would take to ride several floors an elevator. An elevator pitch is an overview usually around 200-250 words that can be expressed verbally in a couple of minutes

Emerging Growth Companies: Companies that grow and expand rapidly due to the development and marketing of highly scalable technological developments. Emerging growth companies and technologies have proliferated as a result of new technical know-how, the Internet and the "new economy."

Entrepreneur: An individual who organizes, manages, and assumes the risks of a business or enterprise. The term is derived from the French word entreprendre, which means "to undertake." It is most frequently used to refer to a person who is starting up a new project or venture.

Environmental factors: The external circumstances and features that determine the concrete opportunities or constraints which individuals and organizations must recognize and to which they must react in order to succeed. Environmental factors relate to where and when actions must be taken.

Field of Innovation: The state of the bigger system or context in which the entrepreneur's passion and intention takes shape. This "field" is a function of the evolving socio-economic dynamics as well as technical developments. Such a field is composed of both latent or developing needs and attitudes as well as existing needs, attitudes and opinions. It is the state of this larger field of possibilities that determines whether an entrepreneur's idea is perceived as feasible and desirable. Those ventures that are most successful are the ones that produce something that is truly a breakthrough and "game changing." This happens when they are able to catch the "crest of the wave" of an emerging trend in the surrounding field.

First Mover Advantage: The competitive advantage gained by a company by offering its products and services into a market in a meaningful way before others focusing on the same market space.

Fund: To finance or underwrite. Also, a collection of money put together by a group of investors, whose purpose is to invest in companies meeting certain criteria (as in an investment company, venture fund or mutual fund).

Funding Gap: An area of investment in early stage companies between early stage and venture funding. This funding satisfies a Company's early need for funding before they are ready or able to attract venture capital investment.

Globalization: The increasing tendency toward an interconnected worldwide technology, investment and overall business environment.

Identity: The sense of who a person or group perceives themselves to be, and who they are perceived as by others. The identity of an individual or venture is related to the unique characteristics of its product, service or business and is what distinguishes a product or company from its competitors; i.e., its branding. Identity organizes the corresponding values, beliefs, capabilities and behaviors into a single system.

Imagineering: A process developed by Walt Disney and his animators by which ideas and dreams are brought into reality. The term is a combination of "imagination" and "engineering." The process of imagineering takes place through the balance and coordination of three fundamental processes: dreamer, realist and critic. Imagineering is the foundation of successful entrepreneurship.

Incubator: A business incubator is a supportive environment designed to assist start-up and early-stage companies to grow successfully. Incubators generally include:

- Pro-active support, access to critical tools, information and contacts which may otherwise be inaccessible or unaffordable
- Shared resources such as lobby/reception, meeting rooms, copy and fax equipment, audio visual equipment, clerical services, and kitchen
- Private offices, cubicles, lab or manufacturing spaces
- Access to business and technical advice and introductions to a range of qualified service providers, potential mentors and financial resources
- An organized program of training, one-on-one counseling, or mentoring

Technology incubators support the growth of companies involved in emerging technologies. These incubators focus on commercialization of technology as well as research and development.

Information Age: Refers to an era in human history characterized by the emergence of information and knowledge as the primary commodity in the economy.

Infrastructure: The resources (as technology, personnel, buildings, or equipment) required for a larger system or activity. Web browsers, transmission lines, search engines, intelligent terminals, back end systems, etc., are all part of the "infrastructure" for the Internet.

Intellectual Property/Patent Protection: The legal rights that an individual or organization can establish with respect to a product, service or expression of an idea. Patents, copyrights and trademarks are all examples of intellectual property. Such legal devices give the holder the exclusive right to apply, sell and benefit from the use of the "property" and to prevent others from using or benefiting without permission or a license. Intellectual property rights are one of the ways start-up companies create "barriers to entry," which help to prevent competitors from encroaching within their target market.

Internet Revolution: A radical shift in economic and social interaction brought about by the emergence of the Internet as a fundamental means of communication and commerce. The Internet revolution is one of the cornerstones of the "new economy." Functioning as both a marketplace and information highway, the Internet allows people from diverse localities to interact rapidly and directly, share large amounts of information quickly, and do business electronically.

Intranet: A private network that uses Internet-related technologies to provide services within an organization.

Intrapreneur: A person within a company who promotes innovative product development and marketing. An intrapreneur is essentially someone who engages in entrepreneurial activities within the context of an organization.

Investor: A person who commits money to a venture in order to earn a financial return. An investor in a start-up is typically someone who has a surplus of money, which he or she wants to make use of to get a longer-term payoff. Investors generally become "stakeholders" by owning some portion of the venture, usually in the form of stock. Getting sufficient investment is a key factor for the success of a new venture.

IPO--Initial Public Offering: Also known as "going public," the term refers to the placement of a company on a public stock exchange (such as the Dow Industrial or NASDAQ). A major milestone for any company, the price of the company's stock frequently increases after a public offering, sometimes dramatically. This is the way that many Silicon Valley entrepreneurs have achieved spectacular financial success.

ISP--Internet Service Provider: A business that delivers access to the Internet, usually for a monthly fee. Some ISPs provide Internet services such as web sites or web site development.

IT--Information Technology: Tools and resources used to send, receive and process information, including personal computers, cell phones, smart phones, tablets, web-cams, Internet related tools and other types of software or electronic devices.

Knowledge Economy: An economy in which the primary products are related to the acquisition and transfer of knowledge. A knowledge economy is characterized by the following trends:

- Rapid Technical Change — Need for the Ability to 'Learn to Learn'
- Increased Speed of Change and Demand for Response — "Internet Time"
- Increased Demand for Innovation
- Flexible Company Boundaries — The Extended Organization
- Emphasis on Relationship Building and Alliances — Creating Win-Win-Interactions

Levels of Learning and Change: Levels of success factors which influence effective and successful performance and change including: our environment (where and when we act), our behavior (what we do), our capabilities (how we think and plan), our values and beliefs (why we think and act the way we do), and our identity (who we perceive ourselves to be) and our sense of purpose (for whom and for what we dedicate ourselves).

Market Channels: Means by which a company's products and product information reach customers.

Market Share: The portion of the current available market for a product that is held by a particular company. Market Share is typically calculated by the percentage of sales of a company's product or service with respect to its competitors in a given market.

Mentoring: In Greek Mythology, Mentor was the wise and faithful counselor to the hero Odysseus. Under the guise of Mentor, the goddess Athena became the guardian and teacher of Odysseus' son Telemachus, while Odysseus was away on his journeys. Thus, the notion of being a "mentor" has come to mean the process of both (a) advising or counseling, and (b) serving as a guide or teacher. In organizations, mentoring typically involves a sometimes informal relationship in which a more senior or more experienced person acts as an advisor to a person to others who are just joining the organization or taking on a position.

Mind Share: The degree of brand awareness a product or company has with respect to its potential customers. Mind share may be contrasted with market share, which relates to the existing percentage of sales a product or company has with respect to an existing customer base. For a start-up company, mind share is more important than market share (e.g., Amazon.com).

Mission: The purpose an individual or group serves in relationship to the larger systems of which they are a part. Our mission relates to our contribution to something beyond ourselves. The mission of an individual, team or organization has to do with the special gifts, resources, capabilities and actions that they bring to the larger system in which they are operating in order to help reach the vision for that system. A clear understanding of mission is essential in order for team members and employees to function effectively.

Modeling: The identification and structuring of features and patterns relevant to achieving some goal or simulating some process. Modeling involves analyzing examples of successful performances (a combination of benchmarking and success analysis); sometimes by comparison to unsuccessful performances. The objective of the modeling process is not to end up with the one "right" or "true" description of a particular phenomenon, but rather to make an instrumental map that allows us to apply what has been modeled in some useful way. An 'instrumental map' is one that allows us to act more effectively—the "accuracy" or "reality" of the map is less important than its "usefulness."

New Economy: A term for the changes brought about in financial and social interactions due to advances in communications technology (such as wireless telecommunications, networking technology, media streaming and business-to-business Internet services) and the explosion in the use of tvhe Internet. The "new economy" is characterized by e-commerce, social media, virtual teams and a global marketplace.

NLP--Neuro-Linguistic Programming: The behavioral science at the basis of Success Factor Modeling. NLP studies the patterns or "programming" created by the interaction between the brain ("neuro"), language ("linguistic") and the body. From the NLP perspective, it is this interaction that produces both effective and ineffective behavior, and is responsible for the processes behind both human excellence and pathology. Many of the skills and techniques of NLP were derived by observing the patterns of excellence in experts from diverse fields of professional communication including: psychotherapy, business, hypnosis, law and education.

Partnership: A win-win relationship that allows an entrepreneur to expand or leverage resources or to increase visibility. Partners are different from team members and stakeholders in that their relationship with the venture is more "arm's length"; i.e., the success of their venture is not dependent on the success of their partner. Thus, the degree of dependency and risk is small compared with the possible benefits. The most successful partnerships and alliances are those in which the roles of potential partners complement each other, creating an effective synergy between their resources. Key partnerships and strategic alliances make up one of the essential quadrants of the SFM Circle of Success™.

Perceptual Position: A particular perspective or point of view that may be taken with respect to an interaction. The most common perceptual positions include First (or Self) position, Second (or Other) position, and Third (or Observer) position. Perceptual positions play a key role in strategic thinking and negotiation.

Portfolio Company: A company among the group of companies in which a particular venture investment fund has invested.

Rapport: The establishment of trust, harmony and cooperation in a relationship.

Revenue Model: The structure plan via which a company expects to make money from its product or service.

Role: The "function assumed or part played" by a person or entity. The role of an individual, team or venture reflects their core competencies and actions. It is related to both the position they occupy with respect to others and the expected capabilities and behaviors attached to that position. People, teams and ventures are most successful in roles that are compatible with their characteristics and competencies, and that support the achievement of their vision, mission and ambition. A clear sense of role allows entrepreneurs to establish win-win partnerships that expand and leverage key resources.

Second Position: A perspective that is taken by putting oneself into the "shoes" or point of view of another person. Second position analysis is a crucial skill of Success Factor Modeling.

Silicon Valley: A section of the San Francisco Bay Area noted for technology development. Named after the silicon used in microprocessor and memory chips, Silicon Valley is the home to companies such as Intel, Hewett Packard, Apple Computer, Cisco Systems, Sun Microsystems, Oracle, and thousands of other technology companies that have brought about the Internet Revolution and the New Economy.

Soul: The deepest part of a person's nature and is expressed as a special quality of "emotional or intellectual energy or intensity." The soul is the unique life force, essence or energy that we come into the world with and that comes into the world through us. In conjunction with the "ego," the soul makes up our sense of identity. Motivations of the soul are directed outward toward the larger systems of which we are a part and include contribution, service, connection and purpose. The "soul" of an organization or venture relates to the contribution or service it provides to its customers and society.

Sponsorship: Sponsorship involves creating a context in which others can act, grow and excel. The sponsor is not necessarily a teacher or a role model for the individual or group being sponsored. Rather the sponsor provides a context, contacts and resources (including money) that allow the group or individual being sponsored to focus on, develop and use their own abilities and skills. It involves the commitment to the promotion of something that is already within a person or group, but which is not being manifested to its fullest capacity.

Stakeholder: Any individual or group related to a project or venture who: affects decisions; is affected—positively or negatively—by the consequences of decisions and the intended results; can either hinder or facilitate reaching the expected results; or has resources or skills which can significantly effect the quality of results. The term comes from the old practice of placing a series of (wooden) stakes to delineate the boundary of a property, claiming it for the "holders" of the stakes. It has evolved to indicate a person or group owning a significant percentage of a company's shares, or a person or group not owning shares in an enterprise but affected by or having an interest in its operations. Typically, stakeholders are individuals or groups who hold the key to essential resources that the company needs in order to succeed. Stakeholders form one of the essential quadrants of the SFM Circle of Success™.

Start-Up: A start-up is a new company that is in its earliest stages. Start-ups typically have good ideas and a small but committed team, but need resources—such as money, business services (legal, financial, marketing, etc.) and coaching in the behavioral skills—in order to grow and become successful.

Strategic Alliance: A formal (and sometimes informal) relationship between organizations through which they coordinate technical and business activities and share resources in order to reach goals more quickly, cheaply and/or easily, and to create competitive advantage.

Success Factor Modeling: A process developed by Robert and John Dilts whose purpose is to identity critical success factors—in the form of business practices and behavioral skills—applied by successful Silicon Valley start-up companies and other successful entrepreneurs. Success Factor ModelingTM is applied to define specific models, tools and skills that will allow entrepreneurs and their companies to greatly increase their chances of success, and which will allow traditional companies to stimulate and support innovation and entrepreneurial spirit within their existing organization.

Team Members: The group of people who work most closely with the entrepreneur to fulfill the mission of the venture. To succeed, entrepreneurs must grow a team of competent individuals aligned with and committed to the mission of the venture. Sustainable success requires continuing to increase the team's competency as the business matures. Team members make up one of the essential quadrants of the SFM Circle of Success™.

Valuation: The process of determining the value of an asset or company. The valuation of a start-up company is expressed in the price of its stock multiplied by the number of shares outstanding and reserved for issuance.

Value Added Investor: An investor, such as an "angel" or strategic investor, that contributes more than money to start-up, such as advice or a business relationship.

Venture: A daring or risky journey or undertaking involving uncertainty as to the outcome. A business enterprise or speculation in which something is risked in the hope of profit.

Venture Capital: Funds made available for startup firms and small businesses with exceptional growth potential. Venture capital is money invested in a company by professional managers of special funds set up to make investments in new ventures or start-ups. Resources for managerial and technical expertise are often also provided.

Venture Capitalist: An individual or collection of individuals (a fund) that puts substantial sums of money into a company in return for ownership, typically in the form of stock shares. Venture capitalists hope to benefit from the increase in value of this stock when it is later sold through an acquisition or public offering.

Venture Catalyst: An individual or collection of individuals (a fund) that puts both money and other resources into a start-up company in order to accelerate its growth and reduce the time it takes the company to reach a viable "exit" (i.e., acquisition or IPO).

Vision: The ability to see beyond the confines of the "here and now" – a mental image of what the future will or could be like. Generally, vision relates to imagining future scenarios and relates to people's view of the larger system of which they are a part. It provides the overall direction for the team and defines the purpose of their interactions; i.e., for whom or for what a particular action step or path has been taken. Vision is essential for entrepreneurs in order to be able to navigate the global marketplace, foresee changes and make adjustments, and to anticipate competition.

Zentrepreneurism: An emerging form of entrepreneurship that combines traditional Western thought with an Eastern philosophy of seeking answers to the daily challenges of business and life. It resonates for people who are experiencing a new direction and purpose in their lives and have made a conscious decision to become a more passionate, purposeful and creative person. Social entrepreneurism and Zentrepreneurism reflect a new entrepreneurial model that shifts from bottom line thinking to one that emphasizes a "blended bottom line" founded on the belief that organizations can and should produce social good and contribute to the sustainability of our planet's eco system while producing financial returns that reasonably reward the risk and commitment of stakeholders.

Bibliography

- *From Coach to Awakener*, Dilts, R., Meta Publications, Capitola, CA, 2003.

- *Tools for Dreamers*, Dilts, R. B., Epstein, T. and Dilts, R. W., Meta Publications, Capitola, CA, 1991.

- *Strategies of Genius Vols I, II & III*, Dilts, R., Meta Publications, Capitola, CA,1994-1995.

- *Alpha Leadership: Tools for Leaders Who Want More From Life*, Deering, A., Dilts, R. and Russell, J., John Wiley & Sons, London, England, 2002.

- *Visionary Leadership Skills*, Dilts, R., Meta Publications, Capitola, CA, 1996.

- *Modeling with NLP*, Dilts, R., Meta Publications, Capitola, CA, 1998.

- *Encyclopedia of Systemic Neuro-Linguistic Programming and NLP New Coding*, Dilts, R. and DeLozier, J., NLP University Press, Santa Cruz, CA, 2000.

- *Effective Presentation Skills*, Dilts, R., Meta Publications, Capitola, CA, 1994.

- *Skills for the Future*, Dilts, R., Meta Publications, Capitola, CA, 1993.

- *NLP II: The Next Generation*, Dilts, R. and DeLozier, J. with Bacon Dilts, D., Meta Publications, Capitola, CA, 2010.

- *The Hero's Journey: A Voyage of Self-Discovery*, Gilligan, S. and Dilts, R., Crowne House Publishers, London, UK, 2009.

- *Innovations in NLP*, Hall, M. and Charvet, S., Editors; Crown House Publishers, London, 2011.

Photos

- John Dilts photo courtesy of Robert B. Diltsv
- Page 27 - Martha Graham by Yousuf Karsh (1948)
  en.wikipedia.org/wiki/Martha_Graham
- Page 30 - Captain Sully Sullenberger
  www.northjersey.com/arts-and-entertainment/sully-s-new-book-a-testament-to-american-values-1.461531
- Page 41 - Elon Musk
  twitter.com/elonmusk
- Page 43 - Walt Disney portrait by Robert B. Dilts
- Page 48 - Richard Branson
  twitter.com/richardbranson
- Page 64 - Jeff Bezos by Amazon Press Room
  phx.corporate-ir.net/phoenix.zhtml?c=176060&p=irol-images_videos
- Page 66 - Muhammad Yunnus
  istock by Getty Images
- Page 68 - Blake Mycoskie
  bteam.org
- Page 82 - Steig Westerberg
  twitter.com/steigw
- Page 86 - Marwan Zebian and Ronald Bur
  wwwwestlakevp.com/
- Page 94 - Ed Hogan
  wwwventurastpatricksdayparade.com/
- Page 102 - Barney Pell
  www.linkedin.com/in/barneypell
- Page 116 - Samuel Parlmisano by IBM News Room
  www-03.ibm.com/press/us/en/biography/36420.wss
- Page 137 - Don Pickens
  twitter.com/donpickens
- Page 156 - Mark Fizpatrick
  linkedin.com/pub/mark-fitzpatrick

- Page 163 - Cindana Turkatte

    Video footage from the interview with John and Robert Dilts
- Page 194 - Steve Artim

    www.linkedin.com/pub/steve-artim
- Page 208 - Martin Luther King Jr

    www.tutufoundationusa.org/
- Page 252 - Steve Jobs

    istock by Getty Images
- Pages 253, 254 - Images from the Macintosh 1984 Superbowl TV Spot

    www.tuaw.com/

"Next Generation Entrepreneurs - Success Factor Modeling Volume 1" was created using:

- Aurulent Sans - by Stephen G. Hartke
- Roman Serif - by Mandred Klein
- COMIC GEEK – WWW.BLAMBOT.COM
- Comic Book – www.pixelsagas.com
- Modern Type Writer – Lukas Krakora
- BADABOOM BB - WWW.BLAMBOT.COM

Robert Dilts – Author

Email: rdilts@nlpu.com
Homepage: http://www.robertdilts.com

Robert B. Dilts - Author

Robert Dilts has had a global reputation as a leading coach, behavioral skills trainer and business consultant since the late 1970s. A major developer and expert in the field of Neuro-Linguistic Programming (NLP), Robert has provided coaching, consulting and training throughout the world to a wide variety of individuals and organizations.

Together with his brother John, Robert pioneered the principles and techniques of Success Factor Modeling^{TM} and has authored numerous books and articles about how they may be applied to enhance leadership, creativity, communication and team development. His book *Visionary Leadership Skills* draws from Robert's extensive study of historical and corporate leaders to present the tools and skills necessary for "creating a world to which people want to belong." *Alpha Leadership: Tools for Business Leaders Who Want More From Life* (with Ann Deering and Julian Russell) captures and shares the latest practices of effective leadership, offering approaches to reduce stress and to promote satisfaction. *From Coach to Awakener* provides a road map and set of toolboxes for coaches to help clients reach goals on a number of different levels of learning and change. *The Hero's Journey: A Voyage of Self Discovery* (with Stephen Gilligan) is about how to reconnect you with your deepest calling, transform limiting beliefs and habits and improve self-image.

Past corporate clients and sponsors have included Apple Computer, Microsoft, Hewlett-Packard, IBM, Lucasfilms Ltd. and the State Railway of Italy. He has lectured extensively on coaching, leadership, innovation, collective intelligence, organizational learning and change management, making presentations and keynote addresses for The International Coaching Federation (ICF), HEC Paris, The United Nations, The World Health Organization, Harvard University and the International University of Monaco. In 1997 and 1998, Robert supervised the design of *Tools for Living*, the behavior management portion of the program used by Weight Watcher's International.

Robert was an associate professor at the ISVOR Fiat School of Management for more than fifteen years, helping to develop programs on leadership, innovation, values and systemic thinking. From 2001–2004 he served as chief scientist and Chairman of the Board for ISVOR DILTS Leadership Systems, a joint venture with ISVOR Fiat (the former corporate university of the Fiat Group) that delivered a wide range of innovative leadership development programs to large corporations on a global scale.

A co-founder of Dilts Strategy Group, Robert was also founder and CEO of Behavioral Engineering, a company that developed computer software and hardware applications emphasizing behavioral change. Robert has a degree in Behavioral Technology from the University of California at Santa Cruz.

Antonio Meza · Illustrator

Antonio Meza has been drawing cartoons ever since he can remember, but his professional cartoonist work started only recently in his life.

A native of Pachuca, Mexico, Antonio is a Master Practitioner and a Trainer of Neuro-Linguistic Programming (NLP). He has a degree in Communication Sciences from Fundación Universidad de las Américas Puebla, a Masters degree in Film Studies from Université de Paris 3 –Sorbonne Nouvelle, a diploma in Cinema Scriptwriting from the General Society of Writers in Mexico (SOGEM), and a diploma in Documentary Films from France's École Nationale des Métiers de l'Image et du Son (La Fémis).

He has recently certified as well in Generative Coaching with Robert Dilts and Stephen Gilligan at the Institut Repère of Paris.

Antonio's career includes work in marketing research, advertising, branding, corporate image, film production, and scriptwriting. His professional photography work has been exhibited in Mexico, Belgium, and France.

He had participated in animated cartoons startups in Mexico before moving to France where he works as a consultant, coach, and trainer, specializing in creative thinking and collective intelligence. He offers his services under his brand: Akrobatas.

His NGO and Foundations clients include the European AIDS Treatment Group (EATG), OXFAM, the European HIV/AIDS Funders Group, the Open Society Foundations (OSF) and the European Public Health Alliance (EPHA). He has conducted training workshops for business schools such as the ESCP-Europe and international organizations such as the IABC (International Association of Business Communicators).

Antonio is also an experienced public speaker member of Toastmasters International. In 2013 he was awarded 3rd best speaker at the International Speech Contest of District 59, covering continental Europe.

His cartoons and illustrations have been published by the Université Pantheon-Assas (Paris 2), he co-authored two books (as illustrator) with Jean-Eric Branaa: "English Law Made Simple" and "American Government Made Simple" published by Ellipses in Paris. He also uses his skills as a cartoonist and trainer to collaborate in seminars, conferences and brainstorming sessions as a graphic facilitator.

He has several illustration projects including the three volumes for the *Success Factor Modeling* series with Robert Dilts.

Antonio Meza – Illustrator

Email: hola@antoons.net
Homepage: http://www.antoons.net